Metaphor in Discourse

'Metaphor' is the phenomenon whereby we talk and, potentially, think about something in terms of something else. In this book Elena Semino discusses metaphor as a common linguistic occurrence, which is varied in its textual appearance, versatile in the functions it may perform, and central to many different types of communication, from informal interaction to political speeches. She discusses the use of metaphor across a variety of texts and genres from literature, politics, science, education, advertising and the discourse of mental illness. Each chapter includes detailed case studies focusing on specific texts, from election leaflets to specialist scientific articles. Also included is a detailed consideration of corpus (computer-based) methods of analysis. Wide-ranging and informative, this book will be invaluable to those interested in metaphor from a range of disciplines.

ELENA SEMINO is a Senior Lecturer in the Department of Linguistics and English Language at Lancaster University. Her previous publications include *Cognitive Stylistics: Language and Cognition in Text Analysis* (2002, edited with J. Culpeper) and *Corpus Stylistics: Speech, Writing and Thought Presentation in a Corpus of English Writing* (2004, with M. Short).

Metaphor in Discourse

Elena Semino
Lancaster University

CAMBRIDGE UNIVERSITY PRESS
Cambridge, New York, Melbourne, Madrid, Cape Town, Singapore, São Paulo, Delhi

Cambridge University Press
The Edinburgh Building, Cambridge CB2 8RU, UK

Published in the United States of America by Cambridge University Press, New York

www.cambridge.org
Information on this title: www.cambridge.org/9780521686969

First published 2008

Printed in the United Kingdom at the University Press, Cambridge

A catalogue record for this publication is available from the British Library

Library of Congress Cataloguing in Publication data
Semino, Elena, 1964–
Metaphor in discourse / Elena Semino.
p. cm.
Includes bibliographical references and index.
ISBN 978-0-521-86730-6 (hardback)
1. Metaphor. I. Title.
PN228.M4S38 2008
808 – dc22 2008014088

ISBN 978-0-521-86730-6 hardback
ISBN 978-0-521-68696-9 paperback

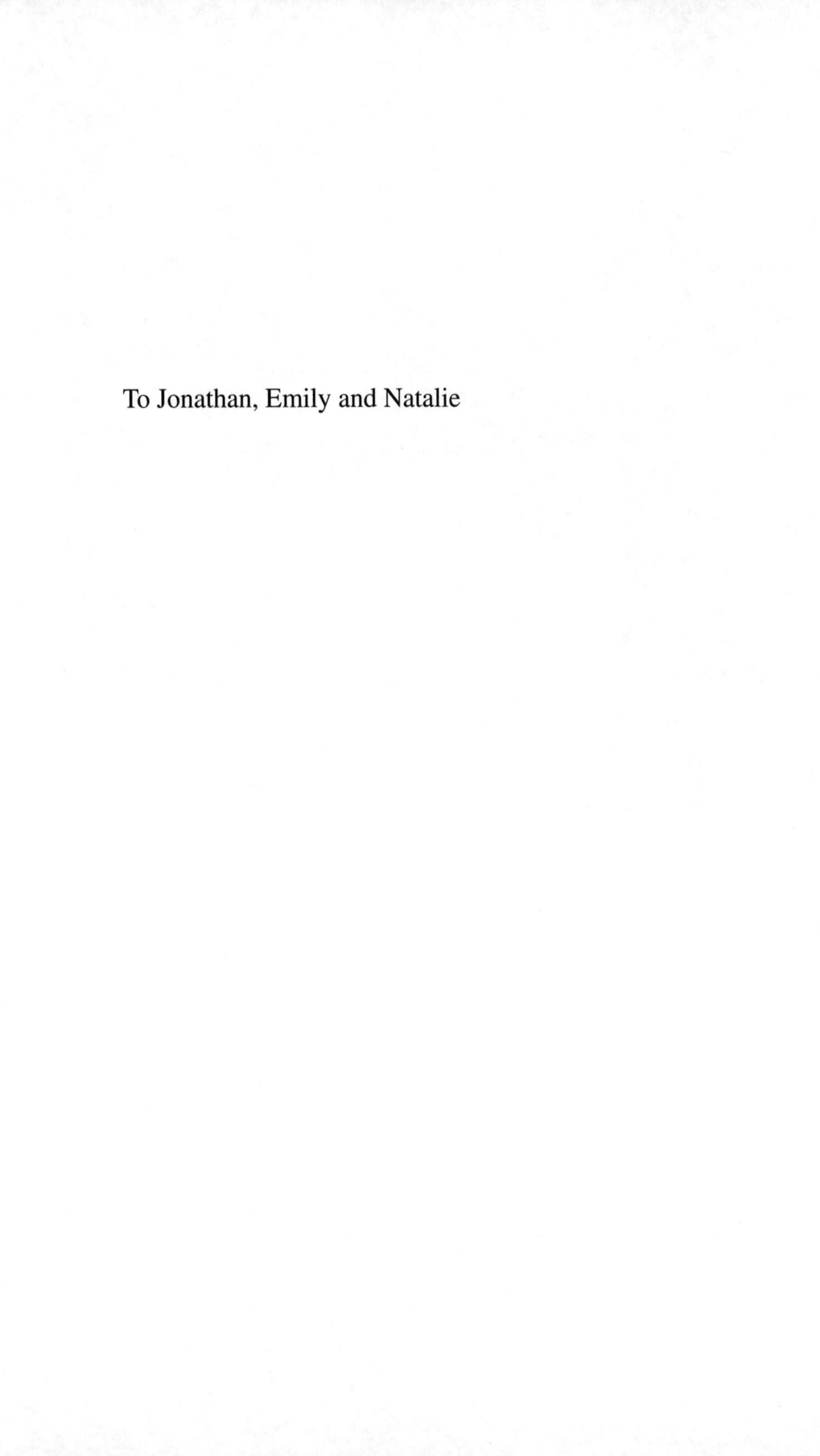

To Jonathan, Emily and Natalie

Contents

Figures

Acknowledgements

I have greatly enjoyed writing this book. In large part, this has been because my ideas have developed in the course of many conversations and collaborations with friends and colleagues at Lancaster University and around the world. I cannot mention everybody here, but a few people deserve special thanks.

Over the last eight years, I have benefited from many hours of discussion with the other nine members of the 'Pragglejaz' metaphor group. I am particularly indebted to Gerard Steen for originally creating the group and inviting me to join.

More concretely, John Heywood patiently read the whole manuscript, made many invaluable comments and, on several occasions, saved me from potential embarrassment. Maria Bortoluzzi, Alice Deignan and Veronika Koller gave me some useful feedback on individual chapters. Sofia Lampropoulou transcribed the radio programme discussed in chapter 5, and Gerard Hearne helped me with the final stages of proofreading. Ben Barton at Billington Cartmell went well beyond the call of duty in order to ensure that I obtained permission to reproduce the advertisement discussed in chapter 5.

The book was completed in reasonable time thanks to a Research Leave grant from the Arts and Humanities Research Council (grant number: AH/E503683/1). I am grateful to Andreas Musolff for his help with the application process.

Helen Barton at Cambridge University Press was exceptionally helpful and supportive at all stages in the development of the book.

Although I enjoyed working on the book, I enjoyed even more taking breaks from it in order to spend time with my extended families in Italy and England, and especially with Jonathan, Emily and Natalie. The girls, in particular, make sure that I never take myself too seriously by being healthily unimpressed with the 'boring' things I write. I will, of course, make it my mission to try to change their minds. In the meantime, I sincerely hope that the readers of this book will disagree with my daughters.

The author and publishers are grateful to the following for permission to reproduce copyrighted materials: Carcanet for permission to reproduce in chapter 2 the poem 'Answers' from: Elizabeth Jennings (1979), *Selected Poems*

(Manchester: Carcanet, p. 32); Steve Bell for permission to reproduce the cartoon discussed in chapter 3; Lucozade for permission to reproduce the advertisement discussed in chapter 5.

Every effort has been made to secure necessary permissions to reproduce copyright material in this work, through in some cases it has proved impossible to trace or contact copyright holders. If any omissions are brought to our notice, we will be happy to include appropriate acknowledgements in reprinting and in any subsequent edition.

Abbreviations

BNC	British National Corpus
CMT	Cognitive Metaphor Theory
MIP	Metaphor Identification Procedure

1 Introduction: studying metaphor in discourse

1.1 Some preliminaries

Let me begin by reflecting on the title of this book, *Metaphor in Discourse*. By 'metaphor' I mean the phenomenon whereby we talk and, potentially, think about something in terms of something else. For example, in the expression 'the war against drugs', the attempt to reduce the number of people who take drugs is talked about in terms of war. This may both reflect and reinforce a particular way of thinking about difficult enterprises (and specifically actions and policies relating to drug abuse) in terms of aggression and military action. I will be more precise about the definition of metaphor below. By 'discourse', as the term is used in the title, I mean naturally occurring language use: real instances of writing or speech which are produced and interpreted in particular circumstances and for particular purposes.

In the course of the book, I discuss metaphor as a pervasive linguistic phenomenon, which is varied in its textual manifestations, versatile in the functions it may perform, and central to many different types of communication, from informal interaction through political speeches to scientific theorizing. More specifically, I explore the forms and functions of metaphor in a variety of texts and genres on a range of different topics; I consider the relationship between individual uses of metaphor in specific contexts and conventional metaphorical patterns in language generally; I emphasize the tendency towards an interaction between conventionality and creativity in metaphor use in a variety of different genres; and I reflect on the important but controversial relationship between metaphorical uses of language on the one hand, and mental representations and thought on the other.

The approach adopted in the book is best introduced with reference to a concrete example. On 8 July 2005, an article by James Landale appeared on the website of the UK version of BBC News with the headline 'Half full or half empty?' (see http://news.bbc.co.uk/1/hi/uk_politics/4665923.stm for the full text). The article is concerned with the aftermath of the G8 summit which had just taken place in Gleneagles in Scotland, and which had been concerned with initiatives to relieve poverty in Africa and to halt climate change. The summit had received unusually high amounts of media attention due to the involvement of rock stars Bob Geldof and Bono, who had been raising public awareness and lobbying governments to ensure that substantial commitments would be made by the G8 leaders (the article was accompanied by a photograph of Geldof and Bono walking with UN Secretary General Kofi Annan). Geldof and Bono had also organized a series of high-profile pop concerts throughout the world on the eve of the summit (Live 8), in order to mobilize public opinion as with the Live Aid concert Geldof had organized ten years before to raise funds for the victims of famine in Ethiopia.

The article focuses particularly on the customary debate that follows events of this kind, in which different people give different assessments of the outcome of the discussions, some more positive, others more negative. I have chosen it for discussion here because of the prominent role that metaphor plays in it. In the opening of the article, the reporter explicitly states that, after all the activities and negotiations, the summit had finally come down to 'a battle of metaphors':

1.1 In the end, after all the talks, the lobbying and the haggling over words, the G8 summit at Gleneagles came down to a battle of metaphors.

> Just how best should the work over the last three days at this Scottish golf course and equestrian centre be characterised?
>
> Was, asked some, the cup half full or half empty?

Indeed, as I will show, the prominent individuals whose statements are quoted in the article use different metaphors to convey their own views and evaluations of what had been achieved. The headline of the article itself also exploits a conventional metaphorical expression ('half full or half empty?') to sum up the way in which the same set of decisions is being presented by some as a success and by others as a failure.

1.1.1 Metaphor and rhetorical goals

The 'story' in the article is represented by the different views expressed by a variety of people about the decisions made by the G8 leaders. In particular, the article includes several direct quotations from statements in which three prominent individuals use different metaphors to express contrasting assessments of the outcome of the summit. In a series of separate quotations, Bono is reported as describing what has been achieved and what remains to be done in terms of the climbing of a series of mountains:

1.2 'A mountain has been climbed,' declared the U2 rock star Bono, who alongside his comrade in alms Bob Geldof, has been lurking on the fringes of this summit.

> But, he said, and it was a big 'but' that was echoed by the army of charity workers and aid lobbyists here.

'A mountain has been climbed only to reveal higher peaks on the other side,' continued Bono.

Not wanting to sound too negative, he continued: 'But let's also look down on the valley from where we've come.'

The expression 'a mountain has been climbed' metaphorically constructs the G8 summit in terms of a difficult, but ultimately successful mountainous ascent, while the following reference to 'higher peaks on the other side' presents the remaining problems as further mountains that need to be climbed.[1] In the invitation to 'look down on the valley from where we've come' Bono constructs the pre-summit situation in terms of the lower position from which the metaphorical climb began, and suggests that it is now appropriate to experience the same sense of achievement that climbers feel when they look at the valley below from the top of a mountain.

The opinions expressed by the British Prime Minister Tony Blair, who was one of the G8 leaders, are also presented via quotations in which he describes what has been achieved in terms of movement. On the issue of climate change, he is reported as saying that there is a 'pathway to a new dialogue', and, on the summit generally, as insisting that:

1.3 'Politics is about getting things done step by step, this is progress, and we should be proud of it.'

Here expressions such as 'pathway to' and 'getting things done step by step' positively construct what has been achieved in terms of movement forward ('step by step') or in terms of entities that make movement forward possible ('pathway'). However, these expressions also suggest that what has been done is part of a longer process rather than the final, desired outcome.

In contrast, a representative of an anti-poverty group is quoted as negatively assessing the G8 summit in comparison with the Live 8 concert via a metaphor to do with sound:

1.4 Dr Kumi Naidoo, from the anti-poverty lobby group G-Cap, said after 'the roar' produced by Live 8, the G8 had uttered 'a whisper'.

The reference to 'roar' could be a nonmetaphorical description of the sound made by the crowd at the concert. However, the use of 'whisper' in relation to the summit is clearly a (negative) metaphorical description of the outcome of the discussions in terms of a sound characterized by lack of loudness. Hence, the contrast in loudness between the sounds indicated by 'roar' and 'whisper'

[1] The noun 'summit' itself derives from the Latin 'summum' (which means 'highest'), and can also mean 'top of a mountain' in contemporary English. In other words, the sense of the noun that is relevant in the article (that of a meeting among leaders) is metaphorically derived from the physical notion of an elevated position. We can only speculate, however, on whether Bono's choice of metaphor was partly inspired by the physical meaning of 'summit'.

is used metaphorically to establish a contrast between the strength of feeling and commitment expressed by the concert audiences and the lack of resolve and effectiveness shown by the G8 leaders.[2]

All three quoted speakers use metaphor to contribute to their own rhetorical goals, which go beyond simply expressing their opinions in an effective way. Both Bono and Blair had been heavily involved in the G8 summit, albeit in different ways, and were therefore faced with a fine balancing act when asked to judge its outcome: on the one hand, they had to claim some degree of success, in order not to lose face themselves and not to damage the prospects of future constructive collaboration with others; on the other hand, they had to recognize that success had not been complete, in order to preserve their credibility and to emphasize that those involved needed to be prepared for further efforts. Interestingly, both achieved this rhetorical balancing act via metaphorical references to having successfully completed *part* of a journey. Dr Naidoo, in contrast, had no direct involvement with the summit, and represented an organization whose goal is to put pressure on governments on the issue of world poverty. Her choice of metaphor, therefore, expresses disappointment, and emphasizes the contrast between the decisions of politicians and the aspirations of ordinary people at the concert.

Aristotle famously described 'a command of metaphor' as 'the mark of genius' (Cooper 2005). While we may hesitate to use the word 'genius' in relation to the three speakers quoted in the article, each of them does show skill and experience in using metaphor to convey their views succinctly, vividly and effectively, and to provide the media with easily quotable material. However, the article also shows that the 'genius' Aristotle talked about is not limited to politicians or media personalities. The article's author, James Landale, does not just notice that a contrast in metaphors would make a nice news story, but also effectively uses metaphor himself: for example, he describes the contrasting metaphors used by different individuals as a 'battle' (see extract above), and exploits the conventional metaphorical opposition between seeing a cup as half full or half empty to provide a catchy headline for his piece. In fact, a closer look at the various metaphorical expressions I have discussed reveals that the 'genius' of their producers lies in exploiting to maximum effect some of the metaphors that are commonly used by speakers of English generally.

1.1.2 Metaphor, conventionality and thought

The metaphorical uses of language that are attributed to Bono, Blair and Dr Naidoo in the article are sufficiently striking for the reporter to have noticed

[2] It is interesting that here the metaphorical noun phrases 'the roar' and 'a whisper' are the only parts of Dr Naidoo's statement that are quoted directly, via a technique that has been described as 'embedded quotation' (see Semino and Short 2004: 153–9).

their metaphoricity and decided that his readers would be able to notice it too. Indeed, we are also likely to conclude that the various metaphorical expressions were used consciously and deliberately by the three speakers, in order to express their views as effectively as possible. Over the last three decades, however, much attention has been paid to the presence of large numbers of highly conventional metaphorical expressions in language, which we often use and understand without being conscious of their metaphoricity. In a series of influential works, George Lakoff and his colleagues (Lakoff and Johnson 1980b; Lakoff and Turner 1989; Lakoff 1993) pointed out that metaphorical expressions are pervasive in language, and that they tend to form systematic sets such as the following:

1.5 Your claims are *indefensible*.
He *attacked every weak point* in my argument.
His criticisms were *right on target*.
I *demolished* his argument.
I've never *won* an argument with him.
You disagree? Okay, *shoot*!
If you use that strategy, he'll *wipe you out*.
He *shot down* all of my arguments.
(Lakoff and Johnson 1980b: 4; italics in original)

1.6 He got a *head start* in life. He's without *direction* in his life. I'm *where* I want to *be* in life. I'm at a *crossroads* in my life. He'll *go places* in life. He's never let anyone *get in* his *way*. He's *gone through* a lot in life. (Lakoff 1993: 223; my italics)

The italicized expressions in list 1.5 describe verbal arguments in terms of physical aggression, including particularly the kind of armed violence associated with war. The italicized expressions in list 1.6 describe various aspects of life in terms of location, movement and journeys.

In *Metaphors We Live By*, Lakoff and Johnson (1980b) famously showed that many such related sets of conventional metaphorical expressions exist in English, and argued that these expressions are not simply ways of *talking* about one thing in terms of another, but evidence that we also *think* about one thing in terms of another. More specifically, in Lakoff and Johnson's view, groups of expressions such as those above reflect conventional patterns of thought, known as 'conceptual metaphors'. Conceptual metaphors are defined as systematic sets of correspondences, or 'mappings', across conceptual domains, whereby a 'target' domain (e.g. our knowledge about arguments) is partly structured in terms of a different 'source' domain (e.g. our knowledge about war) (see also 'basic' metaphors in MacCormac 1985 and 'root analogies' in Goatly 1997). Conceptual domains are rich mental representations: they are portions of our background knowledge that relate to particular experiences or phenomena, and may include elements (e.g. travellers), relations (e.g. that between a traveller and their destination), and patterns of inferences (e.g. if someone reaches the end of a cul-de-sac they cannot continue to move forward) (see Lakoff and Turner 1989: 63–4).[3] Conventional sets of metaphorical expressions such as those given in lists 1.5 and 1.6 are seen as linguistic realizations of conventional conceptual metaphors: the expressions in list 1.5 are presented as linguistic realizations of the conceptual metaphor ARGUMENT IS WAR, where WAR is the source domain and ARGUMENT is the target domain; the expressions in list 1.6 are presented as linguistic realizations of the conceptual metaphor LIFE IS A JOURNEY, where JOURNEY is the source domain and LIFE is the target domain.[4] The ARGUMENT IS WAR conceptual metaphor involves correspondences between participants in arguments and opponents or enemies, strategies in arguments and attack or defence, the outcomes of arguments and victory or defeat, and so on. Similarly, in the LIFE IS A JOURNEY metaphor, people correspond to travellers, actions to forward movement, choices to crossroads, problems to impediments to travel, and purposes to destinations. Importantly, new structure can be projected from source to target domain. Consider, for example, the conventional metaphorical construction of time as a resource, and, more specifically, as money, which is linguistically realized by expressions such as 'You've used up all your time' and 'I've invested a lot of time on that project' (Lakoff and Johnson 1999: 161–4). Some of the material that is projected from the RESOURCE/MONEY source domains is not necessarily part of the TIME target domain independently of the metaphor. This applies, for example, to the notions that time can be 'saved' or 'wasted' (see Lakoff and Johnson 2003: 252–3). This view of metaphor, which is currently the dominant paradigm in metaphor studies, is known as 'Cognitive' or 'Conceptual' Metaphor Theory (henceforth CMT) (see also Gibbs 1994; Lakoff and Johnson 1999; Kövecses 2002).[5]

Cognitive metaphor theorists emphasize that target domains typically correspond to areas of experience that are relatively abstract, complex, unfamiliar, subjective or poorly delineated, such as time, emotion, life or death. In contrast, source domains typically correspond to concrete, simple, familiar, physical and well-delineated experiences, such as motion, bodily phenomena, physical objects and so on. This applies particularly clearly to the LIFE IS A JOURNEY conceptual metaphor, where the target domain (LIFE) is relatively more complex and abstract than the source domain (JOURNEY). Moreover, the

[3] Other terms for general mental representations are roughly equivalent to 'domain', such as 'schema', 'script' and 'frame'.

[4] Small capitals are conventionally used to indicate conceptual metaphors and to refer to conceptual domains. The same convention will be used throughout this book.

[5] In this book I do not have the space to discuss in detail the ways in which CMT has been developed in recent years, but see, for example, Grady (1997a), Lakoff and Johnson (1999) and Lakoff and Johnson (2003: 242–76).

JOURNEY source domain has its basis in the simple and fundamental physical experience of moving along a path from one location to another. Within CMT, such basic experiences have been captured in terms of simple, skeletal mental representations known as 'image schemas'. The LIFE IS A JOURNEY metaphor, for example, is related to the PATH image schema, which is a minimal knowledge structure consisting of two different locations, a path between the two locations, and a direction of movement from one location to the other (see Johnson 1987). In the version of CMT proposed by Grady (1997a; 1997b), conceptual metaphors such as LIFE IS A JOURNEY are seen as the result of the combination of several simpler and more basic conceptual mappings such as PURPOSES ARE DESTINATIONS and ACTION IS SELF-PROPELLED MOTION (Grady 1997a). These basic mappings are termed 'primary metaphors' and are claimed to be grounded in systematic correlations between our tangible, sensorimotor experiences on the one hand (e.g. arriving at a destination) and our intangible, subjective experiences on the other (e.g. achieving a purpose). In other words, the LIFE IS A JOURNEY conceptual metaphor is claimed to derive ultimately from basic experiential correlations between performing actions and moving, reaching destinations and achieving purposes, and so on. In fact, even the conceptual metaphor ARGUMENT IS WAR, where the source domain (WAR) is rather complex, can be seen as arising from the basic experience of physical struggle amongst individuals with contrasting goals (Lakoff and Johnson 1980b: 62; 2003: 265). I will return to this particular metaphor in chapter 6.

Within earlier approaches, metaphor was claimed to be based on similarities between unlike entities, even though it was recognized in some studies that metaphors can create new similarities, rather than simply relying on pre-existing, 'objective' ones (e.g. Black 1962). Within CMT, the notion of similarity plays a more minor role, and conventional conceptual metaphors are often explained in terms of recurring correlations in experience, as I have just mentioned. However, it is also recognized that some metaphors cannot be traced back to experiential correlations, but rather have their basis in *perceived* similarities or resemblances, i.e. in the perception of common characteristics or structures between different entities or areas of experience. This can explain, for example, metaphorical statements such as 'Achilles is a lion' (Grady 1999), or conventional conceptual metaphors such as LIFE IS A GAMBLING GAME, which, according to Kövecses (2002: 71–2) is based on the perception that some aspects of life are similar to some aspects of gambling games (cf. expressions such as 'It's a *toss-up*' and 'Those are *high stakes*', 'If you *play your cards right*, you can do it'; Kövecses 2002: 72; italics in original).[6]

[6] In this book, I do not discuss other theories of metaphor, but see, for example, MacCormac (1985), Kittay (1987), Glucksberg (2001), Sperber and Wilson (1995), Stern (2000) and Gentner and Bowdle (2005).

Let me now return to the metaphorical expressions from the G8 article I discussed in the previous subsection. From the perspective of CMT, the metaphorical use of 'battle' in the expression 'a battle of metaphors' is part of the pattern exemplified in list 1.5, or, in other words, a linguistic realization of ARGUMENT IS WAR: the reporter metaphorically describes the use of different metaphors on the part of people who have different opinions in terms of a stage in a war. In doing so, he exploits a conventional metaphorical sense of the noun 'battle', which is normally included in dictionary entries alongside the nonmetaphorical sense of a fight between opposing armies.

The movement metaphors used by both Bono and Blair are reminiscent of the expressions listed in list 1.6 as linguistic realizations of LIFE IS A JOURNEY. In fact, as I mentioned earlier, they can best be explained in terms of a combination of a small set of primary metaphors, including particularly ACTION IS SELF-PROPELLED MOTION and PURPOSES ARE DESTINATIONS (Grady 1997a: 286–7; Lakoff and Johnson 1999: 52–3). Both Bono and Blair metaphorically construct the G8 summit as part of a difficult journey, and the achievements that have been made as movement forward. In both cases, however, further movement forward is needed, and no explicit reference is made to the end point of the journey, which presumably corresponds to the almost unattainable goals of eliminating world poverty and environmental damage. The metaphorical expressions used by Blair ('pathway', 'step by step'), however, are rather more conventional than those used by Bono: in fact, readers may only become aware of their metaphoricity, if they do, because these expressions occur in close proximity to each other, and possibly also because of the explicit reference to a 'battle of metaphors' at the beginning of the article. In contrast, Bono starts off with a rather conventional expression ('a mountain has been climbed'), and then fleshes out the mountain-climbing scenario by using expressions that are much less conventional ('higher peaks', 'the valley from which we've come', etc.). I will return to the creative exploitation of conventional metaphorical expressions in section 1.2.3 below.

Dr Naidoo's metaphorical use of 'whisper' and, to some extent, 'roar' is not as obviously connected to conventional uses of metaphor. This may explain why it is less likely to be perceived as clichéd as compared with Blair's and, to a lesser extent, Bono's metaphors. However, even Dr Naidoo's choice of metaphor is at least consistent with some conventional metaphorical expressions where loudness is positively evaluated and corresponds to effectiveness, as in the saying 'actions speak louder than words'.

It could be argued that the skill of individuals like Blair and Bono as public speakers lies precisely in their ability to exploit conventional conceptual metaphors for their own rhetorical purposes, by creatively stretching and adapting them to convey particular points. More specifically, the kind of creative exploitation of conventional conceptual metaphors exemplified by Bono's statements achieves an important rhetorical compromise: on the one hand, the conventional basis of Bono's metaphors ensures that they are widely and easily comprehensible; on the other hand, the creative elements add vividness to his statements, and help to convey simultaneously a sense of satisfaction with current achievements and the need to concentrate on future challenges. Within CMT, the different types of phenomena mentioned as evidence for the existence of conceptual metaphors actually include the ability to produce and understand effortlessly creative uses of metaphor such as Bono's 'higher peaks' (see Lakoff and Turner 1989; Lakoff 1993: 205). However, most metaphorical expressions are highly conventional, so that, by and large, we are not consciously aware of their metaphoricity when we produce or interpret them. The G8 article contains many such expressions, such as, for example, the temporal use of the spatial preposition 'over' in 'over the last three days' in extract 1.1 above (I will return to metaphorical uses of prepositions in section 1.2.2 below).

Cognitive metaphor theorists do not normally acknowledge any intellectual debt to previous scholarship on metaphor. Rather, they describe the work of earlier metaphor scholars as entirely misconceived, and present their approach as a radical corrective to the errors of the past (e.g. Lakoff and Turner 1989: 110–39). This is rather unfortunate, in my view. CMT is indeed innovative in many crucial respects, and does contrast with a traditional view of metaphor as a mere decorative device, simply involving the substitution of a literal term for a concept with a nonliteral one. However, the insights and tenets of CMT had been anticipated in many previous studies on metaphor, albeit from different perspectives and with different emphases (for overviews, see Jäkel 1999; Cameron 2003). Aristotle, for example, who is often presented as the source of later misconceptions, did in fact recognize the cognitive dimension of metaphor, as well as its rhetorical power (see Mahon 1999; Cameron 2003). The cognitive implications and linguistic ubiquity of metaphor were also discussed by a number of significant European philosophers and linguists over several centuries including, for example, John Locke, Giambattista Vico, Immanuel Kant and Harald Weinrich (see Jäkel 1999). More recently, prominent Anglo-American philosophers and literary critics such as I. A. Richards (1936) and Max Black (1962; 1993) recognized that metaphor can lead to the construction of new meanings by bringing together different ideas and systems of knowledge. In his work on metaphor, Richards also introduced some influential terms that still have wide currency today. These include particularly the term 'vehicle' to indicate the source-domain meaning of a metaphorical expression (e.g. the 'fight' meaning of 'battle' in 'a battle of metaphors'), and 'tenor' to indicate the element of the target domain that is actually being talked about (e.g. a contrast in the use of metaphor in the expression 'a battle of metaphors').

The overlaps between CMT and earlier work on metaphor do not, in my view, detract from the achievements of Lakoff and his colleagues, but rather provide additional support for their claims. The originality of the contribution of CMT lies particularly in its focus on patterns of conventional metaphorical expressions, its emphasis on the embodied nature of many conventional metaphors, and its account of how metaphors can systematically shape our world-views. On the other hand, classic works in CMT such as Lakoff and Johnson's *Metaphors We Live By* (1980b) also have a number of weaknesses which have direct implications for the concerns of this book.

The notions of conceptual domains and image schemata are not always sufficient to explain the metaphorical phenomena that can be observed in language use. Some recent studies have more successfully accounted for the use of metaphor in language by making reference to mental representations such as 'scenes' (Grady 1997a, 1997b) or 'scenarios' (Musolff 2004), which are smaller and less complex than conceptual domains, but richer in content than image schemata. The notion of metaphorical 'scenario' in particular, will be frequently used throughout the book to refer to mental representations of particular situations, and the settings, entities, goals and actions that are associated with them (e.g. a BATTLE scenario as opposed to the broader conceptual domain of WAR). More crucially for the purposes of this book, CMT is primarily concerned with *conceptual* metaphors, while metaphorical expressions in language are seen as secondary. This results in a general lack of consideration for the textual manifestations of metaphor and for the authenticity of the linguistic data that is adduced as evidence. The main proponents of CMT mostly relied on artificially constructed examples to support their claims, and did not develop an explicit methodology for the extrapolation of conceptual metaphors from linguistic data. This casts doubts on the reliability of claims about conventional conceptual metaphors, and on the exhaustiveness of the CMT account of metaphor in language (Steen 1999; Low 2003; Semino *et al.* 2004; Deignan 2005).

In order to address these weaknesses, in this book I retain the main insights and tenets of CMT but I also build on recent work by a number of scholars who have explored the use of metaphor in authentic discourse (e.g. Cameron 2003; Charteris-Black 2004; Musolff 2004; Deignan 2005). More specifically, when making claims about conventional linguistic metaphors and underlying conceptual metaphors, I frequently use evidence from language corpora (singular 'corpus'), i.e. large machine-readable collections of authentic texts (see chapter 6 for more detail). I also give detailed attention to the formal characteristics of metaphorical expressions, and to the textual and intertextual patterns they are part of. My goal is to combine an awareness of the conventional status of many uses of metaphor with a consideration of the uniqueness and specificity of individual occurrences, as I have briefly demonstrated in relation to the G8 article. As Swan (2002) puts it, the 'disciplinary commitment' of CMT 'to describe what is regular, invariant, and generalizable across an open-ended sample of instances' does not necessarily have to 'prevent a cognitive approach to metaphor from joining a description of its systematic structure with accounts of particular, situated, acts of meaning' (Swan, 2002: 450–1).

1.2 Metaphor in language

In this section, I begin by providing a more precise definition of metaphorical expressions, and then go on to consider the variety of different manifestations of metaphor in language, including particularly: the metaphorical use of different parts of speech and multi-word expressions, the distinction between conventional and novel metaphorical uses of language, and the patterning and possible functions of metaphorical expressions in texts.

1.2.1 Identifying metaphorical expressions

So far, I have operated with a rather general definition of metaphor as the phenomenon whereby we talk and, potentially, think about something in terms of something else. In introducing CMT, I have also implicitly introduced an important distinction between metaphorical expressions in language (e.g. the noun 'battle' in 'a battle of metaphors') and conceptual metaphors (e.g. ARGUMENT IS WAR). Within CMT, the former are seen as linguistic realizations of the latter. It is now time to be more precise about what I mean when I talk about 'linguistic metaphors' or 'metaphorical expressions' or 'metaphorically used words'. This is an issue which metaphor scholars have tended to leave rather vague, but which has recently started to be addressed more explicitly and systematically (e.g. Goatly 1997; Cameron 2003; Deignan 2005).

My approach to the identification of metaphorical expressions is based on the metaphor identification procedure (MIP) proposed by a group of scholars known as the Pragglejaz Group, of which I am a member (Pragglejaz Group 2007).[7] The procedure is as follows:

1. Read the entire text-discourse to establish a general understanding of the meaning.
2. Determine the lexical units in the text-discourse.
3. (a) For each lexical unit in the text, establish its meaning in context, that is, how it applies to an entity, relation or attribute in the situation evoked by the text (contextual meaning). Take into account what comes before and after the lexical unit.
   (b) For each lexical unit, determine if it has a more basic contemporary meaning in other contexts than the one in the given context. For our purposes, basic meanings tend to be
   - More concrete (what they evoke is easier to imagine, see, hear, feel, smell and taste);
   - Related to bodily action;

[7] The name Pragglejaz is formed by the initials of the first names of the ten members of the group: **P**eter Crisp, **R**ay Gibbs, **A**lan Cienki, **G**erard Steen, **G**raham Low, **L**ynne Cameron, **E**lena Semino, **J**oseph Grady, **A**lice Deignan and **Z**oltan Kövecses.

– More precise (as opposed to vague);
– Historically older.

Basic meanings are not necessarily the most frequent meanings of the lexical unit.

(c) If the lexical unit has a more basic current-contemporary meaning in other contexts than the given context, decide whether the contextual meaning contrasts with the basic meaning but can be understood in comparison with it.

4. If yes, mark the lexical unit as metaphorical.

(Pragglejaz Group 2007: 3)

The reference to 'lexical units' in the procedure is an acknowledgment that there is no unproblematic unit of analysis when investigating language generally and metaphoricity in particular. Consider, for example, the expression 'A mountain has been climbed', which is attributed to Bono in the G8 article. It could be argued that the clause should be treated as a whole and analysed as a single linguistic metaphor: it arguably constitutes a semi-fixed expression, and provides a single metaphorical description of the achievements of the summit. On the other hand, it could also be argued that Bono's expression can be analysed word by word: 'mountain', for example, metaphorically refers to the problems facing the G8 organizers, whereas 'climbed' refers to the process of tackling those problems. Indeed, there is some variation in the form of 'mountain-climbing' metaphorical expressions in English. The British National Corpus (BNC), which contains 100 million words of late twentieth-century British English, includes several instances of metaphorical uses of each of the following expressions: 'a mountain to climb', 'have a mountain to climb', 'climb a/the mountain'. Bono's own formulation is slightly unusual in that it is in the passive voice, and has no equivalents in the BNC (see Moon 1998 for a corpus-based study of fixed expressions; see also Gibbs 1994: 265–318).

Different researchers may define lexical units differently, depending on their goals and theoretical assumptions. In this book, I generally assume that decisions on metaphoricity can be made at the level of individual words, even if, as I will often point out, metaphorically used words often occur as part of multiword expressions, rather than singly.[8] Let me now demonstrate the application of the MIP procedure to the use of the word 'battle' in 'a battle of metaphors' (see extract 1.1 above), which is a fairly straightforward and uncontroversial example.

[8] The notion of what counts as 'a word' is problematic, of course. When analysing written texts, I apply the term 'word' graphologically, namely to refer to a string of characters that has spaces on either side. When considering speech, I operationalize the term in a pragmatic way by relating particular strings to lemmas or headwords in dictionaries. There are cases, however, where I consider multiword expressions as single lexical units, namely when the meaning of the whole expression cannot be retrieved from the meanings of the words that compose it, as in the case of 'of course', 'all right' and 'at least' (see Pragglejaz Group 2007). Truly non-compositional expressions, however, are rather rare (e.g. see Gibbs 1994, Moon 1998).

Having read the whole article (step 1), I concluded that it is concerned with different views on the outcome of the recently concluded G8 summit. I then considered the noun 'battle' as a single lexical unit (step 2), and established its contextual meaning, which I would paraphrase as 'contrast/difference/disagreement' (step 3a).[9] I then considered the issue of whether the noun has a more basic meaning in other contexts, and decided that this is indeed the case (step 3b). In the *Macmillan English Dictionary for Advanced Learners* (2002) this meaning is expressed as follows: 'a fight between two armies in a war' (the Macmillan dictionary also includes at least two conventional metaphorical meanings that roughly correspond to the contextual meaning of 'battle' in the G8 article). This basic meaning is more concrete than the contextual meaning (physical fight vs. contrast/difference), as well as more closely related to bodily action and, according to the *Oxford English Dictionary*, historically older. Having identified a different basic meaning, I observed that it contrasts with the contextual meaning (physical battles contrast significantly with differences in the expression of opinions), and that the contextual meaning can be understood in comparison with the basic meaning: verbal disagreements, including in the use of metaphor, can be understood in terms of physical fights between opposing armies (step 3c). As a consequence, I concluded that 'battle' is a metaphorically used word in the second sentence of the G8 article (step 4). I should point out that this conclusion does not mean that I claim that the writer and/or the readers will consciously recognize the word as metaphorical, or even process it via a cross-domain mapping: it simply means that this particular use can be analysed as metaphorical in contrast with other current uses, and that it therefore has the *potential* to be recognized and processed as metaphorical.[10]

Even though the MIP procedure does not explicitly refer to any specific theory of metaphor, step 3 can be rephrased in terms of CMT. The basic meaning and the contextual meaning correspond to elements of different conceptual domains: in this case, the basic meaning of 'battle' can be seen as an element of the WAR conceptual domain, while the contextual meaning can be seen an element of the ARGUMENT conceptual domain. Moreover, the contextual meaning can be understood in terms of a cross-domain mapping from WAR to ARGUMENTS, whereby people with different opinions correspond to armies, and the expression of those different opinions corresponds to a battle. The fact that the contextual meaning also appears in the dictionary confirms the conventionality of this metaphorical expression, which, together with similar

[9] This step in the procedure does not assume that metaphorical expressions have equivalent nonmetaphorical paraphrases. The step simply involves the establishment of what the relevant lexical unit means in the relevant co-text and context, however vague or inexpressible this meaning may be.

[10] In Cameron's (1999) terms, I am defining metaphor in language at the 'theory' level, rather than at the 'processing' or 'neural' levels. For work on the processing of metaphorical expressions, see for example Gibbs (1994), Steen (1994), Giora (2003) and Gentner and Bowdle (2005).

conventional uses of war vocabulary, provides evidence for the conventional conceptual metaphor ARGUMENT IS WAR.

At this point some readers may be thinking that I have just taken a large analytical sledgehammer to crack a very small textual nut, since most people would intuitively agree that the use of 'battle' I have just described is metaphorical. Of course, I rely on my intuitions too in analysing data, and I intuitively identified 'battle' as metaphorically used before I put the noun through the MIP procedure. However, intuitions are not necessarily explicit and systematic, and tend to vary from individual to individual, including from metaphor scholar to metaphor scholar. Moreover, it is generally recognized that metaphoricity is a matter of degree, and that the boundary between metaphorical and non-metaphorical expressions is fuzzy. A procedure such as the one I have just described forces analysts to be as explicit, precise and consistent as possible, and to use sources other than their intuitions to deal with problematic and borderline cases.

Several problematic cases can in fact be found in the G8 article. Consider, for example, the expression 'make progress' in the following sentence:

1.7 And as for trade, even the prime minister conceded that he had failed to make progress.

Here the verb 'make' is used to mean something different from what may be regarded as the most basic meaning of the verb, which the Macmillan dictionary defines as follows: 'to create or produce something by working'. The problem, however, is that 'make' belongs to a group of highly delexicalized English verbs that have lost much of their semantic content, and that can be used to indicate action in a very general, abstract sense (see also the verbs 'take' and 'get'). Hence, it is debatable whether the contextual meaning of 'make' in extract 1.7 can be established clearly enough to identify a contrast with the basic meaning. An analyst could therefore decide that, for the purposes of a particular study, delexicalized verbs lack enough contextual meaning to be analysed for metaphoricity. The opposite argument can also be made, however. It could be argued that, in 'make progress', 'make' has the contextual meaning of achieving something. One could then identify a contrast with the basic meaning of the verb, and decide that achieving something is understood by comparison with the physical action of creating an object (NB: the MIP procedure spells out that basic meanings do not have to be the most frequent meanings of lexical units, and this probably applies here). As such, the use of the verb in extract 1.7 would be seen as metaphorical. In the course of this book, I mostly focus on clearer cases of metaphoricity, but I assume that uses of 'make' such as this are indeed metaphorical, however weakly (see Cameron 2003: 72–3; Pragglejaz Group 2007: 29).

The noun 'progress' in 'make progress' in extract 1.7 exemplifies a different kind of borderline case. The contextual meaning here is to do with positive change, and particularly with persuading others to make decisions on trade that would positively affect poor African nations. This corresponds to the main current meaning of the word, which the Macmillan dictionary expresses as 'the process of developing or improving'. If we regard this as the basic meaning of 'progress', the use of the noun in the G8 article would clearly not be metaphorical. However, the noun 'progress' also has a rather archaic meaning of 'forward movement', which is included in the Macmillan dictionary but with the description 'mainly literary' (the example given in the dictionary is 'the ship's slow progress across the harbour'). If this meaning is taken as the basic meaning of the word, 'progress' would count as a metaphorically used word.

From the point of view of the history of the word, there is no question that the contextual meaning of 'progress' developed as a metaphorical use of the physical meaning of moving forward. Within CMT, this can be explained in terms of the conceptual metaphors CHANGE IS MOTION and PURPOSES ARE DESTINATIONS. The borderline status of 'progress' in terms of metaphoricity is due to the fact that the basic, nonmetaphorical meaning is becoming obsolete, with a consequent loss of the contrast between metaphorical and nonmetaphorical uses in present-day English. If this process continues, the metaphoricity of 'progress' will survive only in the history of the word, as is the case, for example, for 'declared', as used in extract 1.2 above. In present-day English, the verb has no basic meaning to contrast with the contextual meaning of 'saying something in an official manner'. However, the verb derives from the Latin 'declarare', which originally meant 'to make something clear' in a visual sense (the adjective 'clarus' meant 'clear, bright'). In other words, the verb developed its current meaning from a metaphorical construction of communication as enabling vision (see Semino 2005), but has no nonmetaphorical sense in present-day English. Expressions such as these have been described as 'historical' or 'etymological' metaphors (Deignan 2005; Knowles and Moon 2006). The fact that the MIP procedure spells out that basic meanings need to be 'contemporary' or 'current' is aimed precisely at distinguishing the metaphoricity of 'battle' in extract 1.1 from the metaphoricity of 'declared' in extract 1.2. 'Battle' is used metaphorically because its meaning in the article can be contrasted with the meaning expressed by current nonmetaphorical uses. 'Declared' is not used metaphorically because its meaning in the article cannot be contrasted with current nonmetaphorical uses. The use of 'progress' in extract 1.7 lies somewhere in-between.[11]

The use of an explicit procedure such as MIP can help analysts identify the main types of problematic cases, and deal with them consistently and systematically. As I have shown, dictionaries may also be useful in determining

[11] It would be possible, of course, to modify the MIP procedure so that it would include etymological metaphors. It is also worth noting that the tendency for earlier meanings of words to be more concrete than later meanings is well known in historical linguistics (e.g. Sweetser 1990, Traugott and Dasher 2002).

current meanings, in spite of their inevitable limitations. Ideally, however, the dictionaries used for this purpose should be corpus-based, namely they should have been compiled with reference to large, relevant corpora of the language, as in the case of the Macmillan dictionary I have referred to in this section (see Pragglejaz Group 2007). The relevance of corpora for the study of metaphor will be demonstrated throughout this book, and is the topic of chapter 6.

Similes The approach I have just described to the identification of metaphorical expressions does not exhaust all manifestations of metaphoricity in language, or, in CMT terms, all the linguistic phenomena that may realize mappings across different conceptual domains. One such phenomenon that features consistently in this book is simile: an explicit statement of comparison between two different things, conveyed through the use of expressions such as 'like', 'as', 'as if' and so on. Consider, for example, extract 1.8 below, which is taken from Zadie Smith's (2005) novel *On Beauty*. In the extract, Jerome, who has briefly returned home from university, is struggling to keep the conversation going with his younger teenage brother Levi:

1.8 They were both nodding a lot. Sadness swept over Jerome. They had nothing to say to each other. A five-year age gap between siblings is like a garden that needs constant attention. Even three months apart allows the weeds to grow up between you. (Smith 2005: 403)

In the third sentence of the extract, a simile is used to express a particular perception of the reason why the two brothers are finding it difficult to talk: 'A five-year age gap between siblings is like a garden that needs constant attention.' Here the noun 'garden' is not a metaphorical expression according to approaches such as MIP, since it is in fact used in its basic, physical meaning. However, like metaphorical expressions, similes are a way of talking about one thing (a five-year age gap between siblings) in terms of another (a garden that needs to be tended to). Within CMT, they are indeed seen as a type of linguistic realization of cross-domain mappings, although some studies have suggested several important differences between similes and metaphors (Chiappe *et al.* 2003; Gentner and Bowdle 2005).[12] In the extract above, the use of the simile in the third sentence evokes what we may call a GARDEN source scenario, and invites readers to map some material from this scenario onto the target concept of a five-year gap between two brothers. In the following sentence, several lexical items relating to the same source scenario are then used metaphorically

[12] It is important to note that not all statements involving words such as 'like' are similes in the sense intended here. I am concerned with cases where the two elements of the comparison are part of different conceptual domains. This applies, for example, in cases such as 'Encyclopaedias are like goldmines,' but not to cases such as 'Encyclopaedias are like dictionaries' (see Ortony 1993).

to specify what aspects of this scenario are to be mapped onto the target (see 'weeds', 'grow up' and 'between'). In other words, the description of the age gap as a garden is expressed first via a simile and then via metaphorically used words. In the course of the book, I discuss further examples of this kind of textual interaction between similes and metaphorical uses of words, which is particularly common when the metaphorical comparison is rather unconventional, as in extract 1.8.

1.2.2 *Variation in metaphorical expressions: word class, multi-word expressions and conventionality*

I have already begun to show that metaphorical expressions may occur as single words belonging to different word classes, or as groups of related words occurring in close proximity to one another. I have also already pointed out some degree of variation in the degree of conventionality or novelty of individual uses. In this section I consider in more detail these aspects of variation in metaphorical expressions.

Metaphor and word class The most prototypical examples of metaphorical expressions tend to involve nouns, such as 'battle' in 'a battle of metaphors' (see extract 1.1) and 'whisper' in 'the G8 had uttered "a whisper" ' (see extract 1.4). Because nouns typically refer to entities, it tends to be reasonably straightforward to establish, and possibly perceive, a contrast between contextual and basic meanings (see Goatly 1997: 83). However, many metaphorical expressions are in fact not nouns. In her work on classroom interaction, for example, Cameron (2003: 88) found that linguistic metaphors involving nouns or noun phrases only accounted for 13 per cent of all cases. This proportion was lower than that for metaphors involving verbs (47 per cent) and prepositions (34 per cent). Examples of metaphorically used verbs in the G8 article include 'climbed' in 'A mountain has been climbed,' 'look down' and 'come' in 'let's also look down on the valley from where we've come' (see extract 1.2), and the delexicalized use of 'make' in 'he had failed to make progress' (see extract 1.7). In Cameron's data, cases of metaphorically used adjectives were infrequent (just over 3 per cent of all cases), but the G8 article does include several examples, such as 'full' and 'empty' in the headline, and 'big' in 'big "but" ' (see extract 1.2). The metaphorical use of adverbs is even less frequent in Cameron's data, where it accounts for only 1 per cent of linguistic metaphors. The few instances contained in the G8 article include 'longer' in the expression 'African countries should no longer be forced to liberalize their markets' and 'far' in the expression 'The debt relief doesn't go far enough' (see also Koller 2004b; Deignan 2005, who both found that the relative frequencies of metaphorical expressions belonging to different word classes can vary depending on the source domain).

'Closed-class' words (also known as 'function' or 'grammatical' words) vary in their potential for metaphorical uses as defined in this chapter, depending on whether they have enough semantic content to establish a distinction between contextual and basic meanings. Prepositions tend to have well-defined physical basic meanings which have given rise to a wide range of abstract and highly conventional metaphorical meanings. The G8 article contains several instances of metaphorically used prepositions, such as 'over' in 'over the last three days' (see extract 1.1) and 'on' in the sentence 'On trade, the buck was passed onto the trade talks in Hong Kong later this year.' Both prepositions have spatial basic meanings, but in the quotations above 'over' is used in relation to time, and 'on' is used to indicate the topic of discussions and decisions. Other types of function words have very abstract grammatical meanings, which cannot easily be exploited for the kinds of metaphorical uses I consider in this book. The article does, however, contain a few further examples, such as the use of the spatial relative pronoun 'where' to refer to the pre-summit situation in 'the valley from where we've come' (see extract 1.2).[13]

As I mentioned in section 1.1, in this book I do not normally consider 'historical' or 'etymological' linguistic metaphors, namely those cases where the current meaning of a word is metaphorical in origin, but where the word has no current nonmetaphorical uses. This applies, for example, to the verb 'declare', which is discussed in the previous section, and to the verb 'comprehend' which is derived from the Latin 'comprehendere', 'to grasp'. The metaphorical expressions I do consider, however, vary significantly in the degree to which their metaphorical uses are conventional in English. A number of classifications have been proposed to distinguish between different types of conventional metaphorical expressions (see Goatly 1997: 31–5; Deignan 2005: 39–47). Here I assume that conventionality is a matter of degree, but, for the purposes of my analyses, I mostly operate with a broad distinction between conventional and novel

[13] The process of deriving new words from existing words also often involves the creation of metaphorical meanings (see Goatly 1997: 92–106). The verb 'to parrot', for example, is derived from the noun 'parrot'. The noun has a fairly obvious basic meaning to do with the relevant bird. The verb, in contrast, does not have a basic meaning to do with the bird's behaviour, but is used exclusively to describe a particular human behaviour in terms of parrots' ability to imitate human sounds. The Macmillan dictionary defines the meaning of the verb as follows: 'to copy or repeat what someone says without thinking about it or understanding it properly'. All eleven instances of the verb in the BNC are indeed used in this way, as in 'to get on in education you must parrot the latest jargon'. In cases such as this, the verb itself has no basic meaning that contrasts with the contextual meaning. The same applies to other similar verbs derived from nouns referring to animals (e.g. 'to dog', 'to squirrel'), as well as to many other cases of derived words (e.g. 'further' as an adverb and verb, and so on). However, the metaphoricity of such examples can be captured by the MIP procedure by allowing the crossing of word-class boundaries in the search for the basic meanings of lexical units in step 3b (Pragglejaz Group 2007: 27–8; see also Deignan 2005: 48).

metaphorical expressions. I regard metaphorical expressions as conventional when the relevant metaphorical meaning has become lexicalized, so that it is normally included in dictionaries alongside nonmetaphorical (basic) meanings. This applies to almost all of the metaphorical expressions in the G8 article, including 'battle' (see extract 1.1), 'army' (see extract 1.2), etc. Conventional metaphorical expressions will vary, however, in the extent to which they can be readily perceived as metaphorical by 'ordinary' language users: in extract 1.1, for example, the metaphoricity of 'battle' is more easily noticeable than that of 'summit'; similarly, the metaphoricity of 'summit' is more easily noticeable than that of 'on' in 'on trade'. Conversely, I regard metaphorical expressions as novel, creative, or innovative when the relevant metaphorical meaning has not become lexicalized, and is therefore not included in dictionaries. As a result, the metaphorical expressions I describe as novel will also vary considerably in terms of their strikingness, originality and potential aesthetic effects. The G8 article does not abound in novel metaphorical expressions, but the use of 'peaks' in extract 1.2 and 'whisper' in extract 1.4 can be considered as such cases. Where appropriate, I will also carry out corpus searches to establish the degree of conventionality of particular metaphorical uses, since, as Deignan puts it,

> [t]he boundary between innovative and conventionalised metaphors is fuzzy rather than stark . . . Nonetheless in the analysis of concordance citations, the difficulty of deciding on cases of innovative metaphor arises only rarely, because innovative metaphors are infrequent. Corpus frequencies can be used as a rough guide: any sense of a word that is found less than once in every thousand citations can be considered either innovative or rare. (Deignan 2005: 40)

In the next chapter, I also consider the issue of conventionality and creativity in terms of conceptual metaphors.

As I have already mentioned, variation in the degree of conventionality affects the extent to which the metaphorical use of a particular expression is likely to be conscious and deliberate on the part of its user, and recognized and/or processed as such by its receivers. Other things being equal, the more conventional a metaphorical expression, the less likely it is that it will be consciously used and recognized as a metaphor. However, things are not always equal, and co-text (including both language and pictures) may draw attention to the metaphoricity of highly conventional metaphorical expressions. For example, I have already described 'progress' as a borderline case in terms of metaphoricity, since its basic meaning to do with forward movement is becoming archaic. However, in extract 1.3, Blair's use of 'progress' is preceded by another movement metaphor in 'Politics is about getting things done <u>step by step</u>.' This makes it a little more likely that readers familiar with the movement meaning of 'progress' will become aware of its metaphoricity.

It is also possible for someone to draw attention to the metaphoricity of a conventional metaphorical expression to create humorous effects. The extract below is a transcription of part of a conversation that took place in January 2007 between the presenter of a phone-in radio programme on the UK channel *Classic FM* and a caller. The caller has just said that, although she is 62 years old, she is learning to play the piano, and has just passed the Grade 6 exam:

1.9	Radio presenter:	I have always wanted to pick up the piano myself
	Caller:	Not literally

The radio presenter uses the phrasal verb 'pick up' in the highly conventional metaphorical meaning of 'learning something new'. By responding 'not literally' the caller draws attention to the metaphoricity of this use of 'pick up', in contrast with the basic meaning of 'lifting something'. This humorously evokes a scenario where the presenter is lifting the instrument, rather than learning how to play it, and shows how even highly conventional metaphorical expressions have the potential to be consciously recognized as metaphorical. Goatly (1997: 276–7) calls this phenomenon the 'revitalization' of metaphors.

A further, less obvious contrast between the two interpretations of the presenter's utterance concerns the meaning of the noun phrase 'the piano'. If 'pick up' is used metaphorically, 'the piano' does not refer to the instrument as a physical object, but rather to the process of playing it. This is an example of metonymy, which involves talking about something in terms of something else that is closely associated with it, often via a relationship of contiguity. In CMT terms, the two elements of the metonymy (e.g. the piano as an object and the process of playing the piano) are elements of the same conceptual domain, rather than elements of different domains, as is the case with metaphor. In other words, metonymy involves a mapping between elements that can be seen as part of the same conceptual domain, rather than between elements belonging to different domains (Lakoff and Johnson 1980b: 35–40; 2003: 265–6; Kövecses 2002: 143–61). Metaphor and metonymy are separate but overlapping phenomena, and frequently interact in language use (Goossens *et al.* 1995; Deignan 2005: 53–71). Although I do not focus specifically on metonymy, I will discuss some further cases of interaction with metaphor in the course of the book.

Metaphor and multi-word expressions The examples I have considered so far in this section have already shown that metaphorically used words frequently occur as part of multi-word expressions, rather than individually. These multi-word expressions vary in length, structure and degree of fixedness. I have already mentioned how the expression 'A mountain has been climbed' is a rather unusual passive form of a semi-fixed expression which is normally clausal in form and has several conventional variants. The same applies to the expression exploited in the headline ('Half full or half empty?'), which is then reiterated in the body of the article in a fuller form: 'Was, asked some, the cup half full or half empty?' In contrast, 'play ball' in the expression 'Bob Geldof would not play ball', from the G8 article, consists of a verb and its direct object and normally allows for relatively little formal variation, other than the various forms of the verb 'play'.

Deignan (2005) has pointed out that metaphorically used words have a noticeable tendency to occur in fixed or semi-fixed expressions, which often have idiomatic meanings (see also Moon 1998). In some cases, the metaphoricity of these multi-word expressions can be explained in terms of general conventional conceptual metaphors, as in the case of Bono's mountain-climbing metaphorical scenario (see also Gibbs 1994: 290–5; Moon 1998: 202–7). In other cases, these multi-word expressions can only be explained in terms of specific, one-off mappings that rely on very specific source scenarios. This applies, for example, to the expression exploited in the headline ('Half full or half empty?'). Moon also discusses variation in the degree of semantic 'transparency' of metaphorical fixed expressions (see Moon 1998: 22). Some expressions have fairly transparent metaphorical meanings, which can be arrived at on the basis of general world knowledge, as in the case of 'alarm bells ring'. Other fixed expressions are rather opaque, often because the scenario they are based on is no longer familiar to language users. This applies, for example, to 'passing the buck', which originated from a practice used by poker players in nineteenth-century America (in order to avoid cheating, players took it in turns to deal the cards; the player who was next in line to do so would be given a marker, which became known as the 'buck' because it was usually a knife with a handle made of buck's horn; when an individual had taken their turn, or did not want to deal, they passed the buck on to the next person).

The metaphoricity of fixed expressions can be creatively exploited by going beyond the conventional range of variation in form and lexical choices. This is the case in Bono's exploitation of the expression 'have a mountain to climb' in the G8 article: as I have already mentioned, Bono not only uses a passive construction, but goes on to talk about 'higher peaks' and 'the valley from where we've come', which are not part of the conventional linguistic realizations of the mountain-climbing metaphor. The G8 article's author also plays creatively with the fixed expression 'comrade in arms' by turning it into 'comrade in alms' (see extract 1.2), where 'alms' is phonetically similar to 'arms' and semantically appropriate to Geldof and Bono's activities.

Another case of creative exploitation is displayed in extract 1.10 below, which was emailed by one of my colleagues to our staff list in May 2004, after a successful review of teaching quality in our Department. The member of staff who had coordinated the review had just circulated a message of thanks to colleagues for their cooperation. This had triggered a series of emails congratulating the coordinator himself, including the following (the email below also congratulates the Departmental Officer, whose name has here been changed to 'Carol'):

1.10 To keep sight of the wood so clearly when there is just so much growing – and so fast – takes a lot of doing: well done to you, and to Carol.

The writer of the email creatively exploits the conventional expression 'can't see the wood for the trees', in which the negative consequences of an excessive concentration on detail are metaphorically presented in terms of a paradoxical scenario where someone's perception of a multitude of trees prevents him or her from seeing the wood that they form. The email does not just go beyond the normal range of variation of the expression, for example by using 'to keep sight of' instead of 'see'; it also includes some instances of metaphorical lexis that further exploit the WOOD metaphorical scenario by presenting it as growing, and growing fast. This emphasizes the achievement of the coordinator and the Departmental Officer, who are congratulated for having been able to cope with the complexity of an increasing set of tasks without being overwhelmed by them.

So far, I have discussed conventionality and novelty in terms of the lexicalization and formal characteristics of particular metaphorical uses of words or multi-word expressions. In the next chapter, I also consider conventionality and novelty in terms of conceptual mappings (see Lakoff and Turner 1989). In the next section, I turn to the patterning of metaphorical expressions within texts.

1.2.3 The patterning of metaphors in discourse

In order to appreciate the functioning of metaphors in texts, one needs to consider the various kinds of textual manifestations that metaphor may exhibit. In this section, I build on a number of previous studies (notably Goatly 1997, Darian 2000, Cameron and Stelma 2004) in order to introduce the main types of textual phenomena that will be shown to be significant across different genres in subsequent chapters. I should emphasize that the various phenomena I describe do not have clear-cut boundaries, but often overlap and co-occur with one another.

Repetition The simplest kind of pattern involves the repetition of particular metaphorical expressions in the course of a text. The G8 article contains several instances of repetition, which also differ from each other in interesting ways. The noun 'progress', which I have discussed as a borderline case of metaphoricity, occurs four times in the article: two occurrences are attributed to Blair, while the other two are used by the author of the article himself. However, all instances have similar contextual meanings (i.e. that of achieving positive change), and can therefore be explained in terms of the same underlying conceptual mapping of the notion of forward movement onto (positive) development. Similarly, the multi-word expression used in the headline, 'half full or half empty', is repeated in fuller form at the beginning of the article (see extract 1.1), and is used in both cases to capture the fact that there have been both positive and negative assessments of the outcome of the summit. This kind of repetition tends to be closely related to the topic and argument of the text, and to contributes to its internal coherence.

The adjective 'big', in contrast, has four occurrences in the article, at least two of which are metaphorical according to the criteria given above. However, the contextual meanings are different in each case. In 'it was a big "but" ' (see extract 1.2), the adjective is used in relation to the seriousness and importance of the objection introduced by the conjunction 'but' (note that here the conjunction stands metonymically for the objection itself). In the expression 'the write-offs should be bigger', the comparative form of the adjective is used in relation to the amounts of money involved in debt cancellation in favour of African nations. In both cases, the relevant basic meaning is that of large size, but the contextual meanings are different, and can be explained in terms of different underlying conceptual metaphors, namely IMPORTANT IS BIG for the first use above and QUANTITY IS SIZE for the second use (Grady 1997a: 285; Lakoff and Johnson 1999: 50). This kind of repetition tends to be more loosely related to the topic of the text in which it occurs, and is rather indicative of the metaphorical productivity of particular concepts, such as size, which can be applied metaphorically to a variety of other, more abstract, concepts. This example also shows a looser kind of repetition in formal terms, since 'bigger' and 'big' are different morphological variants of the same adjective (see also Goatly 1997: 257–8 and Darian 2000).

Recurrence A similar phenomenon is recurrence, which involves the use of different expressions relating to the same broad source domain in different parts of a text (see also Darian 2000 and Goatly's notions of 'modification' and 'multivalency'). For example, in the G8 article, I have identified three different metaphorical expressions that can be related to the source domain of WAR, namely: '<u>battle</u> of metaphors' (see extract 1.1), '<u>army</u> of charity workers' (see extract 1.2), and '<u>combating</u> climate change'. The latter two expressions, although not explicitly or textually connected, reflect a general conventional tendency to construct difficult enterprises in terms of struggle and military action. In the G8 article, these two expressions contribute to a more specific textual construction of action against poverty and environmental damage in terms of war. The use of 'battle' in extract 1.1, as I have already mentioned, reflects a general tendency to construct arguments in terms of physical conflict, as well as a textual strategy to dramatize and polarize the disagreements over the outcome of the summit.

In other words, recurrence is often an important phenomenon in at least two respects. On the one hand, it is indicative of how some aspect of reality is constructed in a text (or in different texts on the same topic). On the other hand, it can be indicative of the kinds of source domains that tend to be conventionally applied to a range of target domains: WAR, for example, is conventionally exploited not just to construct arguments but also difficult enterprises generally. In Kövecses's (2002: 107–18) terms, source domains such as WAR have a wide metaphorical 'scope'.

As I will show throughout this book, a combination of repetition and recurrence can lead to the formation of 'chains' of connected metaphorical expressions in texts (see also Koller 2003).

Clustering It has been noted that metaphorical expressions are often distributed unevenly in texts, and that some portions of text may display particularly high densities of metaphorically used words. The use of several different metaphorical expressions drawing from different source domains in close proximity to one another can be defined as a 'cluster' of metaphors (see Koller 2003; Cameron and Low 2004; Cameron and Stelma 2004). Clusters are difficult to define and identify precisely, since decisions about clustering involves assumptions or calculations about the 'normal' density of metaphorical expressions in a particular kind of data, and the identification of a portion of text where the density is higher than normal (see Cameron and Stelma 2004). The example below is an extract from the spoken part of the BNC, which immediately follows a woman's announcement that she suffered from postnatal depression after her second child. I have underlined the words that I regard as metaphorically used:

1.11 And I fought it for a long time and I wanted to get kick-started back to where I was before, because I felt under a cloud.

In this stretch of text (which has been transcribed as a single sentence in the BNC), I have identified 9 out of 26 words as metaphorical. This corresponds to approximately 35 per cent of the words, or to 350 words per 1,000. In various studies on spoken data, Cameron has found that the average density of metaphorical expressions varies between 27 and 107 per 1,000 words (see Cameron and Stelma 2004: 20). This suggests that extract 1.11 does have an unusually high metaphorical density.

The importance of clusters, however, goes well beyond their statistical aspect. In the press, for example, metaphor clusters are often used in strategic positions for rhetorical purposes. For example, metaphorical clusters may occur at the beginning of newspaper articles in order to 'frame' the issues under discussion, and at the end of the article in order to summarize the overall argument in a persuasive and striking fashion (see Koller 2003). In speech, metaphor clusters have been found to correspond to particularly significant points, where speakers are doing something that is central to their overall goals, such as providing explanations in lectures, or achieving convergence in conciliation talk (see Corts and Pollio 1999; Cameron and Stelma 2004). In extract 1.11, for example, the speaker is attempting to convey her feelings at a particularly difficult point in her life, when she was going through an experience which is difficult to convey using nonmetaphorical language. Indeed, the metaphorical expressions she uses primarily relate to her mental state during the depression ('under a cloud'), and to her attempt to recover from it ('fought', 'get kick-started back to where I was before'). These metaphorical expressions construct the woman's experience in terms of several different source domains, namely WAR/PHYSICAL CONFLICT ('fought'), MOVEMENT/VEHICLES ('get kick-started back to where I was before'), and DOWN/WEATHER ('under a cloud') (see also Goatly's 1997 notion of 'diversification'). Metaphors for depression are discussed in more detail in chapter 5.

Extension The phenomenon traditionally known as 'extended' metaphor can be seen as a particular type of cluster, where several metaphorical expressions belonging to the same semantic field or evoking the same source domain are used in close proximity to one another in relation to the same topic, or to elements of the same target domain. As with clusters, it is difficult to define and identify this phenomenon with complete precision. Definitions vary, and are not usually fully explicit about how many metaphorically used words need to be involved and what grammatical boundaries need to be crossed in order for extension to apply (see Leech 1969: 159; Goatly 1997: 264–5; Darian 2000). In this book I use the term when at least two metaphorically used words belonging to different phrases describe the same target domain/scenario in terms of the same source domain/scenario. The MOUNTAIN CLIMBING metaphor attributed to Bono clearly involves extension, since several lexical items from the source scenario are used in four different clauses.

Another example is given in the extract below, which is taken from a newspaper article commenting on the UK Conservative party during their 2004 national conference:

1.12 The Tories start their conference . . . desperately sick – and tired. Leading lights in the party are crippled by life-threatening anaemia, loss of appetite and delusions of grandeur. Troops have been laid low by the Ukip superbug, which devastated the Hartlepool byelection and threatens to spread its spores nationwide. (Trevor Kavanagh, *The Sun*, 4 October 2004)

Here the condition of the Tories at the start of their conference is described in terms of physical illness via a number of different expressions in two consecutive sentences. In the extract, I have underlined what I see as the relevant metaphorical expressions (but not *all* metaphorical expressions, which would include, for example, 'lights' in the second sentence and 'troops' and 'devastated' in the third). Decisions about what to underline were not straightforward, and you may well decide that you would have done it differently. Some metaphorical expressions are clearly to do with illness and viruses (e.g. anaemia, superbug,[14] spores), others less so ('loss of appetite', 'delusions of grandeur'); some expressions are highly conventional (e.g. 'crippled'), others less so (e.g. superbug); some expressions refer to illnesses ('anaemia'), others to symptoms ('loss of appetite'), others to causes of illness ('superbug', 'spores'). However, it could be argued that the occurrence of 'sick' in the first sentence of the extract facilitates an interpretation in which all these expressions are part of a single lexical field and evoke a single metaphorical scenario of ILLNESS. Cameron and Low (2004) have suggested that, once textually established, a metaphor can 'attract' other metaphorical expressions that are only loosely connected with it. The use of 'sick' in the first sentence of extract 1.12 arguably 'attracts' into a single extended metaphor expressions that are different in terms of their conventionality and in terms of the strength of their association with illness (for example, the notion of 'delusions of grandeur' as a symptom of mental illness can be made relevant here, in contrast with other contexts).

All this highlights the important point that conceptual 'domains' or 'scenarios' should not be seen as entirely fixed and stable mental representations, but rather as flexible cognitive structures that are partly constructed on the basis of the textual input. Extract 1.12 also shows that extended metaphors often co-occur and interact with other metaphors. The extract can in fact be seen as an example of a cluster which includes an extended metaphor alongside other non-extended metaphors, such as the description of party members as 'troops'. I will return to this example below.

Combination and mixing Metaphorical expressions drawing from different source domains frequently occur in close proximity to one another, and can interact in different ways. The use of 'troops' in extract 1.12 introduces a military metaphor within the 'illness' extended metaphor I have just described. This results in a metaphorical scenario in which party members are soldiers who are progressively falling ill. In other words, the 'troops' metaphor is compatible

[14] The term 'superbug' is well-known to British readers, as it is normally used in the media to refer to particularly powerful bacteria that cause infections among hospital patients. Ukip is the acronym for the 'UK Independent Party', which had undermined Tory support in some parts of the country.

with the 'illness' metaphor and can be combined with it to produce a single more complex metaphorical scenario.

The situation is different, however, for the earlier description of party leaders in 'Leading lights in the party are crippled by . . .'. The metaphorical description of prominent conservatives as 'lights' potentially clashes both with their description as 'Leading' within the same noun phrase and with their description as becoming 'crippled' in the following verb phrase (of which 'Leading lights in the party' is the grammatical subject). The 'lights' metaphor, in particular, cannot be incorporated within the 'illness' scenario. This kind of (potential) clash between different metaphors has been traditionally referred to as 'mixed metaphor', and stigmatized as an indication of a poor command of language. In fact, potentially clashing metaphorical expressions are very frequently used in close proximity to one another, but their mutual incongruity often goes unnoticed, as may well have been the case when you first read extract 1.12. In addition, there is, inevitably, a rather fuzzy boundary between the combination of compatible metaphors and the mixing of incompatible ones.

Literal–metaphorical oppositions The metaphorical and basic meanings of particular expressions may be evoked simultaneously in particular stretches of texts, often to achieve humorous effects (see also Goatly's 'literalization of vehicles'; 1997: 272–9). For example, a newspaper article on the conflict between South Africa and Morocco over control of Western Sahara was introduced by the headline 'Diplomatic desert' (*Guardian Unlimited*, 27 September 2004). Here the noun 'desert' is used metaphorically to indicate the lack of diplomatic relationships between the two countries as a consequence of their disagreements. However, the literal meaning of 'desert' also applies to the situation described in the article, since the disputed land is part of the Sahara desert. This kind of metaphorical punning is particularly characteristic of newspaper headlines. In these cases, the choice of the metaphor can be described as 'topic-triggered' (Koller 2004a): an aspect of the topic under discussion (e.g. the Western Sahara desert) inspires the choice of the metaphorical source domain or scenario that is evoked via the metaphorical expressions used in the text (see also Kövecses 2005: 236–9). In the course of the book, I will show how topic-triggered metaphors can also be used for rhetorical purposes other than the creation of humour.

Signalling Metaphorical expressions may in some cases be accompanied by linguistic devices that draw attention to the presence of metaphoricity in the immediate co-text, and that potentially guide readers' or listeners' interpretations. These linguistic devices have been referred to as 'signals' or 'tuning devices', and include expressions such as 'metaphorically speaking', 'literally', 'as it were', 'so to speak', 'sort of', 'imagine' and so on (see Goatly

1997; Cameron and Deignan 2003: 168). Two examples from the BNC are given below. Extract 1.13 is taken from a lecture in a university law school; extract 1.14 is part of a quotation from a biography of Archbishop Michael Ramsey (signalling expressions are underlined).

1.13. The first session is designed to be one that gives y – gets you accustomed to advocacy, to be non-threatening, and to be one where you can simply literally find your feet and get used to advocating in that way.

1.14 He projected himself as a man who would be worth listening to. He spoke weightily – the words deliberately produced and, as it were, laid on the table.

In extract 1.13, the adverb 'literally' precedes the metaphorical expression 'find your feet', while in extract 1.14 the conditional clause 'as it were' precedes the metaphorical expression 'laid on the table'. In both cases, the signalling devices seem to draw attention to the metaphoricity of what follows. In addition, the somewhat paradoxical use of 'literally' as a signal of metaphoricity often emphasizes the appropriateness of the choice of metaphorical expression, while 'as it were' tends to hedge or tone down the force of the metaphor (see Goatly 1997: 173, 193). These general tendencies arguably apply to the examples above.

Different signalling expressions have different specific effects and patterns of use (see Goatly 1997: 168–97). On the whole, however, they seem to be used primarily to guide the interpretation of metaphorical choices that may be partly unexpected in the particular co-texts and contexts in which they occur (Cameron and Deignan 2003). A variety of different examples are discussed in the course of the book.

Intertextual relations The G8 article shows how (relatively) novel and salient metaphorical expressions often provide quotable material in the production of media texts, and therefore participate in the establishment of intertextual relationships between different texts (e.g. between the G8 article and the original statements by Bono and others). Throughout this book, I will discuss a variety of further and often more complex cases of intertextuality in the use of metaphor (see also Musolff 2004).[15] This requires a few words of clarification on issues of terminology.

I use the term 'text' to refer to individual and relatively self-contained instances of language use. The term applies most straightforwardly to instances of writing (e.g. the G8 article, the email quoted as extract 1.10, Zadie Smith's novel *On Beauty*), but also includes instances of spoken language use (e.g.

[15] I do not have the space to do justice to the different phenomena that can be subsumed under the term 'intertextuality', and to the vast literature that is devoted to it (but see Allen 2000 for an overview).

a speech by Tony Blair, the lecture from which extract 1.13 is taken). More informal instances of spoken language use, such as utterances or turns in conversation, are less easy to include under the term 'text'. In most cases, however, I use 'text' in a broad sense, to include all kinds of instances of language use. In some cases, I mention 'utterances' alongside 'texts' in order to emphasize the applicability of a particular point to both speech and writing. I do not deal systematically with multimodal texts, but I will consider some instances of visual metaphor in the course of the book.

I use the term 'genre' or 'text type' to refer to conventionalized uses of language that are linked to particular activities, such as newspaper articles, novels, print advertisements, lectures, informal conversations and so on (see Fairclough 1992: 126; Wodak and Meyer 2001: 66). I use the term 'discourse' as a count noun (i.e. with 'discourses' as plural) to refer to ways of speaking or writing about particular topics (e.g. medical discourse) or in particular settings (e.g. classroom discourse), usually from particular perspectives.[16] This differs from my use of 'discourse' as a non-count noun (i.e. without a plural) to refer generally to naturally occurring language use, as in the title of this book.

Metaphorical expressions can be part of the intertextual relationships between different texts in a variety of ways. A particularly salient and/or controversial use of metaphor in a particular text may be subsequently exploited and developed in other texts from different genres, in order to express agreement or disagreement with the original producer of the metaphor (see also Musolff 2004). In chapter 3, I show how a salient metaphorical statement produced by British Prime Minister Tony Blair during a conference speech in 2003 was repeatedly exploited by journalists and political opponents to express a range of critical views towards him. In other cases, a specific metaphor may become closely associated with a particular issue, resulting in intertextual connections in metaphor use across texts dealing with that issue, albeit in a variety of ways. In chapter 3, I discuss in detail the metaphor of the 'Road Map' for the solution of the Israeli–Palestinian conflict, which was originally used in a prominent official document, and then became, for a time at least, a central component of the discourse surrounding problems in the Middle East.[17]

[16] The labels that I use to refer to discourses may be more or less descriptive or interpretive, i.e. they may be more or less dependent on my own views and evaluations as an analyst: while the label 'classroom discourse' is largely descriptive, for example, the label 'racist discourse' is interpretive (see Sunderland 2004 for this distinction; see also Fairclough 1992: 127–8, Wodak 2001: 66).

[17] Zinken (2003) has made a distinction between 'correlational' and 'intertextual' metaphors: the former are based in systematic correlations in bodily experience, while the latter are cultural in origin (e.g. 'Scientific progress leads to new Frankensteins'). In his data, Zinken found that purely intertextual metaphors accounted for less than 10 per cent of cases, but they are more frequent in crucial parts of texts, notably headlines, picture captions and beginnings and endings. Here I am concerned with a different phenomenon, namely intertextual connections between different uses of metaphors that are normally 'conceptual' or 'correlational' in origin.

The overview I have provided in this section does not do justice to all the varied types of textual phenomena and patterns that may be relevant to the study of metaphor, but introduces the main notions that are exploited in the course of the book. Some further relevant phenomena are discussed in relation to specific examples in the following chapters (see Goatly 1997: 25–82 for a useful overview). I should also emphasize once again that the types of textual patterns I have discussed are not neatly separate phenomena, but often overlap and co-occur with each other in texts. For example, an instance of extended metaphor may be part of a larger metaphorical cluster, as we have seen, and may in some cases be difficult to distinguish from recurrence: whether two related metaphorical expressions constitute extension or recurrence depends on whether they are analysed as textually close or distant, a distinction that is not always easy to make. In addition, some instances of recurrent metaphor may also be textually extended. Nonetheless, the concepts I have introduced so far will prove useful in discussing the textual manifestations of metaphor in the rest of this book.

1.2.4 The functions of metaphors in discourse

I have already mentioned the most general function of metaphor in language and thought, namely the possibility of talking and thinking about something in terms of something else. Within CMT, it is claimed more specifically that metaphor enables us to think and talk about abstract, complex, subjective and/or poorly delineated areas of experience in terms of concrete, simpler, physical and/or better delineated areas of experience, often connected with our own bodies. This makes metaphor a crucial linguistic and cognitive phenomenon, and explains the amount of attention metaphor has received over the centuries and in recent years. In fact, it has even been suggested that metaphor is an important part of the capacity for creativity and innovation that led to the development of modern humans in the course of evolution (see Mithen 1998).

However, in order to explain the use of metaphor in discourse one needs to consider the range of more specific functions that metaphor can have in communication. This applies particularly when metaphorical expressions are chosen among many possible alternatives, or when creativity and textual patterning are also involved. For example, the temporal use of spatial prepositions such as ‘in’ or ‘on’ (e.g. ‘in 1945’ or ‘on that day’) is not just highly conventional, but almost unavoidable, since in English (and in many other languages), time is consistently structured metaphorically in terms of space (e.g. Lakoff and Johnson 1999: 137–69). By contrast, in the G8 article metaphorical expressions such as ‘battle’ in ‘a battle of metaphor’, or ‘army’ in ‘the army of charity workers’, or ‘combating’ in ‘combating climate change’ were used as alternatives

to other possible metaphorical or nonmetaphorical expressions, such as 'difference', 'large number' or 'dealing with'. As such, they do not just reflect the wide metaphorical scope of the WAR source domain in English and, in the case of 'battle', the conceptual metaphor ARGUMENT IS WAR. They can also be related to a more specific contemporary tendency to construct debates over development and the environment in terms of war, and to the writer's goal to dramatize events and polarize contrasts in order to emphasize the newsworthiness of the contents of the article.

In other words, general theories of metaphor such as CMT consider broad questions such as: *Why do particular metaphorical patterns occur in a particular language or languages?* This kind of question is answered with reference to the role of bodily, physical, concrete experiences such as space in the construction of more abstract, complex and poorly delineated experiences such as time. The role of culture is also increasingly taken into account (see Kövecses 2005). However, the study of metaphor in discourse also involves more specific questions such as: *Why do particular metaphorical choices and patterns occur in particular texts, genres or discourses?* This kind of question is answered with reference to the role, identities and goals of addressers and addressees, their mutual relationships, and the relevant co-text and context, broadly conceived (i.e. including situational, social, political, historical and cultural aspects). These two kinds of questions have different emphases but are also interconnected. In this book, I am primarily concerned with the second kind of question, but I will also consistently consider the relationship between the specific uses of metaphor in the texts I analyse and conventional patterns in language generally.

The main set of functions of metaphors in discourse relates to the representation of (particular aspects of) reality. Since metaphor involves constructing something in terms of something else, the choice of the 'something else' (or source domain) affects how the 'something' (or target domain) is represented. More specifically, metaphors can be used to persuade, reason, evaluate, explain, theorize, offer new conceptualizations of reality and so on. For example, the three speakers quoted in the G8 article use different metaphors to provide different representations of the same event, primarily in order to persuade others to adopt the same views. These representational uses of metaphor can be related to M. A. K. Halliday's 'ideational' function of language, which is to do with the role of language in the understanding and construction of reality (Halliday 1978; Halliday and Hasan 1985). The other main sets of functions of metaphor in discourse can similarly be related to the other two functions of language proposed by Halliday, namely the 'interpersonal' and 'textual' functions. These are to do, respectively, with the construction of personal and social relationships in interaction, and with the construction of texts as coherent units of language use (Halliday 1978, Halliday and Hasan 1985; see also Goatly 1997: 148–67; Koller 2004b: 15–20).

Metaphor can be exploited in the construction and negotiation of interpersonal relationships, for example when it is used to express attitudes and emotions, entertain or involve, reinforce intimacy, convey humour, maintain or attack others' 'faces', manage the transition from one topic to the next in interaction and so on (Brown and Levinson 1987; Drew and Holt 1998). The use of metaphor in the email quoted as extract 1.10 above represents an event in a particular way in order to express gratitude and admiration towards the addressee, and hence to contribute to the congratulatory intent of the message. In several of the examples I have quoted above, metaphor is used to create humorous effects, and thereby to entertain the addressee(s) and reinforce the addresser's relationship with them.

Metaphor can also contribute to the internal structuring and intertextual relationships of a text; it may be used to provide summaries, to draw the addressees' attention to particular parts of the text and so on. For example, I have shown how, in the G8 article, a metaphor is used in the headline and then reiterated in the body of the text. The notion of a 'battle of metaphors' functions as a kind of 'meta-metaphor' and provides the backbone of the article as a whole. In addition, the recurrence of metaphorical expressions to do with movement and war at different points in the article further contributes to its internal coherence (see Goatly 1997: 148–67 for a useful discussion of the functions of metaphorical expressions).

In the course of this book, I exemplify the various functions I have mentioned so far, and consider a range of further representational, interpersonal and textual functions. I emphasize how individual uses of metaphor tend to perform several different functions simultaneously: in the email quoted in extract 1.10, for example, a metaphorical fixed expression is creatively exploited in order to provide a particular representation of an aspect of reality, congratulate the addressee, and structure the text of the email itself. I will consider the dominant functions of metaphor in texts belonging to particular genres (e.g. persuasion in political speeches, explanation in educational texts), but I will also show how metaphor may be used to perform a range of functions within individual texts and genres (e.g. in scientific articles it may be used to generate humour as well as for explanatory purposes).

1.3 Metaphor and ideology

I have already suggested in previous sections that metaphors are seldom neutral: constructing something in terms something else results in a particular view of the 'something' in question, often including specific attitudes and evaluations. In CMT terms, metaphors 'highlight' some aspects of the target domain and 'hide' others.[18] For example, ARGUMENT IS WAR highlights the competitive, aggressive and confrontational aspects of arguments and hides their cooperative, constructive aspects. This may affect not just our ways of talking and thinking about arguments, but possibly even the ways we act during arguments (Lakoff and Johnson 1980b: 10). Does this mean, therefore, that we are completely blinkered and straitjacketed by the metaphors we conventionally use? My answer to this question is: generally not, but in some cases we may be.[19]

On the one hand, we can overcome the slant and limitations of individual metaphors, at least to some extent, by exploiting alternative conventional metaphors for the same target domain, or by creating new metaphors, and hence new ways of making sense of particular experiences. For example, Lakoff and Johnson (1980b: 87–105) point out that, in English, arguments are also conventionally constructed in terms of source domains other than WAR (namely JOURNEYS, CONTAINERS and BUILDINGS), and they explore the implications of a hypothetical alternative conceptualization of arguments in terms of dance (Lakoff and Johnson 1980b: 4–5).

On the other hand, however, when particular uses of metaphor become the dominant way of talking about a particular aspect of reality within a particular discourse, they may be extremely difficult to perceive and challenge, since they come to represent the 'commonsense' or 'natural' view of things. In such cases, conventional conceptual metaphors can be seen as an important part of the shared sets of beliefs, or 'ideology', that characterize a particular social group:

> Both in its neutral and its 'loaded' senses, ideology is a system of beliefs and values based on a set of cognitive models, i.e. mental representations – partly linguistic, partly non-linguistic – of recurrent phenomena and their interpretations in culture and society. (Dirven, Frank and Pütz 2003: 1–2)

Van Dijk similarly views ideology in socio-cognitive terms as 'the basis of the social representations shared by members of a group' (van Dijk 1998: 8), and defines 'social representations' as 'organized clusters of socially shared beliefs', including scripts, scenarios, frames, attitudes, opinions and so on (van Dijk 1998: 46). From a CMT perspective, many of these shared mental representations are structured, at least in part, via conventional conceptual metaphors.

As Dirven, Frank and Pütz (2003) point out, however, it is not simply the choice of a particular conceptual metaphor 'that determines the ideological perspective, but also, and equally decisively, the various linguistic

[18] In their introduction to cognitive linguistics, Croft and Cruse (2004: 55) present metaphor as one of a range of 'construal operations', namely as one of the conceptualization processes that we employ to think and talk about our experiences.

[19] In other words, I espouse a weak version of the Sapir–Whorf hypothesis, which states that the structures of the language we speak constrain our thinking and conceptualization (Whorf 1956).

expressions instantiating the underlying conceptual metaphor' (Dirven, Frank and Pütz 2003: 8). In addition, the ideological implications of particular patterns of metaphorical expressions vary depending on the extent to which those patterns are conventionally used across texts and genres. Cameron makes a useful distinction between three types of 'systematicity' of metaphorical expressions. 'Local' systematicity applies when a particular linguistic metaphor or metaphors are limited to a single text or discourse event. I discuss some literary examples of this kind of systematicity in chapter 2. 'Discourse' systematicity applies when particular linguistic metaphors are used within specific 'discourse communities' (e.g. language teachers, or members of a particular political movement); in the terms used in this chapter, discourse systematicity also applies when particular uses of metaphors are characteristics of certain genres or discourses, such as sports news reports or the discourse relating to the Middle East. 'Global' systematicity applies when particular uses of metaphor occur across many genres and discourses, as in the case of spatial metaphors for time. While all uses of metaphor may have ideological implications, those that are discoursally systematic are particularly significant, since they can be seen as the reflection of the shared beliefs and assumptions of the members of particular social groups (see also Wolf and Polzenhagen 2003). I will return to these different types of systematicity in 3.3 below.

The ideological dimension of conventional patterns of metaphor in particular discourses has recently started to receive considerable attention. Koller (2004b), for example, has shown how contemporary business discourse is characterized by systematic metaphorical patterns drawing from a small set of source domains centring around WAR. This, she argues, reflects a sexist ideology that appears to be shared by journalists and their audience, namely a view of business activities as competitive, antagonistic and aggressive, in which women tend to be marginalized or excluded. Goatly (2002) has discussed the inconsistencies and limitations in the metaphors that characterize official educational discourse in Hong Kong, while a number of studies have considered the central role played by conventional metaphors in the discourses surrounding immigration and asylum in different historical and cultural contexts (see El Refaie 2001; O'Brien 2003). In some cases, metaphor scholars actively suggest new, alternative metaphors, that provide, in their view, more adequate, just and productive approaches to problems and activities (e.g. Goatly 2002, 2007; Koller 2004b). More generally, however, the study of metaphor can raise awareness of the role it plays in our conventional ways of talking and thinking, so that individuals are better able to notice metaphorical expressions and conceptualizations, and to reflect critically on their validity. I will return to the role of metaphor in discourses and ideologies at various points throughout the book (see especially section 3.3; see also Dirven, Frank and Pütz 2003; Goatly 2007).

1.4 The structure of this book

Having provided a general introduction in this chapter, in the next three chapters I discuss the use of metaphor in a variety of texts and genres from four broad areas of socio-cultural activity: literature (chapter 2), politics (chapter 3), and science and education (chapter 4). Each of these three chapters begins with the analysis of a preliminary example, which is then followed by an overview of the uses and functions of metaphor in texts and genres that are associated with the relevant socio-cultural area. Each chapter ends with two case studies, namely extended analyses of specific texts (e.g. a political leaflet), or of particular metaphorical phenomena involving many texts (e.g. the use of the 'Road Map' metaphor in relation to the Israeli–Palestinian conflict). Chapter 5 broadens the discussion to the role of metaphor in other genres and discourses, and contains two further case studies, respectively, on an advertisement and a radio phone-in programme on the topic of depression. Chapter 6 focuses specifically on the use of corpus-based techniques for the study of metaphor, and ends with a case study demonstrating some of these techniques. Chapter 7 provides some conclusions to the book as a whole.

I have strived to write each chapter so that it can be read individually by readers who have specific interests in particular genres, discourses or approaches. Ideally, however, readers with no previous experience of the study of metaphor in language should read this introductory chapter (if they have not done so already) before reading any of the following chapters.

2 Metaphor in literature

2.1 A preliminary example: metaphors for migraine in a novel

In chapter six of Ian McEwan's novel *Atonement* (2001), one of the main characters, Emily Tallis, is presented as suffering one of the frequent migraine attacks that blight her life and that of her family. It is a hot summer day in 1935, and Emily has been overseeing various activities and preparations in the Tallises's mansion in Surrey when she becomes aware of the imminent attack. The chapter begins as follows (in the extract below sentences have been numbered for ease of reference):

2.1 Not long after lunch, once she was assured that her sister's children and Briony had eaten sensibly and would keep their promise to stay away from the pool for at least two hours, Emily Tallis had withdrawn from the white glare of the afternoon's heat to a cool and darkened bedroom [1]. She was not in pain, not yet, but she was retreating before its threat [2] . . . She felt in the top right corner of her brain a heaviness, the inert body weight of some curled and sleeping animal; but when she touched her head and pressed, the presence disappeared from the co-ordinates of actual space [3]. Now it was in the top right corner of her mind, and in her imagination she could stand on tiptoe and raise her right hand to it [4]. It was important, however, not to provoke it; once this lazy creature moved from the peripheries to the centre, then the knifing pains would obliterate all thought, and there would be no chance of dining with Leon and the family tonight [5]. It bore her no malice, this animal, it was indifferent to her misery [6]. It would move as a caged panther might: because it was awake, out of boredom, for the sake of movement itself, or for no reason at all, and with no awareness [7]. (McEwan 2001: 63–4)

The rest of chapter six of McEwan's novel is devoted to a description of Emily's sensations, feelings and thoughts while she is lying in bed waiting for the pain to subside. Here I focus particularly on how the character's experience of pain is conveyed by McEwan via the use of the kind of striking and novel metaphorical expressions that are typically associated with literary writing.

I hope readers will agree that the most salient metaphor in extract 2.1 is the description of Emily's perception of pain in terms of the presence, inside her head, of a sleeping animal that can, at any point, start moving casually around. This metaphor is extended and gradually developed throughout the extract. It begins with the description of what Emily felt as a 'heaviness' in sentence 3. This is immediately qualified, via an appositional noun phrase, as 'the inert body weight of some curled and sleeping animal'. In the following sentence, the temporary relief that Emily achieves by pressing the painful part of her head is described as 'the presence disappear[ing]'. In the final part of the extract the sleeping animal is further described as a 'lazy creature' that can be 'provoked' (presumably by Emily moving), and that will react by 'mov[ing] from the peripheries to the centre', causing excruciating and disabling pain. In sentences 6 and 7, the animal is attributed specific attitudes, namely lack of 'malice' towards Emily and 'indiffer[ence]' to her misery, and its movements are compared via a simile to those of a 'caged panther' that moves for no specific reason. In sentence 4, Emily is presented as imagining a variant of this scenario, in which she (or, rather, a minuscule variant of herself) stands on tiptoe inside her own head and touches the sleeping animal.[1]

Extract 2.1 also contains other, arguably less salient, metaphorical descriptions of pain, which form a cluster with the ANIMAL metaphor I have just pointed out. In sentences 1 and 2, Emily is described as 'withdraw[ing] from the white glare of the afternoon heat' and 'retreating before its [the pain's] threat'. The verbs 'withdraw' and 'retreat' can both be related to the source domain of WAR, and are conventionally used metaphorically to describe the attempt to avoid something unpleasant or unwelcome. In the context of the extract, however, these conventional metaphorical expressions may be partly revitalized due to their occurrence in adjacent sentences and to the personification of the afternoon heat (via 'glare') and of the pain (via 'threat'). A further metaphorical description of pain occurs in sentence 5, where the movement of the animal inside Emily's head is described as causing 'knifing pains' that 'obliterate all thought'. Since the basic meaning of the verb 'obliterate' is to do with physical destruction, its (conventional) metaphorical use here in relation to thought can be seen as consistent with the earlier personification of pain as an enemy. The metaphorical description of the pains as 'knifing' can also be considered as part of the same pattern, but has a further dimension: Emily's migraine pain is described in terms of the insertion of an external object (a knife), even though it has no direct external cause.

In the rest of chapter six of *Atonement*, the metaphors introduced in the opening paragraph recur and are further extended, resulting in two main chains of metaphorical expressions. Emily's anxious awareness of the potential consequences of any movement are conveyed via further metaphorical references to knives:

[1] This particular scenario, where Emily imagines herself inside her own head, would be particularly suited to an analysis in terms of Blending theory (Fauconnier and Turner 2002).

2.2 She lay rigidly apprehensive, held at knife-point, knowing that fear would not let her sleep and that her only hope was in keeping still. (McEwan 2001: 64)

2.3 the fear of pain kept her in her place. At worst, unrestrained, a matching set of sharpened knives would be drawn across her optic nerve, and then again, with a greater downward pressure, and she would be entirely shut in and alone. (McEwan 2001: 67)

In extract 2.2 the expression 'held at knife-point' personifies the pain as a violent attacker clutching a knife.[2] In extract 2.3, Emily's memory of pain from previous attacks is metaphorically presented in terms of 'a matching set of sharpened knives' repeatedly bearing down on her optic nerve.

The ANIMAL metaphor is also further exploited throughout the chapter to convey different stages in the development of the migraine attack:

2.4 Feeling the black-furred creature begin to stir, Emily let her thoughts move away from her eldest daughter. (McEwan 2001: 65)

2.5 It was beginning to fade, the presence of her animal tormentor, and now she was able to arrange two pillows against the headboard in order to sit up. (McEwan 2001: 69)

2.6 And so Emily lay back against the pillow for another several minutes, her creature having slunk away, and patiently planned, and revised her plans, and refined an order for them. (McEwan 2001: 70)

In extract 2.4, Emily's sensation of the pain starting is presented as '(f)eeling the black-furred creature begin to stir'. In extract 2.5, the decrease of pain corresponds to the (metaphorical) 'fad[ing] . . . of her animal tormentor'. In extract 2.6, the expression 'her creature having slunk away' is used to convey Emily's sense that the migraine attack is over.

McEwan's use of these metaphors to convey Emily's experience of migraine exemplifies some important phenomena that are central to this chapter and to the rest of this book. These include: the use of metaphor to express otherwise 'ineffable' subjective experiences; the creative exploitation of conventional metaphors; the use of strikingly novel and arresting metaphors to provide representations of experiences that can be perceived as both original and realistic; the creation of complex textual patterns. Let me briefly consider each of these phenomena.

As I pointed out in chapter 1, metaphor plays an essential role in the expression of our most intimate subjective experiences, such as our emotions, perceptions and physical sensations, including particularly pain (e.g. Kövecses 2000; Lodge 2002; Lascaratou forthcoming). The pain of migraine attacks, in particular, tends to be described as unique and overwhelming by sufferers. However,

[2] I treat personification as a type of metaphor, whereby non-human entities are constructed in terms of (some characteristics of) human beings (see section 3.4.5 for more discussion).

nobody can have direct access to anybody else's pain, and literal language is often inadequate to convey to others what our own pain feels like. In the case of migraine, sufferers sometimes use drawings to express their experiences, and those drawings often involve powerful visual metaphors, such as a stroke of lightning or a hammer hitting the head of the sufferer (you can easily find some examples by entering 'migraine' in an image search engine on the World Wide Web). In addition, literature is particularly associated with the expression of powerful and intimate human experiences, in ways that are highly creative but also feel 'real' and 'true' to those experiences. In chapter six of *Atonement*, McEwan uses metaphors to express something that is in principle inexpressible, namely the subjective experience of a particular character suffering a migraine attack. In doing this he both exploits and transcends conventional metaphorical ways of describing pain.

The metaphorical pattern involving references to knives is fairly closely related to conventional metaphorical expressions for physical pain. Pain with no immediate external cause is conventionally described in terms of external aggression or invasion that involves physical damage caused by objects touching or penetrating the body, as in the following examples: 'like someone has poked a needle in the muscles or in the veins', 'it burns, it burns inside' (from De Souza and Frank 2000: 212–13). In order to investigate this further, I obtained from the 100-million-word British National Corpus (BNC) the collocates of the search string 'pain', i.e. the words that tend to co-occur with it.[3] Among the top forty collocates of 'pain', I noted the following words: 'stabbing', 'stinging', 'sharp' and 'burning'. All these adjectives have basic senses to do with the properties of objects ('sharp') or the effects of objects on the body ('stabbing', 'stinging', 'burning'). In addition, all four expressions have conventional metaphorical senses relating to pain that is *not* caused by contact with sharp or burning objects (e.g. Speaker A: 'What happens if you lift something or pull something?' Speaker B: 'I get a sharp stabbing pain'; from the BNC). The use of 'knifing' in extract 2.1 in relation to pain is not as conventional as that of 'stabbing', for example, but it is also not entirely unusual: two out of seven instances of 'knifing' in the BNC are metaphorical descriptions of pain where no contact with knives or any other objects is involved. As I have shown, however, McEwan creatively develops the KNIVES metaphor throughout his description of the migraine attack: he uses expressions that are not conventionally applied to pain, and creates a richer and more detailed metaphorical scenario in which the pain is a violent attacker (see 'held at knife-point' in extract 2.2) and multiple knives penetrate Emily's head (see 'unrestrained, a matching set of sharpened knives . . .' in extract 2.3).

[3] Collocations were calculated on the basis of mutual information and with a window span of one word on either side of the search string.

The ANIMAL metaphor, in contrast, is much more strikingly novel and, I am tempted to say, unique. It is of course the case that it can be related to the conventional pattern of describing pain in terms of weight (e.g. 'As I moved over the "heart centre" I experienced a heaviness in my chest', from the BNC) and of external entities invading the body. It can also be related more specifically to metaphorical expressions such as a 'gnawing pain', which describe pain in terms of an entity attacking the body from the inside. However, this metaphor has a number of highly original aspects. First, none of the lexical items that outline the animal scenario (e.g. 'animal', 'black-furred', 'creature', 'stir', etc.) have conventional metaphorical senses that relate to pain. Second, pain is not normally talked about or understood in terms of an animal simply *moving* inside our body. Within McEwan's metaphor, the experience of pain does not correspond to the animal entering the body (as is the case with 'stabbing' or 'knifing' pain) or attacking it (as in 'gnawing pain'), but to the animal moving around inside Emily's head. Third, the animal is not presented as a malevolent aggressor, but as acting as it does without malice or awareness. And, lastly, McEwan develops the source metaphorical scenario in great and vivid detail. Emily's head (metonymically referred to via 'mind' and 'brain') is consistently presented as a hollow physical object, and reference is made to particular parts of it (e.g. 'in the top right corner of her brain', 'from the peripheries to the centre'). The animal that is metaphorically presented as causing the pain is referred to via a series of expressions that provide different kinds of details and potential visual images, including: 'the inert body weight of some curled and sleeping animal', 'this lazy creature', 'a caged panther', 'the black-furred creature' and 'her animal tormentor'.

In addition, the ANIMAL scenario provides a narrative frame for the different stages of Emily's experience of the migraine attack (see also Musolff 2006): her awareness of the imminence of pain corresponds to an awareness of the weight of a sleeping creature in her head; movement and its consequences correspond to provoking the creature and waking it up; a feeling of intense pain corresponds to the creature casually moving around in the head; and the cessation of pain corresponds to the creature having moved out of the head. It is also worth mentioning that this metaphorical scenario contrasts with conventional metaphors for pain by being physically impossible. While it is possible to experience the pain caused by stabbing or burning, it is not physically possible to experience a furry creature moving around in our heads, while conscious (or alive!). As a consequence, McEwan's metaphor can be said to require a much greater leap of the imagination (both in production and reception) than more conventional metaphors for pain.

This kind of highly creative metaphor is associated with some potential effects on readers that tend to be regarded as characteristic of literature. On the one hand, it is arguable that, in virtue of its novelty and textual extension, the ANIMAL metaphor is highly foregrounded: the relevant stretches of text are likely to be particularly noticeable and memorable, and may enable readers to arrive at fresh insights into the experience of migraine, or a renewed awareness of it (see Leech 1969; Mukařovský 1970). More specifically, some readers may feel that, thanks to McEwan's description, they *know* what it is like to have a migraine attack, even though they have never experienced one themselves. Conversely, migraine sufferers may feel that McEwan has captured exactly what a migraine attack feels like, and hence go through what is known as an 'Aha! Experience': the sudden recognition, in a fictional representation, of an experience that the reader is familiar with, but has never been fully aware of or managed to express so successfully (Margolin 2003: 285).[4] Of course, other readers may well find the ANIMAL metaphor far-fetched and repulsive: the more creative and audacious the metaphor, the greater the 'risk' that writers may confuse and/or alienate part of their audience (see Toolan *et al.* 1988).

Finally, it is worth reflecting on the way in which different metaphors for pain are textually extended and interwoven in the description of Emily's migraine. The ANIMAL metaphor is initially extended in consecutive sentences in the opening paragraph, and then recurs at different points throughout the chapter, where it is further extended and developed. The KNIVES metaphor first occurs within a description of the ANIMAL scenario, but is creatively and independently re-used and extended in the course of the chapter. The personification of the pain as an enemy begins before the other two metaphors are introduced, and is combined both with the representation of pain as an aggressor with a knife, and, to a lesser extent, as an animal. This results in the presence, within chapter six of *Atonement*, of clusters and chains of creative uses of metaphor which contribute to the power and global coherence of the chapter, and may play a part in readers' perceptions and evaluations of 'style' in relation to the novel and its author.[5]

These phenomena are discussed further in the course of the chapter, alongside a series of further aspects of the use of metaphor in literature. I begin by considering in more depth the notion of metaphorical creativity. I then discuss metaphor as a phenomenon that may characterize particular literary genres, authors or texts.[6] I finish with two case studies, discussing, respectively, a poem by Elizabeth Jennings, and the use of metaphor to convey characters' world-views in a novel by Joanne Harris.

4 Indeed, I have anecdotal evidence of both reactions from readers, as well as a reliable report that, after a public reading of the novel, McEwan said that he had never suffered a migraine attack himself!

5 In fact, the metaphorical 'assault' suffered by Emily may also be seen to anticipate the literal assault against another character which will constitutes a pivotal moment in the novel's plot.

6 For reasons of space and focus, in this book I will not discuss metaphor and iconicity (but see Hiraga 2005), nor will I consider Blending theory as an account of metaphorical creativity (but see Fauconnier and Turner 2002).

2.2 Metaphorical conventionality and creativity in literature

Much debate has taken place in recent years over the existence of a special 'literary' variety of language that can be differentiated from other non-literary varieties of language. In the early and middle twentieth century, some literary scholars and linguists claimed that it was possible to identify the linguistic properties that made literature linguistically different from non-literature, including particularly the use of linguistic deviation (Mukařovský 1970) and linguistic patterns, or 'parallelism' (Jakobson 1960). Nowadays, it is fairly widely accepted that what we call 'literature' is primarily a cultural and social construct, that cannot be straightforwardly distinguished, in linguistic terms at least, from genres and uses of language that are regarded as 'non-literary' (e.g. Carter and Nash 1990; Carter 2004). Carter and Nash (1990), in particular, have attempted to define the notion of 'literariness' as a bundle of properties of texts and readings, and have proposed a 'cline' of literariness, where different texts and genres can be placed in different positions: for example, advertisements tend to have a higher degree of literariness than legal contracts, and lyric poems tend to have a higher degree of literariness than news reports. More specifically, a number of studies have recently shown that uses of language that may be described as 'creative' are not the exclusive property of literature or of any specific set of texts and genres, but rather a pervasive phenomenon within a wide variety of genres and contexts, including informal everyday conversation (Carter 2004; Carter and McCarthy 2004).

Metaphor, in particular, has been traditionally seen as a highly creative linguistic phenomenon, and has been associated with (and studied in) a relatively restricted set of genres, including primarily poetry. This has resulted in many detailed and subtle analyses of particularly salient uses of metaphor in literature, which generally aimed to demonstrate the artistic value, significance and uniqueness of specific metaphorical choices and patterns in specific texts by particular authors (e.g. in Nowottny 1962, Leech 1969). The ANIMAL metaphor from *Atonement* that I discussed in the previous section is an example of the kind of striking and original metaphors that demand and reward close individual attention, and that can be used to argue for the distinctiveness of the style of individual literary authors. Indeed, within this traditional approach, literary writers have been seen as the main creators of metaphors, which then gradually lose their metaphoricity as they are adopted in 'ordinary' language use. As R. W. Emerson put it, from this point of view, '[l]anguage is fossil poetry' (quoted in Leech 1969: 147).

Over the last thirty years, the influence of Cognitive Metaphor Theory (CMT) has shifted attention to patterns of conventional metaphorical expressions in everyday language, which have been seen as evidence of the existence of conceptual metaphors in thought (see 1.1.2). More importantly, Lakoff and Turner (1989) have reconsidered literary metaphors in the light of CMT, and have argued that poets do not tend to invent brand new metaphors, but rather exploit creatively the conventional metaphors of everyday language. Within this view, therefore, metaphors originate in ordinary language and thought, and are then exploited by poets to achieve particular effects:

> General conceptual metaphors are thus not the unique creation of individual poets but are rather part of the way members of a culture have of conceptualizing their experience. Poets, as members of their cultures, naturally make use of these basic conceptual metaphors to communicate with other members, their audience. (Lakoff and Turner 1989: 9)

Lakoff and Turner, however, share the traditional view that the metaphors we find in literature are typically more novel and creative than those we find elsewhere, and hence have the potential to provide us with fresh insights and new ways of thinking about our experiences (Lakoff and Turner 1989: 92). As I have already mentioned, some important recent work on 'everyday' creativity challenges this assumption, and, indeed, I will show in the course of this book that metaphorical creativity can be found in texts belonging to many different non-literary genres. Nonetheless, the creative use of metaphor is likely to play an important part in our conception of 'literariness', and may well be particularly frequent in some literary, and particularly poetic, genres. In a rare quantitative study in this area, Goatly (1997) has compared the proportion of 'active' (i.e. novel) metaphors out of all metaphorical expressions in six different genres. In his data, modern lyric poetry has the highest proportion of active metaphors (58 per cent), while the proportion for modern novels is much lower (28 per cent), and similar to that for magazine advertising (22 per cent). Much more work of this kind is needed, however, in order to be able to make valid claims about the frequency of creative metaphors in different genres, both literary and non-literary (see also Semino and Steen forthcoming).

In this chapter, I consider metaphorical creativity as an important phenomenon in texts and genres that are regarded as literary, but not as an exclusive or defining characteristic of literature generally. My main concerns are the different manifestations of metaphorical creativity, their relationships with conventional patterns, and their potential significance in the texts and genres within which they occur. In the next sub-section, I introduce Lakoff and Turner's account of metaphorical creativity in poetry, which includes a typology of novel metaphors in terms of conceptual mappings. I then relate this typology to the predominantly linguistic approach I adopted in chapter 1, and argue that a proper account of metaphorical creativity needs to consider both the conceptual and linguistic levels of metaphor.

2.2.1 *Lakoff and Turner's typology of novel metaphors in poetry*

In discussing what they call the 'conceptual power of poetic metaphor', Lakoff and Turner (1989: 67) argue that

> [p]oetic thought uses the mechanisms of everyday thought, but it extends them, elaborates them, and combines them in ways that go beyond the ordinary. (Lakoff and Turner 1989: 67)

As the reference to 'poetic thought' suggests, Lakoff and Turner are concerned with creativity as a *conceptual* rather than a *linguistic* phenomenon, even though they inevitably need to refer to texts in order to exemplify various creative phenomena. More specifically, they identify four main ways in which poets may creatively exploit conventional conceptual metaphors. These include the three phenomena mentioned in the quotation above – extension, elaboration and combination – and the 'questioning' of conventional conceptual metaphors (see also Kövecses 2002: 43–53 for an overview of Lakoff and Turner's typology).

When Lakoff and Turner talk about 'extending' a conventional conceptual metaphor, they refer to the mapping of elements from the source domain that are not conventionally mapped onto the target domain. As an example, they quote the following lines from Hamlet's soliloquy, where death is metaphorically described in terms of sleep:

> To sleep? Perchance to dream! Ay, there's the rub
> For in the sleep of death what dreams may come?
>
> (William Shakespeare, *Hamlet*; quoted in Lakoff and Turner 1989: 67)

Here, Lakoff and Turner argue, 'Shakespeare extends the ordinary conventional metaphor of death as sleep to include the possibility of dreaming' (Lakoff and Turner 1989: 67). It should be noted that Lakoff and Turner's notion of 'extension' is defined in terms of novel mappings of elements across domains. This contrasts with the traditional notion of 'extended metaphor' introduced in 1.2.3 above, which is the *textual* phenomenon whereby several expressions from the same source domain are used in relation to the same target domain over a stretch of text. The two types of extension are separate phenomena, but, in practice, Lakoff and Turner's 'conceptual' extension is often linguistically realized via 'textual' extension. This can be seen in the following extract from Ken Kesey's novel *One Flew Over the Cuckoo's Nest*, where the first-person narrator, Bromden, provides a metaphorical description of a category of patients in the mental hospital to which he is confined:

2.7 What the Chronics are – or most of us – are machines with flaws inside that can't be repaired, flaws born in, or flaws beat in over so many years of the guy running head-on into solid things that by the time the hospital found him he was bleeding rust in some vacant lot. (Kesey 1973: 17)

Bromden's description of the Chronics as broken machines can be seen as involving the creative exploitation of the conventional conceptual metaphors THE MIND IS A MACHINE (e.g. 'I'm a little rusty today') and, possibly, PEOPLE ARE MACHINES (e.g. 'I feel all run down') (see Lakoff and Johnson 1980b: 27; 1999: 247; Kövecses 2002: 122). While the mapping of mechanical problems onto mental problems can be seen as conventional (e.g. 'He has a screw loose'), it is not conventional to map the notion of a problem 'that can't be repaired' onto a mental problem that cannot be cured. The same applies to the mapping of physical collision onto the causes of mental problems ('running . . . into solid things'), and the mapping of abandoned rusty machines onto people with serious mental problems ('he was bleeding rust in some vacant lot'). In Lakoff and Turner's terms, the conventional metaphor THE MIND IS A MACHINE (and arguably also PEOPLE ARE MACHINES) is extended via these unconventional mappings, in order to express Bromden's personal view of mental illness (see Semino and Swindlehurst 1996 for an analysis of metaphor in this novel). The *conceptual* extension of these metaphors is linguistically realized via *textual* extension, since the metaphorical description of the Chronics as machines takes place over several clauses that occupy several lines of text.

Lakoff and Turner's notion of 'elaboration' captures those cases of creativity which involve 'filling in slots in unusual ways rather than . . . extending the metaphor to map additional slots' (Lakoff and Turner 1989: 67). Kövecses describes elaboration more explicitly:

> Elaboration is different from extension, in that it elaborates on an existing element of the source in an unusual way. Instead of adding a new element to the source domain, it captures an already existing one in a new, unconventional way. (Kövecses 2002: 47)

For example, Lakoff and Turner argue that Horace's description of death as 'the eternal exile of the raft' can be said to involve the elaboration of the conventional metaphorization of death as departure without return (e.g. 'She's gone' or 'He passed away'): the general notion of departure is made more specific via the notion of exile, and the general notion of a vehicle is made more specific via the reference to a raft. This may evoke associations that conventional realizations of the metaphor do not necessarily have, such as the idea of banishment and, possibly, that of an uncomfortable journey without a destination. In other words, the elaboration of a conventional conceptual metaphor may lead to new ways of thinking about the target concept (Lakoff and Turner 1989: 67–8).[7]

[7] Lakoff and Turner acknowledge that Horace's metaphor may in fact be related to the representation of death in Greek mythology, where Charon ferried the dead across the river Styx to Hades. However, they point out that the reference to exile nonetheless contrasts with more conventional metaphors for death.

The following extract from David Lodge's novel *Thinks* can also be seen as involving elaboration. In the extract, one of the novel's two first-person narrators, Helen Reed, remembers a period in which she suffered from depression:

2.8 the time of my big depression, seven or eight years ago. For six months, I languished at the bottom of a deep hole, like the shaft of a waterless well, while kindly, puzzled people of whom Martin was one, peered down at me over the rim of the parapet and tried to cheer me up, or lowered drugs and advice in a bucket. (Lodge 2001: 202)

Helen Reed's description of her experience of depression elaborates the orientational metaphor HAPPY IS UP/UNHAPPY IS DOWN, which is conventionally realized by expressions such as 'I'm feeling up', 'He's really low these days', and 'I fell into a depression'[8] (Lakoff and Johnson 1980b: 15). These conventional expressions involve a spatial contrast between higher and lower positions, but are otherwise rather generic. In extract 2.8, the general notion of being 'down' or 'low' is specified through a rich and detailed scenario, involving 'the bottom of a deep hole' that is further described via simile as 'the shaft of a waterless well'. This allows the further furnishing of the metaphorical scenario by adding concerned people (including Helen's husband Martin), who look down from 'the rim of the parapet' and try to help via lowering things 'in a bucket'. Lodge's elaboration of the conventional orientational metaphor is much more obviously metaphorical than expressions such as 'up' or 'down', and also richer in terms of potential associations and effects: the description of the 'deep hole' emphasizes the loneliness and discomfort experienced by Helen, as well as her perception of distance from other people, who could not reach her in spite of their helpful intentions. There is also some humorous potential in the image of people peering over the parapet, and in the zeugma 'lowered drugs and advice': drugs can be literally sent down a hole in a bucket, while advice cannot; however, in this case the notion of 'lowering' is itself metaphorical, since it refers to people's attempts to help Helen during her depression.

According to Lakoff and Turner (1989: 70), the most powerful way in which poets can creatively exploit conventional conceptual metaphors is by 'composing' or 'combining' them (see also my discussion of the combination of metaphors in 1.2.3 above). As an example, they discuss the following quatrain from Shakespeare's sonnet 73:

2.9 In me thou seest the twilight of such day
As after sunset fadeth in the west;
Which by and by black night doth take away,
Death's second self that seals up all the rest.

(William Shakespeare, quoted in Lakoff and Turner 1989: 70)

[8] Note that the same orientational metaphor explains the etymology of the word 'depression', which comes from Latin verb 'de-premere', which meant 'to press down'.

Lakoff and Turner argue that the poetic speaker's description of the presage of death in his physical appearance involves the combination of at least five conventional conceptual metaphors: LIGHT IS A SUBSTANCE, EVENTS ARE ACTIONS, LIFE IS A PRECIOUS POSSESSION, A LIFETIME IS A DAY and LIFE IS LIGHT. For example, they argue that the clause 'black night doth take away [the twilight]' contains:

> a composite of the metaphor that lifetime is a day and death is night, that light is a substance, that a life is a precious possession, and that events are actions. The metaphors are composed in such a way that night is identified as the agent who takes away the light, which is understood metaphorically as life, and consequently seen as stealing a precious possession. (Lakoff and Turner 1989: 71)

According to Lakoff and Turner, the combination of conventional metaphors such as in extract 2.9 produces 'a richer and more complex set of metaphorical connections, which gives inferences beyond those that follow from each of the metaphors alone' (Lakoff and Turner 1989: 71).

A particularly complex case of combination of conventional conceptual metaphors can be seen in Elizabeth Jennings's poem 'Answers', which begins as follows:

2.10 I kept my answers small and kept them near;
Big questions bruised my mind but still I let
Small answers be a bulwark to my fear.

In my own reading of the poem, the poetic speaker reflects on how she tried to avoid thinking about fundamental and difficult issues ('big questions') by concentrating on ('kept near') comfortable and relatively straightforward ideas ('small answers'). Although the difficult issues kept affecting her mental life ('Big questions bruised my mind'), she focused on straightforward ideas in order to avoid the fear associated with the 'big questions' ('I let small answers be a bulwark to my fear'). In other words, the poem is concerned with mental activities but primarily consists of words and expressions that have concrete and physical basic meanings (e.g. 'small', 'bruised').

From a CMT perspective, it can be argued that the speaker's mental life is metaphorically described via expressions that bring together a set of conventional conceptual metaphors. In particular, following Lakoff and Johnson (1980b, 1999), the use of the adjectives 'small' and 'big' in relation to questions and answers can be seen as a realization of the conceptual metaphors IDEAS ARE OBJECTS and IMPORTANT IS BIG; the use of the verb 'keep' in relation to answers can be seen as a realization of THINKING IS OBJECT MANIPULATION; the use of 'near' in the first line can be seen as a realization of INTIMACY IS CLOSENESS; and the lines 'Big questions bruised my mind but still I let/Small answers be a bulwark to my fear' can be see as involving realizations of MIND IS A BODY/PERSON, DIFFICULTIES ARE OPPONENTS, and/or HARM IS PHYSICAL INJURY (see Grady also 1997a: 291, 295). Via the combination of these metaphors, the opening stanza of the poem presents a complex mental and emotional experience in terms of a rich and coherent metaphorical scenario, in which the speaker tries to live a quiet life surrounded by small answers, but finds that she is constantly threatened by the aggressive approach of the big questions. This leads to potential inferences and emotional associations that could not be conveyed by each of the metaphors on its own (e.g. the difference in size between the 'big questions' and the 'small answers' makes it difficult for the latter to provide protection from the former, leading to fear and anxiety). The rest of the poem contains further realizations of this set of conceptual metaphors, as well as expressions that evoke other metaphors that further contribute to conveying the speaker's difficulties. I discuss the whole poem in more detail in case study 1 below.

My experience as a reader and student of literature is consistent with Lakoff and Turner's claim that the composition of conventional conceptual metaphors is a powerful and, I would add, frequent mode of metaphorical creativity (note, for example, the combination of different metaphors for pain in extract 2.1, and the metaphorical use of 'big' as pre-modifier of 'depression' in extract 2.8). This contrasts with Lakoff and Turner's notion of 'questioning' conventional conceptual metaphors, which, although potentially powerful, occurs rather infrequently. Questioning occurs when a writer points out the limitations or inadequacy of a particular conventional conceptual metaphor, as in the following extract from a love poem by the Latin poet Catullus:

2.11 Suns can set and return again,
But when our brief light goes out,
There's one perpetual night to be slept through.

(Catullus, quoted in Lakoff and Turner 1989: 69)

Lakoff and Turner comment that 'Catullus is both using A LIFETIME IS A DAY and pointing out the breakdown of the metaphor at the crucial point, namely, mortality' (Lakoff and Turner 1989: 69).

All four modes of creativity introduced so far (extending, elaborating, composing, and questioning) involve exploiting conventional conceptual metaphors in novel ways. According to Lakoff and Turner, most metaphorical creativity in poetry can be explained in this way. The only further source of creativity they discuss in detail concerns what they call 'image metaphors', which involve the mapping of visual images, rather than complex conceptual domains such as JOURNEYS or MACHINES (Lakoff and Turner 1989: 89–96). As such, image metaphors do not consist of systematic cross-domain correspondences that generate rich inference patterns, but rather involve the 'one-shot' superimposition of one image onto another. For example, Rabelais's simile 'His toes were like the keyboard of a spinet' (quoted in Lakoff and Turner 1989: 90), prompts us to map two conventional mental images with similar part–whole structures: a keyboard consisting of many individual keys and a foot containing a set of (five) individual toes.

In some cases, however, the images evoked by a particular expression may not be conventional, and the mapping may 'disturb what we think we know about the target domain' (Lakoff and Turner 1989: 92). Lakoff and Turner discuss (the English translation of) a French surrealist poem by André Breton, 'Free Union', which includes the following lines:

2.12 My wife . . .
Whose waist is an hourglass
Whose waist is the waist of an otter caught in the teeth of a tiger
(André Breton, 'Free Union', translated by David Antin, quoted in Lakoff and Turner 1989: 93)

They point out that the line 'whose waist is an hourglass' evokes a rather conventional image metaphor, since it involves the mapping of visual images that are normally perceived to be similar in shape.[9] In contrast, in the third line of the extract above, the source image is not conventional, and does not straightforwardly map onto the target image of a woman's waist. In this case, Lakoff and Turner suggest that readers will have to construct a novel mapping: they will have to map onto the image of the woman's waist the shape of an otter, whose waist will get progressively thinner in the teeth of a tiger. In the context of the poem as a whole, the life-and-death associations of the source image may contribute to construct the speaker's wife as wild, unpredictable, exciting, vulnerable and so on (Lakoff and Turner 1989: 95).

2.2.2 *Metaphorical creativity beyond Lakoff and Turner's typology*

Lakoff and Turner's (1989) study made an important contribution to our understanding of both metaphor and literature, but did not pay sufficient attention to two phenomena that are important for the concerns of this book, namely: novelty in the choice of source and target domain combinations, and the linguistic and textual dimensions of metaphorical creativity. In this section I deal with each phenomenon in turn.

Novelty at the conceptual level In *Metaphors We Live By*, Lakoff and Johnson (1980b) consider the possibility of entirely novel conceptual metaphors:

[9] Indeed, Breton was born just before the beginning of the Edwardian period in England (1901–10), which is associated with the fashion of using tight corsets to give women an hourglass shape.

We would now like to turn to metaphors that are outside our conventional conceptual system, metaphors that are imaginative and creative. Such metaphors are capable of giving us a new understanding of our experience. Thus, they can give new meaning to our pasts, to our daily activity, and to what we know and believe. (Lakoff and Johnson 1980b: 139)

Lakoff and Johnson discuss the metaphor LOVE IS A COLLABORATIVE WORK OF ART as an example of a novel conceptual metaphor, which can be developed into a set of multiple cross-domain correspondences and give rise to rich inference patterns.

In contrast, Lakoff and Turner (1989) limit their discussion of novel conceptual metaphors to cases involving the mapping of visual images, which are 'one-shot' and 'characteristically do not involve the mapping of . . . rich knowledge and inferential structure' (Lakoff and Turner 1989: 91). This does not do justice to the more radical cases of metaphorical creativity that can be found in poetry, as well as elsewhere. Let me return for a moment to the ANIMAL metaphor for migraine discussed in the opening section of this chapter. It is true, of course, that the scenario that functions as source involves visual images, while the target (the migraine pain) does not. However, it is also the case that what is mapped from the source scenario to the target is more than a visual image. As I have said before, the animal scenario has a narrative structure, which gets mapped onto the different stages of the experience of migraine: the character's awareness of the imminence of pain corresponds to the perception of the weight of the sleeping animal; the sensation of peaks of pain corresponds to the perception of the animal moving around; and the realization that the attack is over corresponds to the perception that the animal is no longer there. While, as I have said, it is possible to establish a connection with conventional metaphorizations of pain in terms of external invasion into the body, it would be reductive simply to categorize McEwan's ANIMAL metaphor as a case of elaboration of a conventional conceptual metaphor: McEwan's metaphor is far too distinctive and idiosyncratic, and its relationship with conventional (conceptual and linguistic) metaphors is far too tenuous for such an analysis. Hence I would argue that here we have the linguistic expression of a novel and highly original conceptual metaphor, which is *consistent* with conventional conceptual metaphors, but cannot easily be subsumed under any of them.

Similar considerations apply to cases such as John Donne's famous metaphor of the compass in 'A Valediction: Forbidding Mourning'. The speaker in the poem describes the 'refined' love that he shares with his addressee as a union of souls, which can continue to persist and flourish even when the two lovers are physically separated. This is expressed via similes and metaphorical expressions evoking the image of a drawing compass, in which the woman is the 'fixed foot' (NB: in the first line of the quotation below, 'they' refers to the souls of the speaker and his addressee):

2.13 If they be two, they are two so
As stiff twin compasses are two;
Thy soul, the fixed foot, makes no show
To move, but doth, if th' other do.

And though it in the centre sit,
Yet when the other far doth roam,
It leans and hearkens after it,
And grows erect, as that comes home.

Such wilt thou be to me, who must
Like th' other foot, obliquely run;
Thy firmness makes my circle just,
And makes me end where I begun.

(quoted in Abrams *et al.* 1979: 1070)

In the scenario that functions as metaphorical source, the fixed foot of the compass does not move, but adapts to the movements of the other arm, ensuring that it draws a perfect circle and that it can return where it started. In the same way, physical separation does not jeopardize the couple's unity, as the woman's spiritual attachment to the man enables him to succeed in what he does and then return to her.

It is possible to argue that Donne's metaphor creatively exploits a conventional tendency to talk about social and emotional relationships in terms of physical links (e.g. in the expressions 'the ties of blood relationships' and 'the mutual bond of friendship' (see Kövecses 2000: 94)). As such, the metaphor would be seen as a case of elaboration of the conventional conceptual metaphor RELATIONSHIPS ARE PHYSICAL LINKS: the general notion of link is elaborated via the specific image of the compass. However, this kind of analysis underestimates the novelty of Donne's image. Unlike physical objects such as ties, compasses are not prototypically seen as involving a connection between separate entities, and their function is not that of bringing about a physical connection. So, while Donne's choice of source concept is again *consistent* with the conventional metaphor RELATIONSHIPS ARE PHYSICAL LINKS, it can be seen as involving an entirely novel cross-domain mapping.

An even more radical case of novelty can be found in the third stanza of Sylvia Plath's poem 'Morning Song', in which a mother addresses her new baby (see Semino 1997: 181–2):

2.14 I'm no more your mother
Than the cloud that distils a mirror to reflect its own slow
Effacement at the wind's hand.

(Plath 1965: 11)

In my reading of this stanza, the relationship between mother and child is metaphorically constructed as being *no more* than that between a cloud and the watery surface it produces on the ground when it rains.[10] More precisely, the cloud corresponds to the mother; rain corresponds to having a child (note that I interpret 'distils a mirror' as a metaphorical description of rain and its watery deposit on the ground); the child corresponds to water on the ground, or a puddle; the way in which a puddle reflects the clouds above it corresponds to the way in which a child may resemble his or her mother (physically or otherwise); and the way in which the puddle reflects the gradual disappearance of the cloud due to the (personified) wind seems to correspond to some awareness, on the mother's part, of her own loss of identity, freedom, youth, etc., due to the birth of the child. In other words, motherhood is here being constructed via an entirely novel conceptual metaphor, that, as far as I can see, has no obvious connection with conventional metaphorizations of motherhood. The result is an original and potentially disturbing representation of a universal experience, which radically departs from conventional and comforting views of motherhood and new mothers (some of which are also present in the poem): the relationship between mother and child is metaphorically presented in terms of purely physical, inanimate, unintentional and unemotional processes, and the mother's perception of herself is presented in terms of dissolution. This is therefore not simply a novel metaphor, but also a metaphor that challenges conventional representations of a particular experience. As such, it runs the risk of not being understood, or of being rejected by readers as inappropriate or outrageous (cf. Toolan *et al.* 1988). On the other hand, it can also be perceived by some readers as a most apt representation of a common personal experience (e.g. during post-natal depression), which is perhaps not sufficiently recognized or expressed.

In Turner and Fauconnier's more recent work, novel metaphors are given greater attention, and are accounted for in terms of the general cognitive phenomenon of 'conceptual integration' or 'blending', a discussion of which is beyond the scope of this book (see Fauconnier and Turner 2002; for literary applications, see the papers in *Language and Literature* 15, 1, 2006). Both the blending approach and the approach to poetry proposed in Lakoff and Turner (1989), however, conspicuously ignore the *linguistic* dimension of creativity, or rather treat linguistic choices simply as prompts for the activation of conceptual metaphorical mappings.

Linguistic and conceptual aspects of metaphorical creativity The typology of novel metaphors proposed by Lakoff and Turner (1989) can be usefully combined with the approach to the analysis of metaphorical expressions in texts that I outlined in chapter 1. Lakoff and Turner (1989: 50) explicitly

[10] I regard the structure used by Plath as a kind of negative simile, since 'I'm no more your mother than' can be paraphrased as 'I'm your mother in the same way as'.

mention the need to distinguish between 'the conceptual level and the linguistic level' in the analysis of metaphor, and between 'idiosyncrasy of language' and 'idiosyncrasy of thought' in the analysis of creative metaphor use. Their main concern, however, is to define creativity in terms of mappings across conceptual domains.

In chapter 1 I proposed a fairly general, and to some extent simplistic, approach to novelty in relation to individual linguistic metaphors (see 1.2.2). I suggested that a metaphorical expression can be regarded as novel when its metaphorical meaning in a particular context of use is not one of the conventional senses of the expression (as determined not just intuitively, but by consulting dictionaries and large electronic corpora). From this point of view, both quotations below from chapter 6 of McEwan's *Atonement* convey the experience of migraine pain via the use of novel metaphorical expressions (the relevant metaphorically used words are underlined):

2.15 'a matching set of sharpened knives would be drawn across her optic nerve'. (McEwan 2001: 67)

2.16 'Feeling the black-furred creature begin to stir'. (McEwan 2001: 65)

None of the underlined expressions in these two short extracts have conventional metaphorical meanings that relate to the experience of pain. However, there is a difference in the degree of novelty of the metaphorical scenarios evoked by each of the two quotations. As I have already mentioned, the novel metaphorical expressions in extract 2.15 can be related to similar expressions that *are* conventionally used metaphorically in reference to pain (e.g. 'stabbing'). In Lakoff and Turner's terms, the expressions in extract 2.15 creatively exploit (largely through elaboration) a conventional conceptual metaphor for pain which can be expressed as PAIN IS THE INSERTION OF A SHARP OBJECT. In contrast, the novel metaphorical expressions in extract 2.16 do not exploit conventional conceptual metaphors, but rather realize, as I have argued, an unconventional conceptualization of migraine pain as the movement of an animal inside the sufferer's head. In other words, a consideration of the conceptual dimension of metaphor allows us to distinguish between different kinds or degrees of creativity in the use of metaphor in language.

It is also the case, however, that by focusing primarily on metaphor as a conceptual phenomenon, Lakoff and Turner (1989) do not do full justice to the role of linguistic and textual phenomena in our perceptions of creativity in metaphor use. As shown in 1.2.2 above, individual words or expressions differ in terms of whether or not they have conventional metaphorical senses, and in the frequency and degree of conventionality of those senses. 'Stabbing' has a conventional metaphorical sense to do with 'internal' pain, for example, while 'black-furred creature' does not. 'Knifing' can be used metaphorically in relation to pain, but this metaphorical use is less frequent than that of 'stabbing' (at least as far as the BNC is concerned). In addition, in McEwan's passage, the use of 'knifing' in the context of the ANIMAL metaphor and of the previous personification of the pain may be perceived as more actively metaphorical and creative than in other contexts. Moreover, both the KNIFE metaphor and the ANIMAL metaphor recur with some variation within McEwan's chapter-long description of Emily Tallis's migraine, thus creating two separate but partly connected metaphorical chains. As I have shown, the ANIMAL metaphor is also textually extended over a whole paragraph when it is first introduced.

Lakoff and Turner focus primarily on the kind of creativity that involves a departure from conventional patterns, or, in their case, from conventional conceptual metaphors. This kind of creativity has been traditionally captured in literary studies by the notion of 'deviation', which results from making choices that go beyond a conventional set of options (see Leech 1969; Mukařovský 1970; see also Carter's (2004) notion of 'pattern-reforming'). However, another important aspect of creativity in language involves the creation of patterns, i.e. the repeated use, throughout texts, of expressions that are similar in terms of sound, lexis, grammar, meaning and so on. This phenomenon has been captured by the notion of 'parallelism', and has been shown to result, like deviation, in the perception of particular stretches of text as 'foregrounded', i.e. as particularly salient, interesting, memorable and so on (see Jakobson 1960, Leech 1969, van Peer 1986; see also Carter's (2004) notion of 'pattern-forming'). This suggests that an important aspect of metaphorical creativity is the production of patterns of related metaphorical expressions, which may occur within a particular stretch of text (e.g. textual extension), throughout a text (e.g. metaphorical chains) or across texts (e.g. intertextual connections).

Metaphorical creativity, therefore, needs to be considered both in terms of the novelty or otherwise of underlying conceptual mappings, and in terms of the salience and originality of individual metaphorical choices and patterns. Throughout this book, I attempt to combine Lakoff and Turner's approach with a consideration of the textual manifestations of metaphor discussed in chapter 1. I will continue to describe individual expressions as conventional or novel in their own right, depending on the existence or otherwise of lexicalized metaphorical senses. However, I will also consider the potential creativity of the patterns within which individual expressions occur, and the conventionality or creativity of underlying conceptual metaphors.

2.3 Literature and variation in metaphor use

Much work on metaphor in literature has focused on the distinctive use of metaphor in different literary genres, in the works of particular literary authors, or in individual literary texts. These studies tend to focus on novel and salient metaphorical choices and patterns, and therefore often treat metaphor as part of the characteristic style of particular genres, writers or texts, rather than as part of general language use (see also Kövecses 2005: 95).

2.3.1 Metaphor and genre

In section 1.2.2 above, I briefly introduced metonymy as the phenomenon whereby we refer to an entity in terms of another entity that is part of the same conceptual domain. For example, in the sentence 'The White House issued a statement,' the noun phrase 'The White House' is used to refer to the US President and administration in terms of the building that is the President's residence and main headquarters. Traditionally, the relationship between the two concepts involved in the metonymy has been described as one of 'contiguity', in contrast with metaphor which has traditionally been seen as involving a similarity between source and target concepts (see also 1.1.2 above).

In a highly influential study, Roman Jakobson (1956) proposed that the distinction between metaphor and metonymy could be used to distinguish between different ways of speaking or writing:

> The development of a discourse may take place along two different semantic lines: one topic may lead to another either through their similarity or through their contiguity. The METAPHORIC way would be the most appropriate term for the first case and the METONYMIC way for the second, since they find their most condensed expression in metaphor and metonymy respectively . . . In normal verbal behaviour both processes are continually operative, but careful observation will reveal that under the influence of a cultural pattern, personality, and verbal style, preference is given to one of the two processes over the other. (Jakobson 1956: 90)

Although he initially developed this distinction in his work on speech disorders, Jakobson went on to argue that it was particularly relevant to the study of 'verbal art'. Different literary schools, he suggested, privilege either metaphor or metonymy as the main organizing principle in the texts they produce: for example, romanticism and symbolism privilege metaphor, while 'realistic' writing privileges metonymy (Jakobson 1956: 91–2).

David Lodge developed Jakobson's intuition into a larger scale approach to the 'discrimination of periods, schools and movements in literature, and the examination of an individual writer's development through his [sic] *oeuvre*' (1977: 124). He suggested that different texts can be ordered along 'a kind of spectrum of discourse extending from the metonymic to the metaphoric poles' (Lodge 1977: 104). For example, Lodge places an encyclopaedia entry at the metonymic end of this continuum, and T. S. Eliot's *The Waste Land* at the metaphoric end. In between, he positions texts such as the following (moving from the metaphoric to the metonymic end): Dickens's *Bleak House*, Forster's

Passage to India and an article from *The Guardian* newspaper. At the highest level of generality, Lodge suggests that literary language is metaphorical, while non-literary language is metonymic. Within literature, he sees poetry as primarily metaphorical, and prose fiction as primarily metonymic. More specifically still, he associates different literary genres and schools with either a metaphorical or metonymic tendency in their writing: for example, he argues that modernist novels privilege metaphors (as can be seen from titles such as *Heart of Darkness* and *Ulysses*), while realistic novels privilege metonymy.

The definitions of metaphor and metonymy adopted by Jakobson and Lodge are rather more general than those used in this book: both scholars are primarily concerned with whether details, images or topics are sequentially organized in texts on the basis of contiguity (e.g. between characters and settings), or similarity (e.g. between a character and a bird). Lodge, in particular, does not consider conventional metaphorical expressions, but primarily focuses on the kind of creative, and often extended, metaphorical expressions that we have already seen in this chapter, such as the simile 'moments like this are buds on the tree of life' from Virginia Woolf's *Mrs Dalloway* (quoted in Lodge 1977: 186).

Overall, from the point of view of current research on metaphor, Lodge's work is limited in several respects: metaphor and metonymy are defined rather generally; no systematic consideration is given to the distinction between novelty and conventionality; no quantitative evidence is provided; and some rather simplistic generalizations are made at times (e.g. on the differences between 'literature' and 'non-literature'). On the other hand, many of Lodge's claims about differences between literary schools and authors are backed up by extensive quotations from literary texts and critical works, and are also intuitively persuasive. The claim that modernist writers employ more novel metaphors than realistic writers is likely to be perceived as valid by readers even in the absence of quantitative evidence. Indeed, many of the claims I make in this book rely on the same combination of representative analyses and intuitive validity, rather than on hard figures.

Most studies of metaphor in specific literary genres are not in fact concerned with the overall frequency of metaphorical expressions, but rather on what *kinds* of metaphors tend to be used. Crisp (1996), for example, has argued that Imagist poetry (associated with writers such as Ezra Pound and Amy Lowell) tends to rely on what Lakoff and Turner (1989) call 'image metaphors', namely metaphors involving the mapping of visual images. Below is one of the best known Imagist poems, by Ezra Pound:

2.17 *In a Station of the Metro*
The apparition of these faces in the crowd:
Petals on a wet, black bough.

The description of faces as petals, Crisp argues, produces an aesthetic effect that is entirely based on a striking visual experience, and cannot be explained or paraphrased in terms of explicit 'meanings' or 'propositions'. This, according to Crisp, is characteristic of the genre of Imagist poetry, and poses some interesting challenges for metaphor theory itself.

Tsur (1992; 2003) applies to the study of poetic genres his distinction between metaphors that have a 'split focus' and metaphors that have an 'integrated focus'. Split-focus metaphors emphasize the incongruous, discordant elements of source and target concepts and, according to Tsur, tend to be perceived as witty, ironic, paradoxical and, in some cases, emotionally disorientating. Donne's use of the compass metaphor in extract 2.13 above is seen by Tsur as one such metaphor: Donne presents a spiritual, emotional relationship in terms of the unemotional workings of a technical instrument, and forces readers to focus on the precise visual details of the image of the moving compass (Tsur 1992: 94–5). Integrated-focus metaphors, in contrast, background the incongruity between source and target concepts, and emphasize the similarity or congruence between them. As a consequence, according to Tsur, they tend to be perceived as emotional, elevated or sublime. As an example, Tsur discusses another compass metaphor, from Milton's description of the creation of the world in *Paradise Lost*:

2.18 Then staid the fervid wheels, and in his hand
He took the golden compasses, prepared
In God's eternal store, to circumscribe
This universe, and all created things:
One foot he centered, and the other turned
Round through the vast profundity obscure;

Here, Tsur (1992: 95–6) argues, the compass metaphor fits into the context of a broader CREATION AS ARCHITECTURE metaphor, and is exploited to provide a grandiose image in which the Creator prevails over shapeless chaos and gives form to the whole earth in a single powerful act. In a study of religious poetry, Tsur (2003) argues more generally that Metaphysical and Modern poetry are characterized by split-focus metaphors, while Renaissance and Romantic poetry privilege integrated-focus metaphors (for work on metaphors in other literary genres see, for example, Hiraga's (1999) study of Japanese haikus and Walsh's (2003) study of science fiction and fantasy novels for young adults).

2.3.2 Metaphor and author

As I mentioned earlier, Aristotle famously described 'a command of metaphor' as 'the mark of genius' (Cooper 2005: 76). Similarly, literary critics often regard the distinctive and creative use of metaphor as an important component of the individual style of great writers. The rise of CMT over the last few decades, however, has focused attention on how we all use (conventional) metaphorical expressions in everyday language, and on how even acclaimed literary authors rely on these conventional patterns in their writings. In his recent work, Kövecses (2002, 2005) has reconnected contemporary metaphor theory with more traditional views on metaphor by recognizing the importance of the 'individual dimension' in metaphor use: he argues that our individual concerns and experiences may result in idiosyncratic uses of metaphor, and that this applies both to great writers and to 'ordinary' individuals (e.g. doctors using medical metaphors or sailing enthusiasts using maritime metaphors).

In *The Modes of Modern Writing*, Lodge (1977) distinguished between 'metaphoric writers', who use metaphors frequently and innovatively (e.g. Dylan Thomas, T. S. Eliot, James Joyce), and 'metonymic writers', who do not rely heavily on the use of metaphor (e.g. William Wordsworth, Ernest Hemingway, Philip Larkin). Although Lodge is obviously concerned with novel metaphors only, he does recognize that they occur even in the writings of 'metonymic writers', but as a less frequent and central component of their style. As I mentioned previously, Lodge does not conduct a quantitative analysis, but his claims are based on a powerful combination of textual analysis, the work of other critics and, in some cases, statements of intent on the part of literary writers themselves.

As with metaphor and genre, however, literary scholars are not, by and large, concerned with frequency in metaphor use, but with the characteristic ways in which metaphors are used by individual writers (e.g. Thompson and Thompson 1987 on metaphor in Shakespeare). For example, Margaret Freeman (1995) explores Emily Dickinson's distinctive and unconventional metaphors for life and death, and claims that these metaphors create the poet's individual world view, or 'conceptual universe'. Freeman argues that Dickinson rejected the dominant religious metaphor of her time, namely LIFE IS A JOURNEY THROUGH SPACE, which involves movement along a linear path, and heaven as the destination. In extract 2.19 below, this metaphor is explicitly questioned:

2.19 Of subjects that resist
Redoubtablest is this
Where go we –
Go we anywhere
Creation after this?

(P1417, quoted in M. H. Freeman 1995: 647)

As an alternative, Dickinson develops a novel conceptualization of LIFE AS A VOYAGE IN SPACE, which reflects her own personal experience and her awareness of the astronomical discoveries of her time. Within this metaphor, air is metaphorically constructed as a sea (see extract 2.20 below), and human beings are constructed as sailors on a perilous, non-linear voyage without a specific destination (see extract 2.21 below):

2.20 A soft Sea washed around the House
A Sea of Summer Air

(P1198, quoted in M. H. Freeman 1995: 650)

2.21 Down Time's quaint stream
Without an oar
We are enforced to sail
Our Port a Secret
Our Perchance a Gale
What Skipper would
Incur the Risk
What Buccaneer would ride
Without a surety from the Wind
Or schedule of the Tide –

(P1656, quoted in M. H. Freeman 1995: 652)

In addition, Freeman argues, Dickinson conceived of both time and space in terms of cyclical, circular movement, which was modelled on the newly discovered movements of the planets in space. Consequently, her VOYAGE metaphor for life does not include a specific, stable destination, and no comfortable 'location' for the dead (M. H. Freeman 1995: 658). Overall, Dickinson's novel and idiosyncratic metaphors can be seen as a reflection of her personal and unorthodox view of the world, which contrasted with the dominant ideology of her time (see also M. H. Freeman 2000; for similar work on other poets, see for example Hamilton's (1996) study of W. H. Auden's use of personification, and Sobolev's (2003) study of Gerald Manley Hopkins's religious metaphors).

2.3.3 Metaphor and text

Much work on metaphor in literature focuses on individual texts, and aims to show how metaphors are used in salient and creative ways in order to convey particular ideas, experiences, emotions, insights, world-views and so on. Consider, for example, Shakespeare's sonnet 73, part of which was quoted earlier as extract 2.9:

2.22 That time of year thou mayst in me behold
When yellow leaves, or none, or few, do hang
Upon those boughs which shake against the cold,
Bare ruined choirs, where late the sweet birds sang.
In me thou see'st the twilight of such day
As after sunset fadeth in the west;

> Which by and by black night doth take away,
> Death's second self, that seals up all in rest.
> In me thou see'st the glowing of such fire,
> That on the ashes of his youth doth lie,
> As the death-bed whereon it must expire,
> Consumed with that which it was nourished by.
> This thou perceiv'st, which makes thy love more strong,
> To love that well which thou must leave ere long.
>
> (quoted in Abrams *et al.* 1979: 806)

Each of the three quatrains that make up the first 12 lines of the poem provides a different metaphorical representation of the speaker in his old age: as a tree in the autumn (first quatrain), as the end of the day (second quatrain), and as a fire slowly going out (third quatrain).

Lakoff and Turner (1989: 26–34) suggest that the complexity and richness of the sonnet results from the way in which Shakespeare brings together different conventional metaphorical conceptualizations of life and death. In the first quatrain, the description of the speaker as a tree with yellowing and gradually falling leaves can be seen as a realization of the conceptual metaphor PEOPLE ARE PLANTS, in which the stages of human life correspond to the stages of the life cycle of plants. However, Shakespeare's description of the boughs as 'shak[ing] against the cold' and as 'Bare ruined choirs, where late the sweet birds sang' can also be seen as involving image metaphors: the image of the tree can be superimposed onto that of a person shivering in the cold, and the image of an empty church choir can be superimposed onto that of a tree with no birds sitting on its branches.[11] According to Lakoff and Turner, the reference to 'time of year' also evokes the conventional metaphor A LIFETIME IS A YEAR, where the seasons correspond to the different ages of human beings. In the second quatrain, the metaphorical description of old age as sunset can be seen as a realization of the metaphor A LIFETIME IS A DAY. Within this metaphor, different parts of the day correspond to different stages in human life, and twilight corresponds to the period that immediately precedes death. In addition, Lakoff and Turner argue, the last two lines of the quatrain exploit a series of further conventional metaphorizations of life as light and a precious possession, and death as night and an agent, to produce an image in which night is 'Death's second self' who takes away the light and the speaker's life (see also my comments on extract 2.9 above). In the third quatrain, the description of old age as a gradually fading fire exploits the conventional conceptual metaphor LIFE IS A FLAME, in which the stages of the burning of a flame correspond to the stages of human life. This quatrain involves a complex image in which the ashes function metaphorically in more than one way:

[11] This line can also be read as alluding to the dissolution of the monasteries during the Reformation.

> Just as the ashes help smother the last embers of a fire, so the speaker sees the residue of his earlier life as diminishing him even further in old age. There is an irony here. The ashes are two things: that which smothers the embers and that which is left over of the wood. Thus, what ultimately consumes his life is what once fed, or 'nourished' the fires of youth. (Lakoff and Turner 1989: 32–3)

As this brief summary of Lakoff and Turner's analysis suggests, it is enlightening to appreciate how poets exploit conventional conceptual metaphors. However, in my view, it is also essential to appreciate what is distinctive and unique about the poet's choice of wording, images and structure in a specific text. Lakoff and Turner's main concern is with the conventional basis of Shakespeare's metaphors, but they do discuss in some detail the way in which different metaphors are creatively extended and combined in the poem, in order to produce a rich, complex and powerful representation of the speaker's perception of his old age and of the imminence of death.

Nowottny (1962: 76–86) had previously gone even further, and suggested that it is not sufficient simply to notice that each of the sonnet's stanzas provides a different metaphorical description of the progressive decline of the speaker's life. She notes that three main metaphors are subtly but significantly different from each other, and that they provide a progression in the poem,

> from a cold, bare, ruined season to a glowing fire, from a time of year to a crucial moment, from what has gone to what is imminent, from the separate perceptions and simple reference in the first quatrain ('yellow leaves' . . . 'boughs that shake against the cold') to the one complex image, highly figurative in expression and irradiated with intellection, in the last quatrain. (Nowottny, 1962: 78)

In addition, there is a gradual increase in what Nowottny calls 'extra figuration' from quatrain to quatrain, namely in the extent to which the source metaphorical scenario is itself described metaphorically (this phenomenon has been referred to as the 'compounding' of metaphors; see Goatly 1997: 271–2). In the first quatrain, the tree's branches are metaphorically described as 'bare ruined choirs'; in the second stanza, night is metaphorically described as 'tak[ing] away' the daylight and as 'Death's second self, that seals up all in rest'; in the third quatrain, the fire is itself personified over three lines which Nowottny describes as of 'unanalysable intricacy' and which Lakoff and Turner take two whole pages to analyse. All of this, Nowottny argues, crucially contributes to the reader's experience in interpreting the poem.

Finally, Lakoff and Turner (1989: 33) make the subtle observation that the poetic speaker's different metaphorical descriptions of himself as old are accompanied by the expressions 'thou mayst in me behold', 'In me thou seest' and 'This thou perceiv'st'. These expressions may suggest that the metaphors only capture how the speaker is perceived, rather than his own perception of himself. Hence, we may wonder whether the metaphors are used rhetorically to obtain reassurance, or to influence the addressee's strength of feeling towards the speaker. In other words, it is only through a detailed analysis of the language of the poem that its creativity, complexity and richness can be fully appreciated (see Crisp 2003, Deane 1995 for further examples of discussions of the use of metaphor in individual poems).

Literary scholars have also explored the phenomenon whereby individual literary texts are characterized by pervasive metaphorical patterns that relate to a particular source domain, or to a small set of source domains. In the terms used in section 1.2.3 above, a combination of repetition, recurrence and extension result in multiple chains of metaphorical expressions that are significant to the overall interpretation of the text. For example, Donald Freeman (1995) shows how the language of Shakespeare's *Macbeth* is dominated by metaphorical expressions that draw from two basic image-schemas: CONTAINER and PATH (see Johnson 1987). Early in the play, Lady Macbeth describes Macbeth's nature as a container that is 'too full o' th' milk of human kindness / To catch the nearest way' (I.v.14–16), and expresses her intention to influence her husband in terms of filling the container with her 'spirits':

2.23 Hie thee hither,
That I may pour my spirits in thine ear
And chastise with the valor of my tongue
All that impedes thee from the golden round.
(I.v.23–26; quoted in D. C. Freeman 1995: 694)

Lady Macbeth also describes herself as a container: she invokes the spirits to 'fill her top-full of direst cruelty', and to 'stop up th'access and passage to remorse' (I.v.38–45). Freeman shows how other characters are similarly described, including particularly Duncan, whose murder involves the breaching of several different, and sacred, containers: the castle in which he was a guest, the room in which he slept, and the king's own body.

Macbeth's life and enterprise are also repeatedly described, by him and other characters, in terms of a variety of metaphors involving movement along a path. For example, Macbeth explains why he killed Duncan's bodyguards after murdering the king by saying: 'The expedition of my violent love / Outrun the pauser, reason' (II.iii. 106–7). Here, Freeman (1995: 700) argues, 'Macbeth conceives of his "violent love" for Duncan as the trajector on a path that travels so rapidly that it "outrun[s]" his reason, which should hold it back.' At the end of the play, Macbeth expresses his predicament in terms of a metaphorical scenario where he can no longer move freely: 'They have tied me to a stake; I cannot fly, / But bearlike I must fight the course' (V.vii. 1–2). Freeman shows in minute detail the uses and development of PATH and CONTAINER metaphors throughout the play. He argues that these two metaphorical source domains contribute to the projection of characters, themes and plot developments, and ultimately to the play's coherence and unity of focus. In fact, Freeman goes as far as suggesting that the two image-schemas influence and constrain readers' interpretations of *Macbeth*, and presents as evidence a large number of quotations from Shakespearean critics, who themselves use PATH and CONTAINER metaphors in their discussions of the play.

Many similar studies highlight the significance of the patterning of metaphorical expressions in individual texts (e.g. Simon-Vandenbergen 1993; Freeman 1999; Popova 2002). Werth (1999), for example, considers the set of interconnected metaphorical patterns that are used in E. M. Forster's *A Passage to India* to describe the Indian landscape and the country's different groups of inhabitants. The different ethnic groups are contrasted fairly conventionally in terms of the metaphor POWER IS UP, with the English colonialists at the top, people of mixed race in the middle, and native Indians at the bottom. Further metaphorical contrasts are less conventional, however. The native Indians are negatively described as 'mud moving', and are said to live in a place which is 'like some low but indestructible form of life' (Werth 1999: 322). The English colonialists are consistently dehumanized via metaphorical associations with geometrical shapes. In contrast, the vegetation is presented as animate and active (e.g. the trees 'rise', 'greet' and 'beckon'), and the sky is personified and attributed divine qualities:

2.24 The sky settles everything – not only climates and seasons but when the earth shall be beautiful. By herself, she can do little – only feeble outbursts of flowers. But when the sky chooses, glory can rain into the Chandrapore bazaars or benediction pass from horizon to horizon. The sky can do this because it is so strong and so enormous. (Forster 1924: 1–4; quoted in Werth 1999: 321)

This results in a 'vitality scale', where the sky is at the top, followed, in decreasing order of animacy, by the vegetation, the native Indians and the English colonials. The fact that vitality comes down from the sky to the land explains why the vegetation is more vital than human beings, and the natives (who are close to the earth) are more vital than the English (who are higher up). The vitality scale, therefore, runs counter to that of social and political power among human beings. All this is conveyed, Werth argues, not by local clusters of metaphorical expressions, but by 'sustained metaphorical undercurrents' which run through the whole novel, and which he calls 'megametaphors' (Werth 1999: 323).

Metaphorical patterns can also be exploited more specifically to convey the world-views and characteristic mental habits of individual characters in literary texts. Let us reconsider for a moment extract 2.7 above, where the first-person narrator in Kesey's *One Flew Over the Cuckoo's Nest* describes the mental patients labelled 'Chronics' as broken machines that cannot be repaired. This metaphor is not an isolated example, but part of a pervasive pattern whereby

Bromden describes various aspects of his world in terms of machinery (see Semino and Swindlehurst 1996). For example, he calls society outside the hospital 'the Combine', and describes the hospital itself as

2.25 a factory for the Combine. It's for fixing up mistakes made in the neighborhoods and in the schools and in the churches, the hospital is. When a completed product goes back into society, all fixed up and good as new, better than new sometimes, it brings joy to the Big Nurse's heart; something that came in all twisted different is now a functioning, adjusted component, a credit to the whole outfit and a marvel to behold. (Kesey 1973: 36)

Of course, Bromden's machinery metaphors have a conventional basis, and can be seen as extensions and elaborations of conventional metaphors such as PEOPLE ARE MACHINES (e.g. 'he is running out of steam', from the BNC) and SOCIETY IS A MACHINE (e.g. 'True, she was important back home, while here she was just a small cog in the wheel of Samana life', from the BNC) (see Kövecses 2002: 122). However, Bromden uses machinery metaphors more frequently and more creatively than normal. He also 'sees' machines at work where, as readers, we are likely to conclude that no machines are involved (e.g. he claims that the hospital's walls contain a 'fog machine' that the staff periodically switch on). Within the world of the novel, Bromden's reliance on machine metaphors has an explanation in his personal life history: when he was younger, he studied electronics at college, and then worked as an army electrician's assistant, until he finally had a mental breakdown as a result of an air raid during World War 2. His familiarity and reverence for machinery can therefore explain why he exploits the MACHINERY source domain to think and talk about the areas of his experience that he finds complex and obscure, such as the workings of society and people's emotions. As such, the pervasive metaphorical patterns that can be found in Bromden's narrative can be related to his particular world-view, and changes in his use of metaphor correspond to changes in his view of himself and others (see Semino and Swindlehurst 1996). At a more general level, it can also be argued that Kesey creates a narrator/character such as Bromden in order to critique the mechanization of 1950s society, and, more specifically, the methods used to treat mentally ill patients, which often included machinery.

A number of other studies have discussed the use of metaphorical patterns to convey the minds and world-views of individual characters in novels and plays, or to set up contrasts between different characters (e.g. Lodge 1977; Black 1993; Freeman 1993; Barcelona 1995; Semino 2002a). I will return to this particular use of metaphor in case study 2 below.

A particularly extreme case of textually extended metaphor is the phenomenon known as allegory, which is associated with literary works such as John Bunyan's *The Pilgrim's Progress*, Edmund Spenser's *The Faerie Queene*,

William Blake's poems and so on. At the beginning of Bunyan's *The Pilgrim's Progress* (written in 1675), for example, the narrator tells us of a dream in which he saw:

2.26 a man clothed with rags, standing in a certain place, with his face from his own house, a book in his hand, and a great burden upon his back . . . I looked, and saw him open the book, and read therein; and as he read, he wept and trembled; and not being able longer to contain, he brake out with a lamentable cry, saying 'What shall I do?' (quoted in Abrams *et al.* 1979: 1815)

The rest of the first part of *Pilgrim's Progress*, narrates the journey that this man, Christian, undertook from the City of Destruction to the Celestial City. On this journey, Christian faces many difficulties and meets characters with names such as Hopeful, Faithful and Giant Despair. Christian's journey is normally interpreted as a metaphor for the process that human beings have to go through, in a Christian world-view, to achieve salvation. In the quotation above, for example, the 'Man clothed with rags' is normally interpreted as corresponding to a man affected by sin; the 'Burden upon his back' is interpreted as corresponding to human beings' tendency to sin; and the book from which the man reads is identified as the Bible.

What distinguishes allegories such as *Pilgrim's Progress* from other cases of textually extended metaphor is that the whole narrative is devoted to the development of the metaphorical source domain (Christian's journey), which can therefore be imagined as an autonomous and fully fledged text world. Crisp (2001: 8) defines allegories as 'radically extended linguistic metaphors' and adds:

> Allegory brings the metaphorical source domain to life in a way that no other form of metaphorical language can. Its peculiar imaginative excitement, for those who find it exciting, resides in the fact that a metaphorical source domain is given its own, strange and fantastic, fictional life, instead of being mapped straight onto a target domain . . . [W]ith allegory the source domain itself . . . attains a unique degree of imaginative life and density. (Crisp 2001: 10)

In the case of *The Pilgrim's Progress*, Crisp points out, Christian and his experiences exist literally in the fictional world (or, rather, in the narrator's dream within the fictional world). However, the entities and experiences within this fictional world can be systematically mapped onto the target domain of the life and experiences of human beings, within Bunyan's particular Christian view of the world.[12] This metaphorical mapping involves inferences that

[12] According to the metaphor identification procedure introduced in section 1.2.1 above, expressions such as 'rags' and 'burden' in extract 2.26 are not used metaphorically. Rather, they are used in their basic meanings to evoke entities that exist in the fictional world. However, in an allegorical reading, these entities (and the world they are part of) are interpreted as metaphors for the human condition and the process of Christian salvation. In other words, in allegory '[m]etaphorical concepts can be found without metaphorical language' (Pragglejaz Group 2007: 24).

are facilitated by a number of factors, including: various 'metaphoric hints' within the text, such as the names of characters and places in *The Pilgrim's Progress*; the existence of conventional conceptual metaphors such as LIFE IS A JOURNEY, which can be said to underlie allegorical narratives such as *The Pilgrim's Progress* and Dante's *Divina Commedia*; and intertextual knowledge of allegories within particular cultures and literary traditions, such as, in Bunyan's case 'the Christian allegorical tradition in general and . . . the allegorical dream vision in particular' (Crisp 2001: 12). However, in allegories the textual extension of the metaphor is so radical that '[a]n absurdly literal-minded person might read The Pilgrim's Progress as being about some oddly named people going on a journey' (Crisp 2001: 7; see Crisp's paper also for an overview of different definitions of allegory throughout the centuries).

2.4 Case study 1: Elizabeth Jennings's 'Answers'

In section 2.2.1 above, I briefly discussed the first stanza of the poem 'Answers' by Elizabeth Jennings (see extract 2.10). Here I provide a more detailed analysis of the whole poem, which is reproduced below.

Answers

I kept my answers small and kept them near;
Big questions bruised my mind but still I let
Small answers be a bulwark to my fear.

The huge abstractions I kept from the light;
Small things I handled and caressed and loved.
I let the stars assume the whole of night.

But the big answers clamoured to be moved
Into my life. Their great audacity
Shouted to be acknowledged and believed.

Even when all small answers build up to
Protection of my spirit, I still hear
Big answers striving for their overthrow

And all the great conclusions coming near.

(Jennings 1979: 32)

Elizabeth Jennings (1926–2001) is a contemporary English poet who lived in Oxford most of her life. The main characteristics of her poetic production have been described as 'flawless traditional verse technique, sharp imagery, logical thought and emotional sensitivity' (Lindop 2001). In the 1950s, her early work was associated with that of a group of poets known as *The Movement*, whose poetry aimed to achieve precision, clarity and elegance via the use of 'everyday' vocabulary and traditional poetic form (Conquest 1962).

Indeed, 'Answers', which was first published in 1954, has a tightly controlled formal structure. It consists of four three-line stanzas and a fifth one-line stanza. The first four stanzas are composed in what is known as *terza rima*: the first line of each stanza rhymes (or half rhymes) with the third line (e.g. 'near'/'fear' in the first stanza); and the middle line of each stanza rhymes (or half rhymes) with the first and third lines of the following stanza (e.g. 'loved' in line 5 rhymes with 'moved' and 'believed' in lines 7 and 9). The first three stanzas end with an 'end-stopped' line, namely with a sentence boundary marked by a full stop. However, the fourth stanza ends with a 'run-on' line: the end of line 13 corresponds to a clause boundary, rather than a sentence boundary. This links the fourth stanza with the final, one-line stanza of the poem, resulting in both continuity and contrast at the end of the poem. The last line is consistent with the poem's rhyme scheme ('near' rhymes with 'hear' in line 11), and is part of the same sentence as stanza 4. However, the fact that it forms a single-line stanza foregrounds the ending of the poem, with its reference to 'all the great conclusions coming near'. These structural contrasts in the poem also correspond to a change in tense: the first three stanzas are written in the past tense (e.g. 'kept', 'bruised') while stanza 4 is in the present tense (e.g. 'hear'), and the last two lines contain non-finite verbs ('striving' and 'coming'), which appear to refer to processes that are currently taking place.

In terms of vocabulary, the poem combines some abstract lexis (e.g. 'answers', 'questions', 'abstractions', 'conclusions') with a variety of expressions that have concrete and physical basic meanings (e.g. 'small', 'big', 'bruised', 'coming'). When I discuss this poem with my students, there is normally agreement early on that the concrete vocabulary is to be interpreted metaphorically, even though several readings are often needed to begin to arrive at possible overall interpretations. As I mentioned earlier, I read the poem as being about the poetic speaker's attempt to focus her attention on issues that she can cope with, or questions that she can easily answer, and to avoid thinking about more complex and troubling issues, i.e. questions that she cannot easily answer.[13] However, this leads to a state of increasing inner conflict: while in the past she managed, with some difficulty, to avoid the more complex issues, it now appears that she will soon have to confront them (note the change in tense I mentioned earlier). Other interpretations of the poem are possible, of course. For example, since Jennings is known to have been a Roman Catholic, the poem can be given a religious reading, in which, for example, the big questions are to do with sin, salvation and the existence of God. Similarly, the fact that Jennings suffered from depression during her life can lead to a reading in which the poetic

[13] Although it is possible to read the poem in autobiographical terms, I will refrain from a straightforward identification between the voice in the poem and Jennings herself. I therefore refer to this voice as the 'poetic speaker', but I treat this speaker as female.

speaker's internal conflict is a symptom or a trigger of mental instability (see Childs 1999). Overall, however, I have always encountered universal agreement on the fact that the poem is concerned with mental experiences, which are described metaphorically in terms of concrete entities and physical processes. I will argue more specifically that Jennings creatively exploits a variety of conventional metaphors in order to produce a rich description of the poetic speaker's mental life (and of an experience that some readers may recognize as familiar).

The concrete vocabulary used in the poem sets up a series of oppositions, which can be related to conventional patterns of metaphorical expressions, and possible underlying conceptual metaphors. Firstly, the contrast between different types of questions and answers is expressed in terms of a contrast in size between big and small objects: e.g. 'Big questions' (line 2), 'Small answers' (line 3), 'huge abstractions' (line 4), 'big answers' (lines 7 and 12). It is indeed conventional to talk about concepts and ideas in terms of physical entities (note also 'Small things' in line 5), and cognitive metaphor theorists have explained this tendency via the conceptual metaphor IDEAS ARE OBJECTS (see Lakoff and Johnson 1980b, 1999). It is also conventional to talk about importance or difficulty in terms of size, as suggested by expressions such as 'She had a big day ahead' or 'you could make a small problem bigger', from the BNC). In other words, important and difficult issues or experiences are conventionally described as large objects, while unimportant or easy issues or experiences are conventionally described as small objects. Within CMT, this pattern is seen as evidence of the general conceptual metaphor IMPORTANT IS BIG (see Grady 1997a: 291; Lakoff and Johnson 1999: 50). In the poem, however, Jennings creates a consistent, and therefore potentially salient, pattern of contrasts between small and large objects: the adjective 'small' is repeated four times, 'big' is used three times, and both 'huge' and 'great' are used once. In addition, in the first two lines of stanza 2, the contrast between 'The huge abstractions' and 'small things' is foregrounded by the fact that the two noun phrases both occur as fronted direct objects at the beginning of consecutive lines. Although the combination of the adjective 'big' with 'question(s)' is rather conventional, some of the other metaphorical uses of adjectives occur in more novel combinations. The BNC, for example, contains seventy-two instances of 'big question' and fifteen instances of 'big questions', but no instances of 'small answer(s)' or 'huge abstractions' and only one of 'great conclusions'.

A second contrast that is established in the poem is to do with distance. In the first line of the poem, the poetic speaker says that she kept her answers both 'small' and 'near'. However, in stanza 3 the 'big answers' are presented as clamouring to be moved into her life, and at the end of the poem the 'great conclusions' are described as 'coming near'. These expressions can be related to a conventional metaphorical pattern in which closeness correlates with intimacy (e.g. 'close friends') and distance with lack of concern or emotional involvement (e.g. 'a distant memory'). Within CMT, this pattern has been seen as evidence of the conceptual metaphor INTIMACY IS CLOSENESS (Grady 1997a: 293; Lakoff and Johnson 1999: 50). It can certainly be argued that the use of 'near' in the first line of Jennings's poem suggests that the poetic speaker feels comfortable and secure thinking about the answers she describes as 'small'. However, in the poem the notion of distance is combined with other metaphorical contrasts, resulting in a more elaborate metaphorical scenario.

The third main metaphorical contrast that can be identified in the poem involves the opposition between light and dark. In the second stanza, the poetic speaker says that she kept the huge abstractions 'from the light' (line 4), and then that she 'let the stars assume the whole of night' (line 6). These expressions can be related to conventional metaphorical expressions that construct understanding as vision, and explanations as the provision of light (e.g. 'Can you see the point I am trying to make?' and 'Recent research has shed light on this disease', from the BNC). Within CMT, such expressions are seen as realizations of the conceptual metaphor KNOWING IS SEEING. More specifically, Grady (1997a) has discussed expressions such as 'You should really take a good look at your own motives sometimes', and related them to a basic conceptual mapping CONSIDERING IS LOOKING AT, which he regards as a 'corollary' of KNOWING IS SEEING. In the poem, the speaker's effort to keep the huge abstractions 'from the light' can be seen as a creative exploitation of these conventional metaphors: the speaker metaphorically constructs abstractions as objects, and her effort not to think about them as keeping them in the dark, so that they cannot be seen. This expression is consistent, within the poem, with the 'near–far' opposition: objects which are close to us are easy to perceive, while objects that are further away are not.

The expression 'I let the stars assume the whole of night' in line 6 can be related to the same linguistic and conceptual patterns, but is much more original and creative. In my reading of this line, the stars stand metaphorically for the things the poetic speaker can understand and comfortably think about (i.e. the small answers), while the night stands for the things she cannot understand (i.e. the big questions). Allowing the stars to 'assume' the whole of night can therefore be interpreted as another reference to her attempt to focus on what she knows and ignore what she does not know. The image of a night sky in which the stars prevail over the darkness, however, is much more visually rich and powerful than conventional realizations of KNOWING IS SEEING.

A further metaphorical pattern that is consistent with the ones I have just described can be observed in the repeated use of 'kept' in the poem and in the use of 'handled and caressed' in line 5. The easy, comfortable issues that the poetic speaker wishes to concentrate on are here constructed as objects that can be easily, and even enjoyably, manipulated. These expressions can be related to those that Lakoff and Johnson (1999: 240–1) cite as evidence of the conceptual metaphor THINKING IS OBJECT MANIPULATION, such as 'grasping' ideas, 'toying' with them or 'tossing' them 'around'. Within the poem, this metaphorical construction of thinking forms a coherent scenario with the metaphorical patterns that are to do with size, distance and light: small objects are easy to manipulate and to be kept near; and, in order to manipulate an object, one needs to be able to see it. All these different metaphorical contrasts combine to represent the speaker's mental effort to concentrate her thoughts on manageable issues only.

However, the situation represented in the poem is not static: the poetic speaker's attempt to achieve a stable and comfortable mental condition is constantly under threat, as she cannot help thinking about the big questions/answers. This is metaphorically expressed via personification: the big questions/answers are presented as shouting for attention in stanza 3 ('the big answers clamoured' and 'Their great audacity Shouted') and as moving towards the speaker and engaging in a fight with the small answers (which are also personified as a kind of defending army). Both of these metaphorical patterns are consistent with those I have already noticed. The poetic speaker describes the small answers as physical entities that she keeps close, while she tries to keep the big questions at bay. However, the big answers are presented as trying to attract her attention by shouting, and as attempting to move closer in order to displace the small answers ('to be moved into my life', 'coming near'). This results in a metaphorical battle that runs through the whole poem, as shown in 'Big questions bruised my mind' and 'bulwark to my fear' in stanza 1, and 'build up to Protection of my spirit' and 'striving for their overthrow' in stanza 4. Within this metaphor, the speaker's mind is metaphorically presented as a body that can be bruised, and as a place that needs to be defended from invasion. However, the big questions appear destined to win the metaphorical battle, due to their larger size. In stanzas 1 and 4, the small answers are presented as attempting to protect the poetic speaker by forming some kind of barrier (see 'bulwark' and 'build up to Protection'). However, due to their small size, they cannot prevent the big questions from breaking through.

The description of the speaker's mental life as a physical struggle can be related to a general tendency to present difficult situations as wars/battles/fights, difficulties as enemies or opponents, and negative effects as physical injuries. In the previous chapter, I have pointed out how the WAR source domain has a wide metaphorical scope. The expressions 'Big questions bruised my mind' can be explained in terms of the conceptual metaphors THE MIND IS A BODY (Lakoff and Johnson 1999: 235–43) and HARM IS PHYSICAL INJURY (e.g. 'Every day people are bruised by the press and they haven't got any recourse,' from the BNC; see Grady 1997a: 295); while expressions such as 'bulwark' and 'striving for their overthrow' can be related to the conceptual metaphor

DIFFICULTIES ARE OPPONENTS (e.g. 'I've been wrestling with this problem all winter'; see Grady 1997a: 291). However, in the poem these metaphors are combined with other metaphors in order to convey a very specific experience which takes place entirely in the poetic speaker's mind. What the poetic speaker calls 'big questions' and 'small answers' are all thoughts that she has, and that she finds more or less soothing or troubling. It is also interesting that the speaker aligns her own self with the small answers, and presents the big questions as alien and external opponents. This results in an implicit metaphorical 'splitting' of the speaker's self between the part that is satisfied with the small answers and the part that cannot ignore the big questions (see Lakoff 1996; Emmott 2002 for discussions of more overt split-self metaphors). This conflict inside the speaker's own mind provides support for those readings of the poem where the poetic speaker is mentally unstable or depressed.

Overall, in 'Answers' Jennings represents particular mental experiences by creatively exploiting a variety of conventional metaphorical ways of constructing our thoughts and feelings. In Lakoff and Turner's (1989) terms, she combines a set of different, but consistent, conventional conceptual metaphors into a single and coherent scenario, involving physical entities and processes. In linguistic terms, she exploits both conventional and novel metaphorical expressions (e.g. 'big questions' vs. 'I let the stars assume the whole of night'), and employs repetition, recurrence and textual extension to develop each of the metaphors, and to weave them together. The result, in my view, is a coherent and powerful representation of a state of inner conflict, doubt, anxiety and insecurity that, to a lesser or greater extent, most human beings experience at some points in their lives. The metaphors help to express subjective and invisible mental processes via concrete, physical images, and to convey the emotions associated with the poetic speaker's predicament: 'fear' is explicitly mentioned in the poem, but the affective component of the speaker's experience is powerfully conveyed by the metaphorical patterns I have described, which present her as being constantly under siege, and without the possibility of escape. The last four lines of the poem, which are written in the present tense, suggest that the small answers cannot succeed in blocking the advance of the big answers; and, in the final line, the speaker can hear the approach of 'the great conclusions', which suggests finality, and, possibly, the imminence of death.

2.5 Case study 2: metaphor and character contrasts in Joanne Harris's *Chocolat*

I have already mentioned that novelists can exploit distinctive and systematic metaphorical patterns in order to project a character's individual world-view and ways of thinking. For example, Bromden's narrative in Kesey's *One Flew Over the Cuckoo's Nest* is characterized by the use of MACHINE metaphors

(Semino and Swindlehurst 1996); Clegg's narrative in Fowles's *The Collector* is characterized by the use of BUTTERFLY metaphors (Semino 2002a); and, in Virginia Woolf's story 'Lappin and Lapinova', Rosalind, the female protagonist, sees the world through a highly idiosyncratic RABBIT metaphor (Semino 2006a). Within the relevant fictional worlds, the dominance of these metaphors in the characters' mental lives can be explained in terms of the two sources of individual variation in metaphor use mentioned by Kövecses (2002; see also 2005): human concern (e.g. one's interests or profession) and personal history (e.g. one's autobiographical experiences). The salience of machines for Bromden, for example, is due both to the fact that he trained and worked as an electrician (human concern), and to the fact that he suffered a mental breakdown during an air raid in World War 2 (personal history). Similarly, Clegg is a passionate lepidopterist (human concern), and Rosalind used to own a pet rabbit (personal history).

In some cases, further dimensions of variation in metaphor use may also be relevant, especially in relation to the overall message that the novelist aims to convey. As I have already mentioned, it can be argued that Kesey presents Bromden as an example of the consequences for the individual of some aspects of American culture of the time. In Kövecses's terms (2005: 111–13), this can be captured via what he calls the 'subcultural', 'diachronic' and 'regional' dimensions of variation in metaphor use. In addition, in all three cases I have mentioned here, characters are, in one way or another, excessively dependent on particular metaphors, so that their use of these metaphors can be interpreted as a symptom of some kind of mental illness: Bromden's obsession with machines can be seen as a sign that he suffers from paranoia; Clegg, who kidnaps a young woman as he would collect a butterfly, is often described as a psychopath; and Rosalind seems to fall into depression as she becomes more and more dependent on a fantasy scenario in which she and her husband are, respectively, a hare and a king rabbit. In this case study I show how metaphorical patterns can be exploited in literature to convey *contrasts* between different characters, including their personalities, world-views and cognitive habits. In doing this, I also point out how the idiosyncratic use of particular metaphors does not necessarily result in the attribution of mental illness or cognitive problems to individual characters.

The works I have mentioned so far do in fact include an element of contrast in the use of metaphor on the part of different characters. In *One Flew Over the Cuckoo's Nest*, Bromden's mechanistic metaphors contrast with the animal metaphors used by McMurphy, the character whose arrival on the hospital ward sets in motion the changes that constitute the core of the novel's plot. In *The Collector*, Miranda, the female protagonist, is aware that Clegg treats her as a butterfly, and uses BUTTERFLY metaphors quite differently from Clegg. In

'Lappin and Lapinova', Rosalind's husband, Ernest, is initially involved in the development of the metaphorical rabbit scenario, but, in stark contrast to his wife, gradually loses interest in it. In some novels, however, metaphorical patterns are used even more systematically to characterize individual characters in contrast with each other. This applies to Charles Dickens's *Hard Times*, for example, where the different ideologies and personalities represented by different characters are partly expressed via distinctive and idiosyncratic metaphorical patterns. More specifically, Bounderby's obsession with social class is reflected in his constant references to the social 'ladder' and to the fact that he is now 'high up' (Dickens 1994: 18) even if he was born in the 'gutter' (or, rather, pretends that he was) (Dickens 1994: 113). Mrs Sparsit, his housekeeper, imagines 'a mighty Staircase, with a dark pit of shame and ruin at the bottom' (Dickens 1994: 181), and enjoys watching Louisa gradually coming down those stairs as the plot unfolds. In contrast, Stephen expresses his helplessness and resignation to the injustices of life by repeatedly describing things as 'a muddle', while the power of Louisa's imagination (in spite of her strictly 'factual' upbringing) is partly conveyed by the fact that she sees the fire in her house as a metaphor for the brevity and inanity of her life (e.g. Dickens 1994: 48).

Here I focus on the use of metaphor for contrastive characterization in a more recent novel, namely Joanne Harris's *Chocolat* (see also Semino 2006b).

2.5.1 Contrasting metaphors in Vianne's and Reynaud's narratives

Harris is a contemporary novelist of mixed French/English descent. Her novels are mostly set in rural France, and often feature food and magic as central elements. This is indeed the case with *Chocolat*, which was published in 1999 and made into a successful film in 2000.

The novel begins on an unspecified Shrove Tuesday when Vianne Rocher and her six-year-old daughter Anouk arrive in the small (and fictional) French village of Lansquenet-sous-Tannes, where Francis Reynaud is the parish priest. Vianne takes over the village's old bakery and within days opens a chocolaterie, *La Céleste Praline*, whose delights are repeatedly described in mouth-watering detail. Reynaud, who is engaged in a strict and difficult Lenten fast, objects to the opening of the chocolaterie in Lent, and to Vianne's unorthodox life style: she is a single mother, wears unusually bright colours and does not attend church. In spite of Reynaud's opposition and condemnation from the pulpit, however, the chocolaterie gradually becomes the centre of village life, and Vianne begins to exert a powerful influence on many of the villagers. This seems to be due, in part, to magical powers that Vianne inherited from her mother, but which she is determined to exploit only in order to guess everybody's favourite chocolate, thereby soothing hearts and minds as well as palates.

In the novel, Vianne and Reynaud alternate as first-person narrator. Consequently, as readers, we experience two versions of the same set of events, and are directly exposed to the two protagonists' different personalities, ways of thinking and world-views. Vianne lives her life in complete freedom and openness to other human beings, rejoices in the richness and variety of nature generally and food in particular, and befriends a group of travellers who moor their boats in the vicinity of the village. She is overwhelmed by love for her young daughter, and by the fear that she might lose her. She refuses to engage in the magical practices her mother taught her, as this sets her and her daughter apart from other people, but is recognized as a 'witch' by one of her friends in the village (Harris 1999: 41, 44, 85–6). Reynaud nurtures aspirations of glory and martyrdom, has a deep contempt for his parishioners, and aims to convert or oppose anybody who does not conform to his rigid and uncompromising version of Catholicism. His narrative suggests that he shares with Vianne a powerful fascination with food (its visual appearance, smell and texture), but sees it as his duty to resist temptation and to deny himself any bodily pleasure. He is determined to stop the Chocolate Festival Vianne is planning for Easter Sunday, and to remove from the village the travellers Vianne has befriended. Not surprisingly, chocolate ends up playing a major part in his downfall at the end of the novel. The two characters clearly perceive each other as enemies, and, at the end of the novel, Vianne seems to have won the struggle between them.

The contrasts and interactions between Vianne and Reynaud that lie at the core of the novel are partly conveyed via the different metaphorical patterns that characterize their narratives.

Vianne's metaphors Vianne's narrative contains many reflections on her childhood and adolescence, which she spent travelling from place to place with her mother. These travels were literal enough, but they are also given metaphorical significance by the fact that Vianne describes them as their 'long flight across the world' (Harris 1999: 191) and that she finally understands that 'it was death we fled' (Harris 1999: 45). In other words, the constant travelling she did with her mother is interpreted metaphorically as an attempt to escape from death. Death, for its part, is also consistently associated with the 'Black Man' of her mother's Tarot card (the Hermit or Priest card), and is then successively embodied by specific, real individuals, who pursue mother and daughter and try to separate them.

When, nine months after her mother's death, Vianne gives birth to Anouk, she begins to question whether she wants the same life for her daughter. By the time she reaches Lansquenet, Vianne and Anouk have been in France for five years, and Vianne has a bank account and a trade. In Lansquenet, she soon identifies Reynaud as the Black Man, and starts to re-experience the fear of death, and, more specifically, the fear of losing her daughter. This time, however, she makes a different decision: 'Well, this time, I swear I will not run' (p. 53). Here 'running' functions both literally as a reference to movement, and metaphorically as a reference to the avoidance of the relationships, responsibilities and risks that come from becoming part of a social group and a community. In order to defeat the 'Black Man', Vianne has to stay in a place and manage to belong, without giving in to the fears triggered by those who oppose her way of living and of raising her daughter. At the end of the novel, it is Reynaud who flees the village, and Vianne burns the Hermit card and realizes that she has defeated the 'Black Man': she has freed herself from the urge to live her life moving around in constant fear of loss and death. Nonetheless, her narrative ends with the suggestion that perhaps she and Reynaud 'are linked' (Harris 1999: 318) and that a new move may be imminent.

It could be argued, therefore, that Vianne's narrative is characterized by a particular version of the LIFE IS A JOURNEY metaphor: in her case, travel is both literal and metaphorical, and death is not the end point of the journey, but the pursuing agent that motivates the journey itself. The personification of death as an adversary is not new of course, and the association of death with darkness (the 'Black Man') is also highly conventional (e.g. Lakoff and Turner 1989: 16, 89). However, Vianne's description of life as a constant flight from death creatively combines and elaborates more conventional metaphors, and is rooted in her lived experience within the text world.

This particular understanding of life came to Vianne from her mother, and the novel chronicles her attempt to develop a different approach to life, for herself and her daughter. Even early on, however, Vianne's interest in food and cooking pervades her descriptions of life as travel, and enables her to develop a world-view that is different from that of her mother:

2.27 My mother always viewed my interest with indulgent contempt. To her, food was no pleasure but a tiresome necessity to be worried over, a tax on the price of our freedom. I stole menus from restaurants and looked, longingly into patisserie windows. I must have been ten years old – maybe older – before I first tasted real chocolate. But still the fascination endured. I carried recipes in my head like maps. All kinds of recipes; torn from abandoned magazines in busy railway stations, wheedled from people on the road, strange marriages of my own confection. Mother with her cards, her divinations directed our mad course across Europe. Cookery cards anchored us, placed landmarks on the bleak borders. (Harris 1999: 62–3)

2.28 They [Vianne's cookery cards] gave weight to my wanderings, the glossy clippings shining out from between the smeary pages like signposts along our erratic path. (Harris 1999: 295)

Due to Vianne's passion for food, recipes and cookery cards acquire metaphorical significance for her within her experience and understanding of life as a constant journey: since they are linked to memories of specific places, they provide 'maps', 'landmarks' and 'signposts', and 'anchor' her and her mother in spite of their wanderings. In other words, Vianne expresses her need for permanence by giving recipes the metaphorical significance of stability within her experience of life as a (literal and metaphorical) journey. While this sets mother and daughter apart, Vianne finds a continuity between her own and her mother's passions by metaphorically describing cooking (particularly with chocolate) as 'also a kind of magic' (Harris 1999: 47).

In addition, Vianne's narrative contains many similes and metaphors (both conventional and novel) in which the domain of FOOD/TASTE functions as source. For example, her daughter's hair is described as 'a candyfloss tangle in the wind' (Harris 1999: 12), her friend Armande's appearance as 'a clever winter-apple face' (p. 81), the smile of Armande's daughter as 'sharp and sweet as icing, setting the teeth on edge' (p. 97), and the faces of the villagers on the street watching the Carnival processions as 'like last summer's apples, eyes pushed into wrinkled flesh like marbles on old dough' (p. 12).

More generally, Vianne rejoices in colour as well as taste, and has a passion for nature in its wild, original state, unaffected by human control. In her first description of the fields around Lansquenet, she observes the consequences of 'the strict apartheid of country farming' (Harris 1999: 12), to which she clearly prefers the free growth of vegetation in the abandoned part of the village:

2.29 Even the derelict houses of Les Marauds are touched with colour, but here the ordered gardens have run to rampant eccentricity: a flowering elder growing from the balcony of a house overlooking the water; a roof carpeted with dandelions; violets poking out of a crumbling façade. Once-cultivated plants have reverted to their wild state, small leggy geraniums thrusting between hemlock-umbels, self-seeded poppies scattered at random and bastardized from their original red to orange to palest mauve. A few days' sunshine is enough to coax them from sleep; after the rain they stretch and raise their heads towards the light. Pull out a handful of these supposed weeds and there are sages and irises, pinks and lavenders under the docks and ragwort. (Harris 1999: 261)

Here flowers and plants are consistently personified, and conventional views on the status of different types of vegetations are questioned by the expression 'these supposed weeds'.

Not surprisingly, Vianne does not use conventional metaphorical expressions in which 'weed' or 'to weed' involve a negative evaluation (e.g. 'once double agents have been weeded out' from the BNC). Rather, when 'weeds' function as metaphorical source concepts in Vianne's narrative, they involve a positive evaluation. In the simile below, for example, the reference to dandelion seeds suggests the freedom, unpredictability and beauty of children running out of the chocolaterie:

2.30 I sent them [a group of children] out with a sugar mouse and watched them fan across the square like dandelion seeds in the wind. (Harris 1999: 37–8)

Overall, the examples and patterns I have described suggest that Vianne's narrative includes some novel and distinctive uses and chains of linguistic metaphors. Within the fictional world, these can be explained in terms of Kövecses's notion of 'personal history' (the experience of constant travel, her mother's magic) and 'human concern' (her passion for food, and for plants/weeds). In the next section I show how similar considerations apply to Reynaud's narrative, and also how Harris uses the notion of weeds in particular to emphasize the differences between the two characters.

Reynaud's metaphors In his narrative, Reynaud repeatedly acknowledges his dislike for animals and people, including particularly his parishioners. He mentions, for example, that he would like to poison the pigeons that fly around his church in the same way as he poisons the rats in the sacristy, and wonders whether this may be a sin against his namesake, St Francis of Assisi. He also finds his parishioners' lives trivial and inane, and often expresses his irritation at the pettiness of the problems and failings that they reveal in the confessional.

All of these attitudes are also expressed via Reynaud's self-conscious and idiosyncratic uses of the conventional metaphor of the 'flock' for his parishioners. Within the Bible and the teachings of the Catholic Church, the metaphorical description of people as 'flock' normally emphasizes their vulnerability and meekness. Hence, the role of the Priest is constructed in terms of that of the shepherd, who lovingly cares for his sheep. Due to the strength of his views on both people and animals, Reynaud has difficulties with the conventional version of this metaphor. In the example below, he openly questions it (see Lakoff and Turner 1989) immediately after an irritated outburst against some of his parishioners:

2.31 Sheep are not the docile, pleasant creatures of the pastoral idyll. Any countryman will tell you that. They are sly, occasionally vicious, pathologically stupid. The lenient shepherd may find his flock unruly, defiant. I cannot afford to be lenient. (Harris 1999: 24)

Here Reynaud replaces the representation of sheep in the 'pastoral idyll' with a more negative and realistic view that he attributes to '[a]ny countryman'. Within his description, sheep are personified via adjectives that also apply to his perception of his parishioners, such as 'sly' and 'stupid'. He then goes on to justify his uncompromising behaviour towards the villagers by constructing himself as a shepherd whose flock would become 'unruly, defiant' if treated with leniency. In other words, Reynaud adopts a variant of the conventional SHEPHERD AND FLOCK metaphor of the classical and Biblical tradition in order to express and justify his view of his role as a priest. Even on a rare occasion when he is moved by the villagers' (temporary) obedience to his teachings, he acknowledges that they do this out of instinct rather than 'out of any great feeling of contrition or spirituality', and comments that 'sheep are no great thinkers' (Harris 1999: 266).

Reynaud's attitude to vegetation is consistent with his attitude towards animals and human beings. In contrast with Vianne, he objects to weeds and any plant growing freely and luxuriously, and is disturbed by the scent of flowers. He spends any spare moment furiously weeding and digging in the churchyard, in an attempt to impose order on what he sees as an 'irreverent' profusion of vegetation. His abhorrence of weeds is such that he feels deeply frustrated by their resilience, and metaphorically describes them as an inexorably advancing army:

2.32 What I feel is a kind of helplessness, for as I dig and prune and cut, the serried green armies simply fill the spaces at my back, pushing out long green tongues of derision at my efforts. (Harris 1999: 235–6)

Here the weeds are not just personified as an enemy, but also as people laughing at Reynaud's inability to control them, possibly suggesting that his attitudes border on obsession.

Not surprisingly, Reynaud repeatedly uses metaphorical expressions relating to weeds, and particularly dandelions, in reference to people whom he perceives as threatening outsiders, notably Vianne and her 'gipsy' friends. Reynaud adopts the conventional negative evaluation of WEED metaphors, but often produces creative extension and elaborations:

2.33 What can she [Vianne] *do*? It is merely my sense of order which is offended, as a conscientious gardener might take offence at a patch of seeding dandelions . . . Remember Les Marauds, and the gypsies we ousted from the banks of the Tannes. . . . But at last, we uprooted them all . . . A single dandelion seed, *mon père*, would be enough to bring them back. (Harris 1999: 67–8)[14]

2.34 [In reference to Vianne's influence on the villagers] And yet the Bible tells us quite clearly what we must do. Weeds and wheat cannot grow peacefully together. Any gardener could tell you the same thing. (Harris 1999: 163)

Reynaud's strict and uncompromising attitude towards literal weeds and gardening is metaphorically projected onto his view of strangers ('weeds', 'dandelions') and of his own role (that of a gardener uprooting weeds and maintaining

[14] Reynaud's narrative is addressed to an elderly former parish priest of Lansquenet, who lies in a coma, as a result of a stroke that he first suffered when a young Reynaud discovered him having sex with Reynaud's mother. Reynaud and the old priest had in the past collaborated to oust a group of travellers from the village.

order). In his view, this justifies the use of all means of expelling strangers from the village, including setting fire to the travellers' boats or destroying Vianne's window display in the chocolaterie.

As will have by now become clear, Harris attributes to her two protagonists diametrically opposed views towards nature, which result in different uses of metaphors involving weeds, and particularly dandelions. Interestingly, towards the end of the book, this contrast surfaces in a conversation between the two characters, recounted in the Priest's narrative. He has been digging the beds in the churchyard when she suddenly approaches him:

2.35 'You've got a lovely garden,' she remarks. She lets one hand trail across a swathe of vegetation; she clenches her fist and brings it to her face full of scent.

'So many herbs,' she says. 'Lemon balm and eau-de-cologne, mint and pineapple sage –'

'I don't know their names.' My voice is abrupt. 'I'm no gardener. Besides, they're just weeds.'

'I like weeds.'

She would. (Harris 1999: 236)

This piece of dialogue makes explicit the difference in attitudes between Vianne and Reynaud, which explains the different uses of WEED metaphors in their narratives.

In conclusion, an analysis of metaphorical patterns in *Chocolat* provides a further example of how individual variation in metaphor use can be exploited by novelists to project characters' world-views, and specifically to convey contrasts between different characters. In Kövecses's terms, both 'personal history' and 'human concern' function in the novel as causes of variation in individual metaphor: Vianne's and Reynaud's different metaphorical patterns can be traced back to their life histories (Vianne's itinerant youth, Reynaud's training as a priest), interests and attitudes (Vianne's love of food and nature, Reynaud's dislike of animals and nature). However, it has also become clear that attitudes and value judgements need to be considered in order to explain idiosyncratic metaphorical patterns. More generally, in spite of their individuality, both characters can be seen as representatives, and victims, of broader ideologies: a repressive Catholic education for Reynaud, and a 'pagan' belief in magic and the supernatural for Vianne.

2.6 Summary

In this chapter I have argued that a proper account of metaphorical creativity in general, and in literature in particular, needs to include both the conceptual and the linguistic levels of metaphor. Following Lakoff and Turner (1989), I have shown how literary metaphors often have a conventional basis, but I have also discussed cases of entirely novel cross-domain mappings. I have provided an overview of how variation in the creative use of metaphor can characterize different genres, the works by particular authors and individual texts. The two case studies have demonstrated the power of metaphorical choices and patterns in conveying particular mental experiences and in projecting contrasting world-views.

3 Metaphor in politics

3.1 A preliminary example: Tony Blair's 'reverse gear'

On 30 September 2003, the British Prime Minister, Tony Blair, delivered the traditional leader's speech at the Labour Party Conference in Bournemouth. Prior to the speech, there was much speculation as to whether Blair would apologize for taking the country to war in Iraq, and give any indications of a shift to a different kind of leadership, one more in tune with public opinion and with the traditional principles of the Labour Party, which many had accused him of betraying. Perhaps unsurprisingly, Blair did nothing of the sort: on foreign policy, he defended the decision to invade Iraq; on the Labour Party front, he expressed the choice facing the party leader as follows:

3.1 Get rid of the false choice: principles or no principles. Replace it with the true choice. Forward or back. I can only go one way. I've not got a reverse gear. The time to trust a politician most is not when they're taking the easy option. Any politician can do the popular things. I know, I used to do a few of them.

What Blair presents as 'the false choice' is, I would argue, the opposition between traditional Labour principles and the 'lack' of principles that his New Labour government was accused of by some sections of the party. The 'true choice' for the party leader, in contrast, is metaphorically expressed in terms of movement in opposite directions: 'Forward or back'. Having set up this metaphorical opposition, Blair builds on it by implying that he can only move in one of the two directions, namely forwards: 'I can only go one way. I've not got a reverse gear.'

As we have seen in previous chapters, JOURNEY metaphors are highly conventional and pervasive in English. More specifically, purposes are conventionally constructed as destinations to be reached, so that movement forward tends to correspond to positive change, development and success (e.g. 'We must move forward with a positive and radical agenda', from the BNC). In 1.2.1 above, I also pointed out how the main current meaning of the word 'progress' derives from an earlier and more basic meaning to do with movement forward, which is currently becoming obsolete. In contrast, movement backwards conventionally corresponds to lack of success, negative change, change to an earlier stage of development and also, in some cases, to changing one's mind (e.g. 'But (the GDR) is sliding ever backwards in relation to the West', from the BNC; see also the use of the verb 'backtrack' to indicate the expression of a change of mind) (Lakoff and Johnson 1999: 60–9; Kövecses 2002: 134–8). In addition, the passing of time is conventionally constructed in terms of movement in space, with the future ahead of us and the past behind us (e.g. 'I'm looking forward to my future' and 'Those years are gone', from the BNC) (see Lakoff and Johnson 1999: 137–53; Kövecses 2002: 33).

In the specific context of the conference speech, therefore, Blair probably intended to associate movement forward with the 'new' philosophy and policies which he had developed for the party he had relabelled 'New Labour', and which he had led to election victories in 1997 and 2001. On the other hand, he probably intended to associate movement backwards with the party's traditional but, in his view, outdated, philosophy and policies (which, some would argue, had kept Labour out of power for nearly two decades prior to 1997). Interestingly, the use of a metaphorical opposition enabled Blair to avoid using more openly evaluative terms, which might have directly antagonized part of his audience, such as 'old' vs. 'new', 'traditional' vs. 'modern', 'regressive' vs. 'progressive' and so on. Instead, in the highly charged context of the end of the party conference, the forward–back opposition might be sufficiently vague and ambiguous to allow superficial identification and agreement from conference participants with very different views. The basic physical opposition between forward and backward movement also simplifies what is in fact a highly complex, abstract and nuanced set of choices facing a left-of-centre party in a country such as the UK at the beginning of the twenty-first century.[1]

After metaphorically introducing what he sees as the 'true choice', Blair states that he 'can only go one way', and justifies this via the most novel of the metaphorical expressions in extract 3.1, in which he describes himself as a motorized vehicle, the prototypical example of which is a car: 'I've not got a reverse gear.'[2] Different receivers of the speech will of course (have) interpret(ed) and respond(ed) to these lines differently. The specific choice of a motoring metaphor may be perceived to have a masculine bias, and even be negatively evaluated by some sections of the audience for potentially evoking the private car, one of the symbols of capitalist societies and one of the main causes of environmental damage. However, given the identity and role of the

[1] Chilton (2004: 202–3) has also pointed out that politicians tend to use binary oppositions (rather than more nuanced and scalar expressions) in their representations of the world, and of political issues in particular.

[2] Note that Blair's statement here is in the negative, so that, unlike some prototypical metaphorical statements (e.g. 'Juliet is the sun'), it is literally true: Blair does not have a reverse gear, because he is a human being rather than a vehicle. Although, on a superficial level, this statement is uninformative, in context, it will be interpreted as both informative and relevant, i.e. as a metaphorical description of Blair himself as a vehicle without a reverse gear (see Glucksberg 2001: 47).

speaker, and the nature of the event, it can be safely assumed that Blair intended to portray himself in a positive light.

Since it is structurally impossible for a vehicle without a reverse gear to propel itself backwards, Blair presumably aimed to suggest that he would continue to opt for the 'forward' option in the metaphor opposition he had just set up: he would not change his mind, his philosophy, policies, leadership style and so on. In addition, the REVERSE GEAR metaphorical suggests that Blair's attitudes and actions are due to his intrinsic nature and character. A favourable interpretation of this is that Blair has the strength, integrity and conviction of character to continue what he has started and what he thinks is right, even though this may be the less popular and therefore the more difficult option.

In the days following the speech, the 'reverse gear' statement was the most frequently quoted part of Blair's speech in the media, especially in news headlines.[3] There was also ample evidence, however, that the use of striking metaphors such as Blair's can be a risky enterprise in politics: several media commentators and politicians exploited the conventionality and versatility of JOURNEY metaphors to turn the REVERSE GEAR metaphor against Blair.[4] Here I consider two examples.

A few hours after Blair's conference speech, the anchorman on the BBC evening news prefaced a question to one of the BBC's political commentators with the words:

3.2 but when you're on the edge of a cliff it is good to have a reverse gear.

The journalist's utterance evokes a different JOURNEY scenario from Blair's general opposition between forward and back. Here a vehicle has reached a point in a journey where further movement forward would result in a fall down a cliff and, consequently, irreparable damage. In this context, having a reverse gear is therefore necessary to avoid a catastrophic end to the journey. The expression 'the edge of a cliff' is conventionally used in English to refer metaphorically to a particularly difficult and dangerous situation. In this specific context, the suggestion is of course that Blair is in such a difficult and precarious position that continuing to act in the same way could be seriously damaging for him as

[3] Amongst other things, commentators also pointed out an intertextual parallel with a similar metaphor used by Margaret Thatcher in her 1980 Conservative Party Conference speech, when she was under pressure from sections of her own party to change her controversial economic policies:

To those waiting with bated breath for that favourite media catchphrase, the U-turn, I have only one thing to say: You turn if you want to. The lady's not for turning!

In particular, one newspaper headline ran: 'The man is not for turning' (*Guardian Unlimited*, 1 October 2003).

[4] This is a different kind of risk from the one I mentioned in chapter 2 in relation to radically novel conceptual metaphors in literature, where the risk lies in the possibility of confusing or alienating readers.

party leader and Prime Minister. Within the journalist's metaphorical scenario, moving backwards corresponds to the ability to change one's mind and one's actions as in Blair's speech, but it is positively evaluated ('it is good'), since it may be politically expedient, and may also reflect honesty, flexibility, modesty and the willingness to acknowledge one's mistakes. Humorous effects can also be generated by the contrast between Blair's confident statement and the image of a vehicle without a reverse gear on the edge of a cliff.

A few months after Blair's speech, on 20 April 2004, the leader of the opposition Michael Howard evoked the REVERSE GEAR metaphor again in a House of Commons debate. Blair had just announced that a referendum would be held over the European constitution, even though the government had previously claimed that a referendum would not be necessary. Howard then said that he welcomed the government's decision, and went on to add:

3.3 Six months ago, the Prime Minister stood before his party conference and said, with all the lip-quivering intensity for which he has become famous:

> 'I can only go one way. I've not got a reverse gear.'
>
> Today, we could hear the gears grinding as he came before us, lip quivering once again, to eat all those words that he has pronounced so emphatically for so long. Who will ever trust him again? (*House of Commons Hansard Debates*, 20 April 2004)

Although he agrees with the decision to hold a referendum, Howard exploits the contradiction between the government's change of policy and what is suggested by Blair's 'reverse gear' statement. After quoting Blair's own words, Howard metaphorically describes Blair's behaviour during the announcement in terms of a vehicle audibly struggling to come to a halt or change of direction. The expression 'gears grinding' is clearly meant as an extension and parody of Blair's own conference speech metaphor. Interestingly, empirical studies have shown that, in political debates, metaphorical expressions that extend an opponent's metaphor have a particularly high persuasive power (Mio 1996, 1997). Indeed, Howard's statement, which was widely quoted in the media, was generally regarded as a small victory for the Opposition in the parliamentary debate.

This particular example demonstrates many of the phenomena that I will consider in this chapter on metaphor in politics, including: the use of metaphors on the part of politicians for rhetorical and persuasive purposes; the exploitation of highly conventional metaphors, which tend to simplify abstract and complex issues in order to make them accessible to the public; the dominance of particular wide-scope source domains, including that of PATH/JOURNEY; the creative extension of conventional metaphors to make particular points and produce striking 'quote-worthy' expressions, which are often described as 'soundbites'; the use of metaphorical expressions to achieve humorous effects; the exploitation of the vagueness and ambiguity of metaphorical expressions;

the ideological implications of metaphorical choices; the possibility of 'against the grain' interpretations of particular metaphorical expressions and the strategic extension or evocation of others' metaphors; and the establishment of intertextual chains of metaphorical statements by different speakers on different occasions.

I will now discuss all these issues in more detail, before presenting two specific case studies on the use of metaphor in political discourse.

3.2 Metaphor and persuasion in politics

The domain of 'politics' is not easy to define or delimit (see Chilton 2004 for an overview of different definitions). Here I will assume that it includes a wide variety of individuals (e.g. private citizens, political journalists, party members, Heads of State), groups (e.g. political parties, pressure groups), institutions (e.g. local councils, parliaments, governments, international bodies), activities (e.g. demonstrations, elections and electoral campaigns, decision-making and legislating at different levels) genres (e.g. political speeches, media reports), and discourses (e.g. to do with nationhood, taxation, education). At the core of politics, however, are processes that involve the acquisition, maintenance, negotiation, exercise and loss of power in local, national and international contexts. As Chilton suggests, power can be thought of 'in terms of capability and resources, which include the discursive power to promote and impose concepts as the basis of preferred policies' (Chilton 1996: 6).

One of the main ways in which power can be gained, maintained or undermined is by affecting others' views and behaviour, i.e. by getting others to hold views (that may lead to actions) that are advantageous to a particular individual, group or cause. The general rhetorical goal of persuasion, in other words, is central to much political action, and language is one of the main tools for the achievement of this general goal. It is therefore not surprising that language plays a central (if not always recognized) role in politics, and that much political action is, either wholly or partly, linguistic action (see Chilton 1996: 47; van Dijk 2002; Wodak 2002; Chilton 2004: 3–15). This may take a variety of forms: it may involve speech or writing (e.g. speeches and parliamentary debates vs. leaflets, manifestos and laws); it may be more or less interactive (e.g. speeches and written documents vs. debates and interviews); it may be more or less formal and codified (e.g. informal gatherings vs. political ceremonies); and it may be more or less public (e.g. behind-closed-door negotiations vs. press conferences and media interviews).

As I mentioned in 1.1.1 above, metaphor is a particularly important linguistic and conceptual tool for the achievement of persuasion. In the Western rhetorical tradition, the persuasive use of metaphor in political discourse has been recognized since Greek and Roman antiquity, in the writings of classical rhetoricians such as Aristotle and Quintilian. Many contemporary political theorists and psychologists also claim that metaphor is often used in politics for persuasive purposes, and indeed often attribute to metaphor strong persuasive effects (see Mio 1996 for an overview).[5] Generally speaking, this is explained as a result of the fact that, by metaphorically talking about something in terms of something else, speakers/writers foreground some aspects of the phenomenon in question and downplay others, and therefore potentially affect receivers' views.

The recent emphasis on the pervasiveness and centrality of metaphor in both language and thought has led to more comprehensive accounts of the role of metaphor in politics, which include both its uses in political discourse and its functions in the cognitive processes and representations that are involved in the production and reception of (political) texts. Charteris-Black (2004), for example, has showed how the metaphors used by successful political leaders exploit both conscious beliefs and unconscious emotional associations in order to project particularly powerful representations of the speakers themselves and of the nations or groups they lead. Chilton has developed a cognitive approach where political discourse is considered 'as necessarily a product of individual and collective mental processes' (Chilton 2004: 50), and metaphor as an important part of these processes (Chilton 1985, 1996; Chilton and Schäffner 2002; Chilton 2004). Chilton recognizes the need to consider the social dimension of political behaviour and practices, but stresses the fact that 'language and political behaviour can be thought of as based on the cognitive endowments of the human mind' (Chilton 2004: 28).

Chilton (2004: 45–7) identifies three main strategic functions that linguistic expressions may be used for in politics: coercion; legitimization and delegitimization; and representation and misrepresentation. Coercion is to do with affecting others' behaviour, for example by issuing commands, setting agendas or passing laws. (De)legitimization is to do with establishing or undermining one's own or others' credibility as holders of power, people worthy of being obeyed and so on. (Mis)representation is to do with controlling the amount and nature of information that others receive, and with evoking particular views of 'reality' (note the similarity between Chilton's function of (mis)representation and Halliday's ideational function of language, which was mentioned in 1.2.4 above).

According to Chilton (2004: 51–2), metaphorical expressions are particularly involved in the function of representation, since their interpretation involves the projection of material from source to target domains, including particularly

[5] Only a handful of studies have investigated the actual persuasive effects of metaphorical expressions in politics, and the results have not been conclusive (see Mio 1996, 1997 for overviews). However, these studies have investigated the effects of individual (and mostly creative) uses of metaphor on hearers or readers. Here I am mostly concerned with the cumulative effect of repeated uses of particular metaphorical expressions, including both conventional and novel instances.

patterns of inferences. For example, Blair's use of the metaphorical opposition between 'forward and back' evokes a particular representation of the choice facing the party and its leader, in which one option is conventionally associated with success in achieving goals (and the future), and the other with lack of success in achieving goals (and the past). The REVERSE GEAR metaphor conveys a particular representation of Blair himself, who may be positively constructed as a strong, committed leader who is not influenced by difficulties and opposition. This example also shows how, as Chilton points out, the three main strategic functions of language in politics are closely interconnected: by evoking a particular representation of the party and of himself, Blair presumably also aimed to legitimize his continued leadership of the party and the country, which was being questioned at the time. This simultaneously delegitimizes those who disagree with his policies and actions, since their views are negatively evaluated by being metaphorically presented as involving a backward movement. However, as I have suggested, neither the conventionality of the forward–back opposition nor the strikingness of Blair's 'reverse gear' image can constrain the representations that receivers will actually form in processing the speech, or indeed prevent further exploitations of Blair's metaphors that evoke very different representations from what Blair is likely to have intended.

3.3 More on metaphor, discourse and ideology

In this section, I build on my comments in section 1.3 in order to consider in more detail the relationship between metaphor, discourse and ideology with particular reference to politics.

A proper account of the role of metaphor in language and thought needs to distinguish between two main types of cognitive structures or mental representations, namely: (a) the short-term mental representations that we form while processing a particular text, and (b) the long-term mental representations (such as 'schemata' or 'conceptual domains') that make up our background knowledge and world-view. These two types of mental representations interact with each other: short-term mental representations are partly formed on the basis of long-term representations, and may in turn become part of long-term memory.[6]

Consider the extract below, which is taken from an article on asylum published in a British newspaper at the end of 2003:

3.4 Britain faces a fresh flood of asylum seekers in the New Year, because of an immigration crackdown in France. ('Asylum hordes bound for Britain', *News of the World*, 28 December 2003)

[6] Here I have adopted a simple distinction between short-term and long-term mental representations for the sake of simplicity. Cognitive approaches to political communication such as Chilton's (2004) and van Dijk's (1987, 2002) make finer distinctions between different types of mental representations in both short-term and long-term memory.

There are several conventional metaphorical expressions in this extract (e.g. 'faces' and 'fresh'), but here I am particularly concerned with the metaphorical use of the noun 'flood' to refer to the alleged imminent arrival in Britain of larger-than-usual numbers of asylum seekers. Floods are natural disasters whereby large amounts of water invade inhabited or cultivated areas causing damage and, potentially, death. Since the metaphorical use of 'flood' in extract 3.4 is rather conventional, readers may or may not process this expression via a cross-domain mapping: it is possible that they may access directly the metaphorical meaning of the noun that relates to the movement of large numbers of people or things (see Gentner and Bowdle 2005). Either way, however, the metaphorical use of 'flood' in extract 3.4 contributes to the representation of the situation as particularly serious and threatening: it may suggest that asylum seekers will try to enter Britain in large numbers, that their arrival will be very difficult to stop, that it will cause major disruption for the local population and so on. Some of the negative emotional associations of the concept evoked by 'flood' may also be projected onto asylum seekers and their arrival. In other words, the metaphorical use of 'flood' has significant potential consequences for the short-term mental representation of the particular situation which readers will form while reading the article.[7]

It also needs to be taken into account, however, that the expression 'flood' is conventionally used metaphorically (both as a verb and as a noun) in relation to immigration, particularly in contexts where anti-immigration measures are being advocated.[8] Indeed, the top fifteen collocates of the word 'flood' in the written part of the BNC (90 million words) include both the words 'immigrants' and 'refugees'[9] (see also Baker and McEnery 2005). Other lexical items referring to the movement of large amounts of water are also conventionally used to talk about economic migrants and asylum seekers, such as the nouns 'wave' and 'tide' and the verb 'inundate'. This pattern has been noted in a number of studies, both in relation to English and other languages (van Dijk 1987: 372–3; van Teeffelen 1994; El Refaie 2001; O'Brien 2003; Chilton 2004: 110–34). It can therefore be argued that a conventional metaphorical use of expressions relating to the movement of water, and 'flood' in particular, is part of the discourse of immigration and asylum generally, i.e. it is part of the dominant way

[7] The negative implications of the metaphorical use of 'flood' are reinforced by other linguistic choices in the text, including the metaphorical description of groups of asylum seekers as 'hordes' in the headline.

[8] More precisely, 'flood' metaphorical expressions are conventionally used in English to talk about uncontrollable and overpowering phenomena involving large numbers of entities or events, as in the following examples from the BNC: 'A flood of sell orders from investment trusts redeeming funds for clients brought a sharp fall in the Nikkei average, down 256.6 to 35,366.37' and 'Yesterday's sharp rise in Saatchi's shares, up 40p to 340p in a falling market, was spurred by a flood of rumours.'

[9] Collocations were calculated in terms of mutual information and with a window span of three words to the left and three to the right of 'flood'.

of talking about immigrants and asylum seekers in, minimally, contemporary British English.

I will return to the patterning of metaphorical expressions across texts in section 3.5 below. An important distinction needs to be made here, however. In extract 3.4, the metaphorical use of 'flood' appears to reflect the writer's own views, which are presented as the 'natural', 'common-sense' view that readers will also share. This contrasts with examples such as the following, from the BNC:

3.5 Support for anti-immigrant politics in many west European countries grew in late 1991, fuelled by the belief that a 'flood of immigrants' posed an economic and cultural challenge.

Here the expression 'flood of immigrants' is placed within scare quotes, in order to disassociate the writer from it and to suggest that the metaphorical description of the movement of immigrants as a 'flood' reflects the views of others. In the terms used by Eubanks (2000: 27–8), the FLOOD metaphor is 'claimed' by the writer in examples such as extract 3.4 and 'ascribed' to others in examples such as extract 3.5. Although the metaphorical use of 'flood' is generally conventional in talking about immigration, therefore, individual instances of the general pattern are more likely to be claimed within anti-immigration discourses, which may be negatively described as racist and xenophobic (e.g. van Dijk 1987). As several studies have shown, such discourses are also characterized by other negative metaphorical patterns that are consistent with the metaphorical use of 'flood'. For example, in (British and American) English, immigration is also conventionally described as an invasion, a disease, or as different types of disasters, such as eruptions and explosions (see van Dijk 1987: 372–5; van Teeffelen 1994; O'Brien 2003; Chilton 2004: 110–34).

As far as long-term mental representations are concerned, the linguistic pattern I have noted can be seen as evidence for a conventional conceptual metaphor whereby the target domain of IMMIGRATION is partly constructed in terms of the source domain of FLOOD(ING). This conventional conceptual metaphor may therefore be part of some English speakers' long-term mental representation of immigration, asylum, foreigners and so on. More precisely, the pattern exemplified in extract 3.4, where the metaphor is 'claimed', may reflect a particular negative mental representation of immigration, while the pattern exemplified in extract 3.5, where the metaphor is 'ascribed', may reflect a 'meta-representation', namely a representation of others' view of the world (see Chilton 2004: 202). In the former case, the FLOOD conceptual metaphor may be combined with other negative mental representations of immigration (such as other conceptual metaphors to do with natural disasters) and negative attitudes, opinions and schemata relating to different national and racial groups (see van Dijk 1987 for a more detailed typology of relevant long-term mental representations). The combination of different types of long-term mental representations of (particular aspects of) 'reality' constitutes a particular ideology, which will be socially shared by the members of particular groups (see van Dijk 1987: 202–22; Chilton and Schäffner 2002: 29; Dirven, Frank and Pütz 2003: 1–2).

As I mentioned in chapter 1, I treat 'discourses' as linguistic phenomena, i.e. as particular ways of talking about particular aspects of reality within particular social contexts and practices; and I treat 'ideologies' as cognitive phenomena, i.e. as (shared) conceptualizations of particular aspects of reality, which include conventional conceptual metaphors alongside other long-term mental representations. The relationship between discourses and ideologies is a dynamic one: discourses reflect particular ideologies, but also contribute to shape them and change them; ideologies result from discoursal and social practices but also determine and constrain these practices.[10] Conventional metaphorical patterns, I have argued, can be an important element of discourses, and conventional conceptual metaphors can be an important element of ideologies (see also Koller 2004b, Goatly 2007).

3.4 Source and target domains in politics

It is often claimed that the use of metaphor is particularly necessary in politics, since politics is an abstract and complex domain of experience, and metaphors can provide ways of simplifying complexities and making abstractions accessible:

> Metaphorical processes are one of the most important means by which human minds form concepts of, and reason about, their spatial and temporal environments. This is especially the case for conceptualization of abstract, unfamiliar, or complex domains. Such domains include, for instance, social and political institutions, international relations, strategic doctrines. (Chilton 1996: 48)

> The world of politics is complex, value-laden and both cognitively and perceptively removed from everyday experience . . . The dynamics and consequences of politics are neither tangible, self-evident, nor simple. A major function of political metaphor is to link the individual and the political by providing a way of seeing relations, reifying abstractions, and framing complexity in manageable terms. (Thompson 1996: 185–6)

[10] As I mentioned in chapter 1 (note 18), my approach to discourse and ideology corresponds to a 'weak' version of the Sapir–Whorf hypothesis, which states that the language we speak constrains our thinking. In my view, conventional metaphors significantly affect our world-views, but we can, in principle at least, break out of the constraints of a particular conventional metaphor by exploiting a different one, or by creating new metaphors. The scope for alternative conceptualizations varies, however, depending on the target domain and on the degree of basicness of different metaphors. For example, the metaphorical conceptualization of time as movement in space (e.g. 'time passes') is arguably more basic and generally entrenched than the metaphorical conceptualization of immigration as flood.

In addition, as we have already seen, the choice of one metaphor rather than another has consequences for how a particular issue is 'framed' or structured, which aspects are foregrounded and which backgrounded, what inferences are facilitated, what evaluative and emotional associations triggered, what courses of action appear to be possible and so on (Fairclough 1992: 194–7; van Teeffelen 1994; Allbritton 1995; Deignan 2000; Nerlich and Halliday 2007).

The potential consequences of the 'framing' of particular events (including via the choice of metaphor) is made particularly strongly by Lakoff (2001), in his discussion of the American administration's reaction to the terrorist attacks of 11 September 2001:

> The administration's framings and reframings and its search for metaphors should be noted. The initial framing was as a 'crime' with 'victims' and 'perpetrators' to be 'brought to justice' and 'punished.' The crime frame entails law, courts, lawyers, trials, sentencing, appeals, and so on. It was hours before 'crime' changed to 'war' with 'casualties,' 'enemies,' 'military action,' 'war powers,' and so on. (Lakoff 2001)

Chilton (1996) also shows in detail how the choice of particular metaphors contributed to shape the dominant view of international politics in the USA and its allied countries during the period of the Cold War. Although, as Chilton (1996: 58, 329) points out, it cannot normally be claimed that metaphorical choices directly cause actions and events, 'the way people conceptualize and communicate is an intrinsic part of policy and action' (Chilton 1996: 320), and, as we have seen, metaphor is an important element both in conceptualization and communication.

The elements or aspects of the political domain that tend to be constructed metaphorically (i.e. function as target domains) are numerous and varied, and include the following:

- The current state of affairs, and particularly the problems that need to be solved;
- Causes and solutions to problems;
- Plans and policies;
- Future states of affairs, including positive scenarios (resulting from one's policies), and negative scenarios (resulting from opponents' policies);
- Various types of participants and entities in the political domains (including private citizens, parties, organizations, institutions, states);
- The 'in-group' (oneself, one's party, government, social group, nation or race), as opposed to the 'out-group' (other individuals, other parties, social groups, nations or races);
- Politics and political action themselves.

Most of these entities and phenomena are clearly rather complex, since they consist of many interconnected individuals, elements and relations (e.g. a country's current political or economic situation); and they are abstract, since they cannot be directly perceived or clearly delimited (e.g. a future state of affairs resulting from a party's proposed policies). This contributes to explain why they are often constructed metaphorically. In addition, all of these entities and phenomena are controversial and disputed, so that the choice of metaphor in each particular context will partly depend on the speaker/writer's role, views and goals.

While any area of experience can potentially function as metaphorical source domain in politics, some source domains have been found to be particularly dominant in studies of Anglo-American and generally Western politics. These include the domains of PATH/JOURNEY, CONTAINERS, SPORTS, WAR and PEOPLE (i.e. personification). These are all wide-scope source domains that are conventionally applied to a very large variety of experiences (see Kövecses 2002: 108–9). Each of them, however, has particular applications in relation to politics.

3.4.1 PATH/JOURNEY metaphors

As I mentioned in 1.1.2 above, JOURNEY metaphors can be traced back to the PATH image schema, which is based in our physical experience of motion in space. Its component elements are a starting point, a destination, a path connecting the two, and a direction of movement. This image schema provides a way of metaphorically constructing goals as destinations, ways of reaching goals as movement forwards, problems as obstacles to movement, and success or failure as reaching, or failing to reach, a destination. The PATH schema therefore tends to be used, as Chilton has pointed out, in order to represent 'policies, plans, national history and grand ideas like "progress" ' (Chilton 2004: 204; see also Chilton 1996: 52–3). This schema can be seen as providing the basic structure of the more complex JOURNEY domain, which contains richer and more culture-specific knowledge about travellers, vehicles, modes of travel, impediments to travel and so on. Grady (1997a, 1997b) similarly traces JOURNEY metaphors back to experiential correlations between our sensorimotor experiences (e.g. arriving at a destination), and our more abstract, subjective experiences (e.g. achieving a goal). He therefore sees metaphors such as LIFE IS A JOURNEY as deriving from the combination of more basic 'primary' metaphors, such as PURPOSES ARE DESTINATIONS and ACTION IS SELF-PROPELLED MOTION. What is particularly important, in the context of this chapter, is that any type of purposeful activity can be metaphorically constructed as a journey.

In extract 3.1 which I discussed at the beginning of this chapter, Blair clearly uses several metaphorical expressions to do with movement in order to provide a particular representation of the choices facing him as party leader (and Prime Minister), of his future intentions and of his own personality. This example, however, is by no means the only instance of JOURNEY metaphors in Blair's 2003 Labour Conference speech, which opened as follows:

3.6 It's my privilege to be the first Labour leader in 100 years to speak to our conference six and half years into Government. We've never been here before. We've never come this far. Never governed for so long. Now with the prospect of a full third term.

Here the present situation (in which, for the first time in a hundred years, the Labour party has been in power for over six consecutive years) is presented as a point in a journey: 'We've never been here before. We've never come this far.' The inclusive use of 'we' suggests a collective effort, and, consequently, a collective success, even though, as is often the case with the use of this pronoun, it is not clear exactly who is included in the reference (see Wodak *et al.* 1999: 45–7). Blair's choice of metaphorical expressions also has potential implications for emotional involvement: being in a place never reached before may be associated with exhilaration and excitement, which are the kind of positive emotions that a party leader may well wish to stir up in the audience at the end of a party conference. The expression 'this far', however, also suggests that the current situation is not the end of the journey, but a point in a longer journey: while presenting the party's/government's achievements to date as exceptional, Blair also wants to focus the audience's attention on the future, and especially the possibility of winning another election ('Now with the prospect of a full third term'). Indeed, Chilton and Schäffner (2002) have suggested that, in Western politics in particular, political speeches often achieve internal coherence via JOURNEY metaphors. In Blair's case, JOURNEY metaphors do indeed form a chain that runs throughout the speech, and that contributes to its overall coherence (see Charteris-Black 2004: 152–4 for a discussion of Blair's use of JOURNEY metaphors).

In section 3.6, I will discuss in detail a much more prominent example of the metaphorical construction of a plan as a journey, namely the so-called 'Road Map' for the solution of the Israeli–Palestinian conflict in the Middle East, which was originally launched in 2002. Here I will concentrate on a more specific and creative rhetorical use of a JOURNEY metaphor to make a particular point and provide coherence to a whole text.

On 1 January 1999, the euro became the official single currency of eleven countries within the European Union, collectively known as 'Euroland'. Not surprisingly, this event received considerable attention in the media, and was greeted with both positive and negative evaluations and predictions by media commentators. A particularly pessimistic view was expressed in an article entitled 'Now we have the euro, it is time to prepare for full political union,' which appeared in the 'Comment' section of the UK newspaper *The Independent* on 1 January 1999. The main points of the article are that it will be impossible for the countries of Euroland to function successfully as separate states without controlling their own monetary, budgetary and fiscal policies, and that serious conflicts will arise if some countries do not follow the rules of Euroland. The author therefore argues that monetary union will fail without further political union. This argument is partly made via a metaphor that presents European monetary union as a train. This metaphor is first introduced in the sixth paragraph of the article (extract 3.7 below), further extended in the course of the piece and then used again as a conclusion (extract 3.8) (see also Semino 2002b):

3.7 Think about Emu as a train where all the cars must move at the same speed in the same direction at all times. Unless they do, the train will derail. That is the greatest test faced by a monetary union without political union. (*The Independent*, 1 January 1999)

3.8 Think about trains where each car has its own engine and engineer. Either they all act as one, or the couplings will break and the train will derail. (*The Independent*, 1 January 1999)

The author's explicit invitation to readers to '[t]hink about' European monetary union (Emu) in a particular way is a 'signalling device' (Goatly 1997: 187), i.e. a linguistic expression that may be employed to indicate the use of metaphor, or, in this specific case, to invite readers to set up a particular cross-domain mapping. In extract 3.7 the author introduces a specific metaphorical scenario, in which Emu is seen as a train, and its success in terms of a train moving without accidents. The source scenario is further developed by spelling out one of the default conditions for the successful movement of trains (namely that 'all the cars must move at the same speed in the same direction at all times') and the inevitable consequence of this condition not being met ('Unless they do, the train will derail'). In extract 3.8, readers are invited to imagine a set of hypothetical and highly unusual trains, where 'each car has its own engine and engineer.' Presumably, each car in the source domain corresponds to each nation state in the target domain; each car's separate engine corresponds to each nation's economy, and each car's separate engineer corresponds to each nation's government. This hypothetical source scenario is absurd and potentially catastrophic: if different cars have separate engines and engineers, and are made to run at different speeds, they will become detached, resulting in the derailment of the train. The choice of this particular scenario as source domain suggests that the current situation of Euroland is equally absurd, and, potentially, equally catastrophic. In particular, we are invited to apply to the target domain the inferences that so obviously apply to the source domain: it does not make sense to have states that share a currency but have separate governments, since, unless all governments strictly follow the same rules, monetary union will fail catastrophically.[11]

In other words, the author of the article uses a concrete and highly visual scenario to present a set of problems and issues that are complex, abstract and

[11] Note that the notion of a train where each car has a different engine and engineer is not part of our background knowledge about trains but rather comes from the target scenario. This kind of phenomenon can be accounted for in terms of Fauconnier and Turner's (2002) notion of blending. See also section 7.1.2 below.

quite distant from the average European citizen. It can therefore be argued that here metaphor helps to make the topic and problems under discussion accessible to the audience. However, the train scenario also provides a very specific and clear-cut view of a situation that was, and still is, highly controversial (see Chabot 1999). The metaphorical correspondence between each nation state and one of the train's cars, for example, presents each country as a homogeneous entity, and does not recognize that there are often significant economic differences among different regions *within* each country. Similarly, the correspondence between derailment and the consequences of differences in different countries' economic policies suggests that the outcome of these differences will be the failure of Emu and a return to separate currencies. This does not allow for the fact that, for example, individual countries may be allowed to break the rules of the Emu's 'Stability pact' for a period of time, without catastrophic consequences for the single currency. In other words, the rhetorical use of a very specific JOURNEY metaphor in the article demonstrates particularly well how metaphorical choices may contribute to the 'framing' of issues in particular ways, facilitating some inferences and making others more difficult to draw (see Musolff 2004: 30–62 for a discussion of JOURNEY metaphors for the European Union, including some cases involving train journeys). This example also shows how JOURNEY metaphors often also involve MACHINE metaphors: here the countries of the Eurozone are presented as a train, while, in extract 3.1 above, Blair presented himself as a motorized vehicle.

3.4.2 CONTAINER metaphors

The very basic CONTAINER image schema has three main component elements: an interior, an exterior and a boundary surface. It is used to conceptualize a wide variety of entities (e.g. our bodies), and the main consequence of its application is the creation of a contrast between what is 'inside' and what is 'outside'. This schema also has specific applications in the political arena (see Chilton 1996, 2004: 204, Mio 1997). Groups, institutions, and particularly nation states, are conventionally constructed as containers, so that belonging (to a group, institution, nation, etc.) corresponds to being 'inside' and not belonging to being 'outside'. In the case of monetary union, for example, participating countries were described as 'entering the euro/Emu' and non-participating countries as 'staying out'. In the example below, a pro-euro politician used the metaphorical 'in–out' opposition to warn that a delayed decision to participate could cause difficulties for the UK in future.

3.9 The longer we spend outside, the more difficult we may find to get in. (*The Independent*, 31 December 1998)

The application of the CONTAINER image schema may emphasize the difference between what is 'inside' and what is 'outside', and may also involve the notion of resistance and protection against pressure from entities outside the container (see Chilton 1996: 50–1). CONTAINER metaphors are therefore often used when there is conflict or opposition between groups or countries, so that one or both sides feel threatened by whoever is perceived as 'other'. In such cases, the threat can be metaphorically constructed as the possibility of others entering the container that is associated with one's group, country, etc., causing problems that may then be described as 'bursting' or 'overflowing'.

One such context is one I have already discussed, namely immigration. The FLOOD metaphor, and other water-related metaphors more generally, often present the arrival of immigrants and refugees in terms of the entrance of (excessive amounts of) liquid into a container, as in the following example from the BNC:

3.10 Most of the refugees flowing into Tuzla . . .

In the example below, also from the BNC, refugees are presented as objects which are being placed into a container in large quantities:

3.11 Hundreds of thousands of refugees are packed into over-crowded towns and villages.

Metaphorical expressions such as 'flowing' and 'packed' in these examples do not just dehumanize the people involved, but also present large areas such as towns or countries as bounded containers with a limited capacity, that can be filled until no more space is available. This considerably simplifies the relationship between people and inhabited areas, and contributes to the 'common-sense' view that some areas cannot accommodate any more newcomers because they are (becoming) 'full' (see van Teeffelen 1994; El Refaie 2001).

Chilton (1996) has shown how, in the second half of the twentieth century, CONTAINER metaphors played a central role in international relations. In particular, the notion of 'security' was primarily constructed in terms of 'containment': this involves seeing nation states as separate containers, so that one's own nation needs to be protected from any infiltration or invasion from outside, and other 'threatening' nations need to be forced to remain within the boundaries of their own container. This view, Chilton argues, was at the centre of the policies adopted in the West towards the Soviet Union, which was perceived as a state that was not properly constrained within its national boundaries, and which therefore had to be actively contained by the USA and its international allies. This policy of 'containment' was generally regarded to have 'worked' after the end of the Cold War, but, Chilton suggests, '[a]n alternative interpretation might have been that it had created the conceptual division of East and West, delayed cooperative solutions for some forty years, legitimated internal repression, and produced a dangerous arms race' (Chilton 1996: 354–5).

Both the PATH and CONTAINER image schemata are simple and basic mental representations. Although, as I have shown, both can underlie very specific and elaborate metaphorical scenarios (e.g. the train example), their simple schematic structure can explain the most conventional metaphorical patterns, such as the opposition between 'in' and 'out' in relation to groups and organizations, and that between forward and backward movement in relation to the achievement of goals. I will now consider some more complex source domains, which are also particularly productive and versatile in political discourse.

3.4.3 SPORTS metaphors

Many scholars have noted that politicians and political commentators often use metaphorical expressions that draw from the source domain of SPORTS (e.g. Balbus 1975; Lipsky 1981; Howe 1988; Lakoff 1991; Ching 1993; Gibbs 1994; Jansen and Sabo 1994; Segrave 1994). Expressions such as 'team' and 'player', for example, are conventionally used, in English, in reference to participants in a wide range of non-sporting activities, including political activities. The particular sports that function as source domain, however, vary depending on the cultural context and the nature of the topic under discussion.

It has often been argued that American politics, in particular, is dominated by SPORTS metaphors, and specifically by metaphors where typically American sports function as source domains, such as American football and baseball (see Balbus 1975; Howe 1988; Lipsky 1981; Ching 1993). A number of studies have shown, for example, how SPORTS metaphors, and particularly American football metaphors, were systematically used to justify the First Gulf War to the general public (e.g. Lakoff 1991; Ching 1993; Jansen and Sabo 1994;). In a study spanning the period 1980–5, Howe (1988: 91) noted that different sports are used to construct different aspects of politics. He found that metaphorical expressions drawing from American football tend to be used '[w]hen political professionals refer to the inner workings of their occupation, its subtle manoeuvres, its specific figures, and the like'. For example, support for a policy can be metaphorically talked about as 'carrying the ball', and deflecting opposition as 'being a blocking back' (Howe 1988: 92). In contrast, 'political professionals use baseball metaphors to denote status or assess performance' (Howe 1988: 93). The expression 'big league' for example, is used to refer to the national political scene, while '[a] minor diplomat is '"*a utility ball-player*", rather than an all-star' (Howe 1988: 93; italics in original). Boxing metaphors, on the other hand, are more appropriate when discussing prominent politicians and their confrontations: the most powerful and influential figures in politics can be described as 'heavyweights', and face-to-face debates between presidential candidates as boxing matches. For example, one of President Reagan's aides described the first presidential debates between Reagan and Mondale as follows:

3.12 I think that the President won, quite frankly, because Mondale had to score a knockout to win the debate. Even if we did as poorly as a draw, we won. (quoted in Howe 1988: 94)

As Howe (1988: 94) points out, in presidential debates it is more crucial for the challenger than for the current incumbent to appear to prevail. In the quotation above, this is metaphorically expressed in terms of the boxing rule that, in the case of a draw, victory is awarded to the title-holder.

Since countries and cultures differ in their sporting preferences, different SPORTS metaphors tend to dominate in different languages and countries. For example, the ascent to political power of Italian media tycoon Silvio Berlusconi in 1994 was partly based on a consistent and strategic use of football (soccer) metaphors (see Semino and Masci 1996). The name of Berlusconi's party, *Forza Italia* ('Come on Italy'), is a chant commonly used by supporters of national teams, and especially the national football team. The expression used to refer to party members, 'gli azzurri' ('the blues') is the same as that used to refer to the players of the national football team, who wear blue shirts. The same colour is often used on the party's flags and promotional material. In his election campaign, Berlusconi consistently used conventional metaphorical expressions to do with football in talking about his activities: for example, he referred to his decision to stand for election as 'scendere in campo' ('enter the pitch') and to the successful right-wing coalition he aimed to form as 'una squadra vincente' ('a winning team'). More importantly, he frequently produced more creative metaphorical expressions drawing from the FOOTBALL source domain, in order to achieve particular rhetorical effects in particular contexts. For example, he justified his decision to form a political party as follows:

3.13 Così ho sentito cha la partita si faceva pericolosa, che era tutta giocata nelle aree di rigore e che il centrocampo era desolatamente vuoto . . . E ci siamo detti che non potevamo lasciare quell'immenso spazio libero.

(So I felt that the match was becoming dangerous, that it was all being played in the penalty areas and that the midfield was sadly empty . . . And we said to one another that we could not leave that vast space free.)

Here Italian politics is represented as a football match where most of the action takes place in the penalty areas. Within this representation, the two opposite sides of the field can be taken to correspond to the two opposite ends of the political spectrum, the left and the right. In the source domain, the fact that the midfield is 'vuoto' ('empty') is explicitly negatively evaluated ('desolatamente'/ 'sadly'), presumably because it suggests that there are no strong midfielders.[12]

[12] In fact, in the source domain, a match that tends to be played in the penalty areas is more exciting and entertaining than one where most of the action is in the midfield. However, Berlusconi's aim clearly was to suggest that the match lacked balance because of the absence, or inadequacy, of midfield players. In other words, the main inference he wishes hearers to draw actually results from the metaphorical notion of an empty space (see 'spazio vuoto') which needs to be filled.

By stating that 'ci siamo detti che non potevamo lasciare quell'immenso spazio libero' ('we said to one another that we could not leave that vast space free'), Berlusconi clearly aimed to suggest that he was creating a moderate, centrist force in Italian politics, which would balance the political spectrum (even though, in fact, he made an alliance with right-wing parties). His particular use of the football source domain provides a simple, visual representation of the political situation, and helps to generate an inference whereby Berlusconi's intervention was aimed at solving an existing problem.

Semino and Masci (1996) argued that Berlusconi's strategic use of football metaphors was not simply due to the popularity and positive associations of Italy's national sport, or to the existence of conventional metaphorical expressions drawing from the FOOTBALL source domain. We also argued that Berlusconi aimed to exploit his personal association with football as the successful owner of AC Milan, one of the oldest and most prestigious Italian club teams. While talking about his efforts to give Italy a good Government 'team' in 1994, for example, he mentioned the celebrations for AC Milan's success in the Italian Premier league, and added 'Gli italiani dovrebbero prendere esempio dai miei giocatori' ('The Italians should follow the example set by my players'). This may be interpreted as an invitation to work hard in order to succeed, but also to trust Berlusconi's own judgement, since it is well known in Italy that he has an unusually strong influence (for a club Chairman) on team tactics.

The popularity of SPORTS metaphors in the language of politics can be explained in several related ways. Sports provide familiar and clear-cut scenarios, with clearly identifiable participants aiming for an unambiguous goal (winning). The use of SPORTS metaphors, therefore, can simplify the complexities of politics, and make them accessible to the general public (e.g. see Lipsky 1981; Ching 1993; Segrave 1994). The risk of oversimplification, however, is particularly strong. For example, SPORTS metaphors tend to emphasize inter-party or international competition, at the expense of other goals of politics, such as governing for the common good (see Balbus 1975, Lipsky 1981). Similarly, the metaphorical use of 'team' emphasizes the importance of loyalty and group effort, but may also be used to construct disagreement (which is an essential part of politics) as disloyalty (see Howe 1988).

Due to the popular appeal of sports, SPORTS metaphors potentially create or reinforce a sense of common ground with the general public, especially where citizens are uninterested in politics or disillusioned with politicians. They may also be used to transcend divisions by fostering feelings of national identity, and generally to generate enthusiasm and emotional involvement (see Lipsky 1981; Ching 1993; Jansen and Sabo 1994). On the other hand, however, SPORTS metaphors may also have the effect of emphasizing the distance between politicians and ordinary citizens, since the latter are often constructed as spectators, rather than participants (see Thompson 1996). In addition, SPORTS metaphors involve a marked gender bias, since sports tend to be dominated by men, both as players and as spectators. The widespread use of these metaphors can therefore contribute to maintaining male dominance in politics, particularly by emphasizing competitiveness, physical strength and aggression, and by pervading political discourse with expressions that may alienate or exclude women (see Howe 1988; Ching 1993; Jansen and Sabo 1994).

3.4.4 WAR metaphors

The WAR domain is closely connected with the general SPORTS domain. War and sports are intertwined in cultural history, and are conventionally metaphorized in terms of each other (e.g. Lakoff 1991; Jansen and Sabo 1994; Kövecses 2002: 75; Ritchie 2003; Charteris-Black 2004: 114–5). Like SPORTS, the WAR source domain has a very wide scope in (Anglo-American) English, since it can be metaphorically applied to any domain of experience that involves difficulties, danger, effort and uncertain outcomes. Conventional target domains include, for example, verbal arguments, illness, and business mergers and acquisitions (e.g. Sontag 1979: 64–5; Lakoff and Johnson 1980b: 4; Koller 2002; Kövecses 2002: 5; Ritchie 2003). In politics, metaphorical expressions drawing from the WAR source domain are conventionally used in relation to conflict between individuals, groups, parties, and governments and oppositions. Common conventional expressions include ‘battle’, ‘snipers’, ‘offensive’ and so on (e.g. Gibbs 1994: 140–5). The use of WAR metaphors tends to dramatize the opposition between different participants in politics (who are constructed as enemies), and to emphasize the aggressiveness and seriousness of political debates, conflicts or elections.

In addition, WAR metaphors are often used in relation to particularly serious and intractable problems, and to the initiatives and strategies that are developed in order to solve them. This leads to expressions such as ‘war against crime’, ‘war against inflation’, ‘war against drugs’, ‘combating unemployment’, ‘combating the drugs trade’ and so on. Metaphors such as these emphasize the gravity and urgency of the problem in question, and the seriousness of the effort that is being made to solve it. On the other hand, however, the problem to be solved, and the people involved with it, may be constructed as enemies to be defeated, with potentially negative consequences:

> Which metaphor comes to govern a situation has consequences for both what is to be done and who is to do it. Defining the use of illegal drugs as a *‘problem of addiction’* or *‘symptom of social dysfunction’* directly implies strategies to deal with the situation of the individual drug abuser and to assign pride of place to counselors, therapists and social reformers. Declaring a *‘war’* on drugs leads to strategies to interdict supply or punish demand, highlighting the role of law enforcement and quasi-military techniques and agencies and legitimating their involvement. (Thompson 1996: 190; italics in original)

A particularly salient and controversial example of the use of WAR metaphors in relation to difficult problems is the controversial 'war on terrorism', that became a central part of US foreign policy after 11 September 2001. As I have already mentioned, Lakoff (2001) traces the origin of this particular WAR metaphor in the immediate reaction of the American administration to the terrorist attacks, and points out the different consequences of treating the attacks within a 'crime' frame as opposed to a 'war' frame. The latter frame prevailed, and this resulted in an on-going ambiguity in the meaning and implications of 'war' in the expression 'war on terror'. On the one hand, this particular use of 'war' appears to share some of the characteristics of the more clearly metaphorical uses of 'war' (e.g. 'war against drugs', 'war against inflation'): it does not, strictly speaking, involve a military conflict against a particular country, and it includes non-military initiatives (such as criminal intelligence operations and the freezing of bank accounts of suspected terrorist groups). On the other hand, the use of 'war' in the expressions 'war on terror' or 'war against terrorism' appears to have become increasingly literal, insofar as military action against particular regimes in particular countries has become the USA's main strategy in their attempt to defend themselves from the activities of terrorists. I cannot do justice to these issues here, but see, for example, Silberstein (2002: 1–17) and Chilton (2004: 154–72) for more discussion and analysis.

3.4.5 Personification

Personification is a particularly important and pervasive type of metaphor, since it involves the use of our experience and knowledge of human beings as source domain (e.g. see Lakoff and Johnson 1980b: 33–4; Lakoff and Turner 1989: 72, Goatly 1997: 52; Kövecses 2002: 49–50). Within CMT, personification is primarily treated as a type of 'ontological' metaphor, whereby non-human, often abstract entities (such as life or death) are talked about in terms of human actions and characteristics (e.g. 'Life has treated me unfairly', 'Death arrived unexpectedly') (see Lakoff and Johnson 1980b: 33–4; Kövecses 2002: 35, 49–50).

In political discourse, personification is also widely used, particularly in relation to entities and institutions such as nation states (e.g. Lakoff 1991; Rohrer 1991; Chilton 1996: 142–3; Thompson 1996; Wodak 2002). The following extract from an article in the BNC is concerned with a Swedish diplomat who played a leading role in rescuing Jews from Nazi persecution in Hungary during World War 2, but disappeared while in Russian custody at the end of the war:

3.14 America, which supported Wallenberg's activities in Budapest, quietly forgot, while Israel did little to honour him and even less to secure his release.

Here 'America' is presented as the agent of the actions referred to by the verbs 'support' and 'forget', while 'Israel' is similarly presented as doing little to 'honour' Wallenberg and 'secure his release'. Since all these actions are prototypically associated with human beings, it can be argued that both the referents of 'America' and 'Israel' are personified, namely represented as individual human agents.

This example shows how the personification of nations and countries can represent in relatively simple terms a wide variety of actions and processes involving large numbers of people (see Thompson 1996: 188). The actions and processes represented in extract 3.14, for example, would have involved many different individuals, at different levels of government, doing, or failing do to, particular things over a long period of time. Personification simplifies both the writer's and the reader's task, by allowing the attribution of actions and processes to single individual agents. On the other hand, however, the use of personification in such cases also results in some degree of vagueness: in the extract above, for example, it is not clear who exactly is presented as responsible, in America, for supporting and then forgetting Wallenberg, and who is presented as responsible, in Israel, for doing little to honour him.

Examples such as extract 3.14 also show how personification often overlaps with metonymy, which, as I have already mentioned, exploits 'real-world' associations between entities. In CMT terms, metonymy involves mappings *within*, rather than *across*, conceptual domains. For example, in the sentence 'In Washington, the White House said the coup attempt appeared to have ended in failure' (from the BNC), the noun phrase 'the White House' is not used to refer to a particular building, but to the people who are prototypically associated with that building: the US President and his cabinet. In political discourse, metonymy can also contribute to making complex entities and processes simple and accessible, as well as to focus attention on particular, salient aspects of complex phenomena (see Chantrill and Mio 1996). Examples such as extract 3.14, can therefore also be interpreted as cases of metonymy, since it can be argued that 'America' and 'Israel' are used to refer to the individuals and groups who held power in those particular nations at the relevant points in history.

In the most prototypical cases of personification, however, nations are clearly presented as individual, anthropomorphic entities. For example, in his second inaugural address in January 2005, George W. Bush issued the following invitation to the 'leaders of governments with long habits of control':

3.15 To serve your people you must learn to trust them. Start on this journey of progress and justice, and America will walk at your side.

Here the process of making regimes more democratic is presented as a 'journey', and the USA's promise of help is presented via the personification of America as a fellow traveller for governments who are willing to embark on this journey.

In his 1994 election campaign, Silvio Berlusconi frequently talked about Italy as a sick person, whom he was determined to help by standing for election. In the example below, the state of Italy's economy and politics is described in terms of a patient whose ECG suggests lack of brain activity:

3.16 l'encefalogramma dell'economia e della politica italiana era piatto
(the ECG of the Italian economy and politics was flat)

In cases such as this, personification can also have an important function in constructing and maintaining a sense of national identity. The presentation of nations as anthropomorphized entities may facilitate a sense of identification and emotional involvement on the part of citizens, promote feelings of sameness and homogeneity, and play down differences and dissent (see Rohrer 1991; Wodak *et al.* 1999: 44–5; Wodak 2002). Examples such as extract 3.16 can also be historically related to the metaphor of the nation state as a 'body politic', which originated during the Renaissance and continues to be reflected in conventional expressions such as 'Head of State', and 'the health of the nation'. Musolff (2004: 83–114) has recently noted how 'body politic' metaphors are still systematically used in English and German in relation to the European Union as a confederation of states.

Personification can also be used more generally in political discourse to present abstract and complex processes in terms of relatively simple human scenarios. For example, expressions such as 'the birth of the euro' and 'the euro is born' were widely used by European politicians and journalists at the beginning of 1999, when the single currency was officially introduced. The culmination of the complex political, economic and financial processes whereby eleven different nations adopted the same currency is presented in terms of the much more familiar and accessible process of birth, which applies to all living creatures, but is prototypically associated with human beings (see Semino 2002a; see also Musolff 2004). Expressions such as 'the birth of the women's movement' or 'the death of Communism' similarly personify abstract concepts, and present in simplified human terms large numbers of processes and events occurring over long periods of time and involving large numbers of people.

3.4.6 Other source domains

I could not do justice, in this single chapter, to the variety of metaphorical source domains that are conventionally applied to different aspects of politics, even if I was to limit myself to a single country, language and historical period. In this section I will therefore briefly mention a few of the patterns that have been discussed in more detail in other studies.

Chilton (1996: 54–5) considers the role of other image schemas beside PATH and CONTAINER, which have been discussed in sections 3.4.1 and 3.4.2 above.

Among these is the LINK image schema, which is based in the physical experience of connections between bodies and objects, and is conventionally applied to abstract concepts and relationships. These include the notion of freedom, for example, which is conventionally constructed as lack of bondage or physical constraints. The same image schema is also central to the conceptualization of relationships between people and organizations, as shown by expressions such as 'binding agreements' and 'ties of friendship' (Chilton 1996: 55). The UP–DOWN image schema, in contrast, is particularly involved in the construction of the concepts of power and control (e.g. 'upper/lower classes', being 'under' someone's authority; Chilton 1996: 55).

In British and American English, HEALTH/ILLNESS metaphors are also frequently applied to political issues (e.g. the presentation of social problems as 'cancers' to be 'prevented' or 'cut out') (Mio 1997), and to economic problems and policies (e.g. 'a healthy/ailing economy') (e.g. Boers 1999, Deignan 2000; see also the 'body politic' metaphor in Musolff 2004). Religious metaphors are also significant, particularly considering the central role that religion has come to play in world politics at the beginning of the twenty-first century (see Chilton 2004: 173–93). In Italy, for example, Silvio Berlusconi often draws from the New Testament for his metaphors. One of the ways in which he described himself in his first election campaign in 1994 was as a 'Good Samaritan' figure, and as 'l'unto del Signore' ('he who is anointed by the Lord') (see Semino and Masci 1996). Clearly, the use of religious discourse in the political domain is a significant and complex phenomenon, which has different manifestations and implications in different languages, countries and cultures (see Charteris-Black 2004: 171–240). The systematic use of religious metaphors on the part of politicians, in particular, may not just be an expression of religious beliefs, but also a strategic way of representing one's own identity as a (potential) leader, establishing common ground with some parts of the public and lack of common ground with others, and exploiting some of the emotional associations of religious images for rhetorical ends.

3.4.7 Topic-triggering and situational triggering in the choice of source domain

As I mentioned in chapter 1 (section 1.2.3), the choice of metaphorical source domain may in some cases be triggered by some aspect of the target domain itself, or, more generally, by the topic of the relevant stretch of text. Koller (2004a) uses the term 'topic-triggered metaphors' to capture this phenomenon. In 1.2.3 above, I suggested that topic-triggered metaphors are often used in newspaper headlines for humorous purposes, since they involve puns between literal and metaphorical senses of particular expressions. In politics, however, topic-triggered metaphors may be used to exploit the strength of the 'literal' associations between source and target domain, and hence to strengthen the persuasive potential of one's claims.

Extract 3.17 below is taken from the speech that Rudolph Giuliani gave at the 2004 convention of the US Republican party. As is well known, Giuliani was mayor of New York at the time of the 2001 terrorist attacks on the World Trade Centre, and was widely acclaimed for his handling of the situation at the time. In his 2004 speech, he vigorously defended the US administration's decision to go to war in Iraq in 2003, even though it subsequently proved impossible to find the weapons of mass destruction that were used to justify the necessity of toppling Saddam Hussein's regime. The following is an extract from Giuliani's speech:

3.17 In any plan to destroy global terrorism, removing Saddam Hussein needed to be accomplished. Frankly, I believed then and I believe now that Saddam Hussein, who supported global terrorism, slaughtered hundreds of thousands of his own people, permitted horrific atrocities against women, and used weapons of mass destruction, was himself a weapon of mass destruction.

At the end of this extract, Giuliani turns the controversial notion of weapons of mass destruction into a metaphorical source concept that is applied to Saddam Hussein himself. 'Literal' weapons of mass destruction are of course central to his speech, but more for their *absence* than for their presence. However, the real-world connection between Saddam Hussein and weapons of mass destruction remained strong, particularly for a Republican audience, and Giuliani emphasizes that Saddam had used such weapons in the past. This gives added strength to the metaphorical description of Saddam as 'himself a weapon of mass destruction', which, in Giuliani's argument, counts as sufficient justification for the war. As George Lakoff has commented in relation to Giuliani's speech, '[w]hen the literal isn't there, the metaphorical will do' (www.berkeley.edu/news/ media/releases/2004/08/31_lakoff_gop1.shtml).

In cases such as Silvio Berlusconi's use of FOOTBALL metaphors (see 3.4.3 above), the notion of 'topic-triggering' for metaphor needs to be broadened to what I will refer to as 'situational triggering' (see Kövecses 2005: 236). As I explained above, FOOTBALL metaphors were particularly appropriate in Berlusconi's case, since he was the owner of AC Milan, which, by 1994, had won several prestigious national and international titles. As I have already mentioned, Berlusconi very consciously exploited his association with football, in order to suggest that he could do for Italy what he had done for AC Milan, and that the citizens of Italy should trust him in the same way as the members of his football team:

3.18 Se sarò chiamato da Scalfaro spero di dare al paese un buon governo. Soprattutto una buona squadra. Per ora festeggio lo scudetto del Milan. Gli italiani dovrebbero prendere esempio dai miei giocatori.

> (If I am called by Scalfaro [the Italian President] I hope I will give the country a good government. Most of all a good team. For the moment I am celebrating the victory of Milan in the League. The Italians should follow the example set by my players.)

The notion of 'situational triggering' may be used to capture any nonmetaphorical connection between a particular metaphorical source domain and some aspect of the relevant situational context, including the speaker (as in Berlusconi's case), the setting and so on.[13]

Both topic-triggered and situation-triggered metaphors exploit and potentially reinforce existing nonmetaphorical associations of the source domain or scenario. As such, they may lend additional rhetorical strength to the speaker's or writer's arguments, by triggering particular inferences, evaluations, emotional associations and so on. Such choices of metaphor may also be perceived as particularly apt or 'common sense', and may also be strategically used to blur the boundary between the literal and the metaphorical. The latter point is relevant to the cases of both Giuliani and Berlusconi, who attempt to blur the boundary between, respectively, literal and metaphorical weapons, and football and politics. I will discuss further cases of topic-triggered and situation-triggered metaphors in the course of the book.

3.5 Metaphorical choices and patterns within and across texts in politics

Chilton and Schäffner (2002: 29) point out that, in political discourse, metaphors can provide both 'intertextual coherence' and 'intratextual coherence', namely contribute to the achievement of coherence both *across* texts (intertextually) and *within* texts (intratextually). As far as intertextual coherence is concerned, they suggest more specifically that metaphor 'can provide a conceptual structure for a systematized ideology that is expressed in many texts and much talk' (Chilton and Schäffner (2002: 29). The role of conventional metaphors in discourse and ideology was discussed in section 3.3. Here I will build on my earlier discussion of metaphorical patterns in 1.2.3 above, in order to consider the role of textual and intertextual patterns of metaphor use in politics in particular.

At the broadest level, there are metaphorical patterns that pervade a particular language generally, regardless of genre, register or situational context. For example, in the English language generally, purposes are conventionally talked about as destinations, and the achievement of purposes in terms of movement. In Cameron's (1999) terms, these patterns exhibit 'global systematicity', since they occur '[a]cross texts from a range of discourse types and content'

[13] What I call 'situation-triggered' metaphors provide further evidence for the claim that metaphors often have a metonymic basis (e.g. see Goossens *et al.* 1995).

(Cameron 1999: 16). These conventional pervasive patterns provide the main type of evidence for the postulation of conceptual metaphors such as Lakoff and Johnson's (1980b) LIFE IS A JOURNEY and Grady's (1997a) ACHIEVING A PURPOSE IS ARRIVING AT A DESTINATION.

Some metaphorical patterns, in contrast, are more specifically associated with particular discourses and discourse practices (even though they may have connections with globally systematic patterns). For example, I have argued that metaphorical patterns drawing from the source domain of FLOODING and (NATURAL) DISASTER are characteristic of the discourse of immigration, and particularly of discourses that may be described as anti-immigration, racist or xenophobic. In Cameron's (1999) terms, these patterns exhibit 'discourse systematicity', since they are systematic '[w]ithin language use in specific discourse communities' (Cameron 1999: 16).

A related type of systematicity not explicitly considered by Cameron concerns the level of the individual language user. As I have already mentioned, Kövecses (2005) has noted how the experiences and interests of individuals may affect the ways in which they use metaphor. In chapter 2, I showed more specifically how the writings of individual authors may be characterized, amongst other things, by strikingly idiosyncratic uses of metaphor. In the political sphere, it has been shown that the speeches given by individual politicians can display salient and distinctive rhetorical strategies, including distinctive patterns in the choice and combination of source domains and in the use of particular sets of metaphorical expressions (Charteris-Black 2005).[14]

At the lowest level, metaphorical patterns may exhibit 'local systematicity' (Cameron 1999: 16), when a particular metaphor is locally extended and recurs throughout a text to talk about a particular topic. For example, the idiosyncratic EURO AS TRAIN metaphor I discussed earlier is used repeatedly within a particular newspaper article to support a particular argument. It is this kind of pattern that contributes to what Chilton and Schäffner (2002: 29) call 'intra-textual coherence', namely the overall coherence of the representation of (an aspect of) reality which is put forward in a particular text. These intratextual patterns often involve the creative exploitation of conventional metaphorical patterns. The EURO AS TRAIN metaphor, for example, elaborates via a specific scenario the general tendency to talk about successful enterprises in terms of successful movement or travel. Linguistically, therefore, some metaphorical expressions are novel (e.g. 'the couplings will break'), while others are more conventional (e.g. the use of the expression 'on track' to refer to the fact that the currencies involved in monetary union had not been affected by problems in the South East Asian markets just before the introduction of the euro).

[14] Political speeches are, of course, often the result of teamwork, but it is nonetheless the case that they strongly reflect the views, goals and personality of the political figure who delivers them.

Chilton and Schäffner (2002: 29) indeed emphasize that intertextual and intratextual coherence may result from both conventional and novel metaphorical expressions. I would add that the more conventional metaphorical choices and patterns (whether at the global or discourse level) tend to reflect shared, 'common sense' ways of talking and thinking about particular topics and issues (see van Teeffelen 1994). On the other hand, more novel expressions and patterns (such as the EURO AS TRAIN metaphor) exploit conventional ways of talking and thinking to argue particular points and achieve particular rhetorical effects (see also Semino 2002b). Chilton and Schäffner (2002: 29) use the term 'rhetorical metaphor' precisely to refer to metaphorical expressions that are novel, extended, and therefore (likely to have been) deliberately and consciously used by speakers or writers to obtain particular effects.

As I have already mentioned, individual uses of metaphorical expressions may be 'claimed' as a reflection of one's own views or 'ascribed' to others, namely presented as a reflection of others' views (Eubanks 2000). Eubanks also points out that, in actual discourse contexts, metaphors may be 'attenuated' or 'intensified':

> Conceptual metaphors and instances of conceptual metaphors vary in their degree of rhetorical provocation or controversy. In order to adjust a metaphor's likely rhetorical effect, writers and speakers select alternate metaphors or variant renderings of a given metaphor, thus attenuating or intensifying rhetorical impact. (Eubanks 2000: 28)

For example, Eubanks compares the relative intensity of different instantiations of the conceptual metaphor TRADE IS WAR. He suggests that the expression 'storming the beaches of a competitor's market' is an intensified instance of the metaphor, since it 'evokes blood and violence'; in contrast, the expression 'outflanking' (a competitor) is an attenuated instance of the conceptual metaphor, since it involves 'manoeuvring' (Eubanks 2000: 28).[15]

In his discussion of TRADE IS WAR, Eubanks (2000) also emphasizes a point that is central to this book: metaphorical expressions need to be discussed within their specific contexts of use, since general patterns cannot predict or preclude 'important patterns of variation' at the level of individual examples (see Eubanks 2000: 21). This variation applies both to the linguistic characteristics of individual examples and to the context in which they occur (including both the rest of the text and the discoursal, political and cultural context). When dealing with discourses that involve the mass media, it is also important to bear in mind the amount of public exposure that individual expressions may receive. Individual utterances of prominent politicians, in particular, often receive so much media attention that they may have a disproportionate influence on public

[15] As Eubanks recognizes, however, the relative intensity of specific examples may be perceived differently by different hearers/readers, depending on their familiarity with and understanding of the discoursal and textual context (Eubanks 2000: 28–9).

opinion, political debate and subsequent usage. This applies, for example, to George W. Bush's (in)famous metaphorical description of North Korea, Iran and Iraq as an 'axis of evil', in his 2002 State of the Union address, which caused considerable international controversy and triggered many subsequent uses, whether claimed or ascribed to Bush.

Having discussed a number of general aspects of the use of metaphor in politics, I will devote the rest of this chapter to two specific case studies.

3.6 Case study 1: the Middle East 'Road Map'

In April 2002, seven months after the 11 September terrorist attacks on the USA, the American President George W. Bush announced a new initiative aimed at resolving the Israeli–Palestinian conflict in the Middle East. As part of this initiative, Secretary of State Colin Powell visited the region and held talks with representatives from the European Union, the United Nations and Russia. The talks resulted in the formation of the so-called 'Quartet Group' (consisting of the USA, the EU, the UN and Russia), which, later in 2002, launched a new plan for the achievement of peace in the Middle East. This plan was officially described as a 'Road Map to a Permanent Two-State Solution to the Israeli–Palestinian Conflict' (www.un.org/News/dh/mideast/roadmap122002.pdf) and has since become commonly known as 'the (Middle East) Road Map'. It involved, amongst other things, the cessation of all violence, the recognition of Israel on the part of the Palestinian leadership, Israel's withdrawal from territories occupied from September 2000, the reform of Palestinian institutions, and the final creation of an independent Palestinian state by 2005.

As we have now seen many times, the source domain of JOURNEYS has a very wide scope in English (Kövecses 2002: 107). More specifically, purposes are conventionally constructed as destinations to be reached, so that actions and strategies aimed at the achievement of goals are conventionally constructed in terms of movement forwards or travel. Political negotiations, in particular, are one of the many types of purposeful activities that are conventionally constructed as journeys. This can explain why a particular, detailed plan for the achievement of a shared goal was metaphorically referred to as a 'road map'. Road maps provide information that facilitates travel towards a destination, and are particularly necessary when one has not travelled to a particular place before. In the case of the Middle East conflict, many previous attempts had been made to achieve a solution, but none had been successful.[16]

In this section I am going to begin by discussing the way in which JOURNEY metaphors were used in the original, official formulations of the 'road map'. I

[16] Several colleagues and students have suggested that the ROAD MAP metaphor is not entirely apt, however, since road maps do not prescribe a particular route to a destination, and obviously rely on the previous existence of roads linking different locations.

will then consider how JOURNEY metaphors have subsequently been used by politicians and journalists to express particular opinions and views concerning the Middle East peace process and the Quartet Group initiative in particular. My goal is to show how, when a particular metaphor occupies a prominent position in the public domain, it can be used in different ways by different people in different contexts to achieve different rhetorical goals.

The ROAD MAP metaphor in official speeches and documents Some of the metaphorical expressions used by President Bush in the speeches that announced the new diplomatic initiative can be said to anticipate the official use of the ROAD MAP metaphor by the Quartet Group. For example, in his April 2002 State of the Union speech, Bush outlined what he saw as the 'elements of peace in the Middle East', and then added: 'we must build the road to those goals.' In June 2002, he then talked about the possibility that 'all parties will . . . set out on a new path.' Although expressions such as these are both generally conventional and characteristic of Bush's speeches, the emphasis on a new 'road/path' is intertextually coherent with the later description of the new international plan for the Middle East as a 'road map'.

In the official document which was produced by the Quartet Group (and which has since gone through several re-drafts), the expression 'Road Map' was first used in the title to introduce the new plan that was being proposed. The text of the document contains several further uses of JOURNEY metaphorical expressions, including the following (all examples are taken from the version of the Road Map published on the United Nations web site at: www.un.org/News/dh/mideast/roadmap122002. pdf):

3.19 The destination is a final and comprehensive settlement of the Israel–Palestinian conflict by 2005

3.20 Israel takes all necessary steps to help normalize Palestinian life.

3.21 As comprehensive security performance moves forward,

3.22 progress toward a comprehensive Middle East settlement between Israel and Lebanon and Israel and Syria,

All of these examples involve highly conventional ways of metaphorically describing goals as 'destinations', actions as 'steps', and positive change or success as 'moving forward' and 'progress'. Expressions such as these are particularly common in the context of political policies, plans and strategies, and could therefore have been used independently of the overarching ROAD MAP metaphor. However, the use of the ROAD MAP metaphor in the title (and in the opening of the document) emphasizes the role of JOURNEY metaphors in the overall intratextual coherence of the document.

Examples such as extracts 3.19 to 3.22 evoke a scenario where the two parties travel together towards a mutually agreed destination. This partly contrasts with the reality of the situation, where there is mutual suspicion and mistrust, continued conflict, and disagreement over what counts as a solution to current problems (i.e. the 'destination' of the journey). Not surprisingly, however, in the period 2003–4 the US President and the UK Prime Minister repeatedly echoed the Quartet Group document in their official speeches, and did not use the ROAD MAP metaphor to refer to potential complications. In March 2003, for example, Bush reiterated the USA's commitment 'to implementing our road map toward peace' (*Guardian Unlimited*, 23 March 2004). Around the same time, Tony Blair echoed the official document's wording when he said that 'The destination is a final and comprehensive settlement of the Israel–Palestinian conflict by 2005' (*Guardian Unlimited*, 29 March 2003). In another speech, he said that 'The road map . . . provides the route to a permanent two-state solution (and) a final and comprehensive settlement of the Israel–Palestinian conflict by 2005' (*Guardian Unlimited*, 23 March 2004). In all such cases, the emphasis is on the end-point of the journey and on the route by which to reach it, which is supposed to be provided by the Road Map.

Problems on the journey The detailed timetable that was set out in the Quartet Group document was not followed in the subsequent months and years. At the time of writing, the situation in the Middle East does not appear to have improved from that of 2002, and has in fact been complicated by the 2003 invasion of Iraq and the subsequent, continuing war and violence in that country.

Not surprisingly, therefore, many references to the Road Map in the period following its initial formulation involved descriptions of problems, and of hypothetical catastrophic scenarios if the Quartet Group's plan was not followed by both parties. In the following two examples, the US Secretary of State (Colin Powell) and the UK Foreign Secretary (Jack Straw) exploit the ROAD MAP metaphor to represent the potential consequences of recent, renewed violence in the Middle East:

3.23 'The peace process is at a fork in the road,' Mr Straw warned. 'There is a real risk that people on both sides become so hardened . . . that they stumble down the other road towards more violence, towards unilateral efforts to redraw borders.' (Jack Straw, reported in *Guardian Unlimited*, 23 March 2004)

3.24 'The end of the road is a cliff that both sides will fall off.' (Colin Powell, reported in *Guardian Unlimited*, 21 August 2003)

Both statements rely on some fairly conventional mappings from the JOURNEY source domains to aspects of purposeful, goal-directed activities. Straw's reference to 'a fork in the road' exploits the conventional construction of choices as points in a journey where one has to choose between different possible roads.[17] Straw then describes what he sees as a current 'risk' via a metaphorical scenario in which two parties do not take the road indicated by the Road Map, but another road, which leads to a different destination ('more violence . . . unilateral efforts to redraw borders'). The use of the expression 'stumble down' in reference to movement on 'the other road' may suggest that the road is difficult to walk on, and also that travel down this road may not be the result of a deliberate decision, but the accidental consequence of further, mistaken actions. Powell's statement in extract 3.24 similarly focuses on the destination of the road that the two sides seem to be travelling on in the light of their current actions. In this case, the end point of the road is not a destination as such, but a type of landscape that is lethal for travellers: 'a cliff that both sides will fall off' (see also the CLIFF metaphor discussed in section 3.1 above).

As these examples show, the conventionality, richness and flexibility of JOURNEY metaphors result in many and varied uses of the ROAD MAP metaphor, to argue particular points in different contexts. Although Powell's and Straw's statements went beyond the conventional mappings and expressions used in official documents and speeches, however, they did not question the validity of the plan itself: in extracts 3.23 and 3.24 the ROAD MAP metaphor is exploited in order to dissuade the two parties from taking different directions from that indicated by the Quartet Group. Political commentators, however, have extended and stretched the metaphor in much more creative ways, often in order to question the validity of the plan itself.

An issue that is often raised is whether the plan formulated by the Quartet Group can realistically result in the achievement of peace in the Middle East. Doubts on the actual efficacy of the plan are often expressed metaphorically by questioning the destination that the Road Map is supposed to help the two parties to reach. For example, a 2003 newspaper article expressing scepticism on the chances of success of the whole initiative was entitled 'Road to nowhere' (*Guardian Unlimited*, 23 March 2004). Here the idea that the plan cannot succeed is metaphorically expressed via the notion of a road without an end point.

The issue of what counts as an appropriate destination for the Road Map is developed in a more complex way in another 2003 newspaper article entitled 'The map must show a way home' (*Guardian Unlimited*, 6 June 2003). In the article, the author, Ghada Karmi, questions the solution proposed by the Quartet Group, namely that a separate Palestinian state should be created alongside Israel. She argues that this would not solve what she sees as the most fundamental problem: that the creation of Israel in 1948 displaced many Palestinians whose original home is inside the current boundaries of Israel. Within the

[17] Here the peace process itself is personified, or mentioned to refer metonymically to the Israelis and the Palestinians (see also 3.4.5 above).

solution proposed by the Road Map, Karmi points out, these people would never be able to return to the places they came from. She therefore argues for a different solution to the Middle East conflict: the creation of a single state, that would enable 'both peoples to share the territory that is now Greater Israel and that was the original Palestine' (*Guardian Unlimited*, 6 June 2003). In the headline of the article ('The map must show a way home'), this solution is metaphorically justified by exploiting a particular aspect of (road) maps which is not included in the official formulation of the Road Map: that (road) maps should enable you to get back to your original starting point, which is prototypically associated with one's 'home'. By mapping this particular aspect from the source domain, Karmi exploits for her own rhetorical purposes the emotional associations of the concept evoked by 'home' as well as some inferences derived from the source domain, namely that a road map that does not show the way home is unsatisfactory and inadequate.

A different critique of the Quartet Group plan can be found in an article published around the same time, where the ROAD MAP metaphor is exploited in a more systematic and elaborate way. The headline is 'A rocky road to peace' (*Guardian Unlimited*, 4 May 2003), and the article's lead paragraph[18] summarises the author's overall argument as follows:

3.25 The Middle East 'road map' does not quite match the existing brick and mortar of the old neighbourhood that it is designed to change. What are the potholes ahead?

In the first paragraph of the article, the ROAD MAP metaphor is also used creatively:

3.26 The Middle East 'road map' is a re-drawing of a bendy road to an old neighbourhood which was first visited in late 1991, in the aftermath of another war involving Iraq, and revisited several times since.

Generally speaking, the author of this article, Anoush Ehteshami, welcomes the Quartet Group's initiative as a positive development. However, he points out that similar attempts had been made before (notably after the first Gulf War), and warns against some of the possible difficulties in the process. Both parts of this argument are partly expressed via extensions and elaborations of the ROAD MAP metaphor.

The idea that a similar plan for the solution of the Israeli–Palestinian conflict had been made before is metaphorically expressed via the notion of a 're-drawing' of a road leading to 'an old neighbourhood' which has been visited several times before. The description of the destination as an 'old neighbourhood' makes the abstract notion of peace more concrete, and may be perceived

[18] A 'lead' is an introductory paragraph which is placed below the headline and above the beginning of the body of an article. The lead is often in italics or boldface.

as particularly appropriate because of its literal relevance: a successful solution to the Middle East problem partly involves the establishment of geographical boundaries, often in highly populated areas, which would enable people to live their daily lives in their own neighbourhoods without fearing bomb explosions or tank attacks.

The difficulties involved in realizing the Quartet Group plan are metaphorically expressed by describing the 'road' as one that is potentially treacherous and difficult to travel on: the author uses adjectives such as 'rocky' and 'bendy', and wonders about the possibility of 'potholes ahead'. More importantly, in the course of the article, the author points out that the Road Map 'cannot lead to final peace without the presence of other fellow travellers, notably Syria and its allies in Lebanon'. Here the crucial issue that the Middle East conflict involves several parties within the region is metaphorically expressed in terms of a journey that necessarily has to involve other travellers beside the Israelis and the Palestinians. In addition, the author raises the fundamental issue of whether the proposed plan properly takes into account the realities of the situation it is supposed to resolve. This issue is metaphorically expressed (in the lead and in the final paragraph) as a lack of fit between the Road Map and 'the existing brick and mortar of the old neighbourhood that it is designed to change'. In this case, the 'old neighbourhood' seems to correspond to the current situation in the Middle East, which is supposed to be changed for the better by the plan. In other words, the author does not concentrate on the map as a tool for reaching a destination, but as an accurate reflection of the area it represents. The reference to 'brick and mortar', in particular, is suggestive of the problem posed by the current position of Israeli and Palestinian settlements. Interestingly, in the source domain, maps normally *reflect* geographical and physical regions, rather than aiming to change them. However, in context, the idea that the Road Map is an imperfect representation of the current situation is sufficient to suggest that the plan may not succeed as a result of its own inadequacies.

This article is also typical in terms of the positioning and clustering of the various instances of the extended ROAD MAP metaphor: the most novel and elaborate metaphorical expressions are used in the headline, lead and first paragraphs to introduce the author's argument, and then in the final paragraph to reiterate and summarise the article's main points (see also the 'euro as train' article in section 3.4.1 above). In this case, part of the overall rhetorical effect is also the creation of humour, for example via reference to 'potholes ahead', 'a bendy road' and an 'old neighbourhood'.

Humour is more clearly involved in the final examples I will consider in this section. Figure 3.1 is a black-and-white reproduction of a cartoon that appeared in the online version of the UK *Guardian* newspaper on 12 June 2003. The cartoon was produced by the *Guardian* cartoonist Steve Bell immediately after a renewed worsening of the situation in the Middle East, involving Palestinian

Figure 3.1 Cartoon by Steve Bell

suicide attacks and military retaliation from Israel. Indeed, the background shows the aftermath of explosions, with burned-out cars and buses, and helicopters beaming searchlights from the sky. The foreground shows a caricature of George W. Bush (whom Bell conventionally represents as a monkey in a suit), holding a map labelled 'Road Map to peace', as if he was trying to consult it. The map has a large hole in the middle, which includes the point that an arrow on the top of the map describes with the words 'You are here.' In the cartoon, Bush metonymically stands for his administration and for the Quartet Group which was formed on the US initiative. Bush was also associated with the Iraq war that had started a few months before, and that was seen by many as a contributing factor to the intractability of the Middle East conflict. In the cartoon, the Road Map is represented as a literal, physical map, which Bush is holding in his hands. Within the visual representation, we can infer that the explosions that have occurred in the background have damaged the map to such an extent that the Bush character can no longer use it to locate his own position, and, by inference, to know how to reach his destination.[19] The cartoon can therefore be

[19] The fact that, in reality, only fixed, stationary maps include the expression 'You are here' is unlikely to interfere with the inference that the map is now useless.

interpreted as a visual metaphor: the physical map corresponds to the Quartet Group plan; damage to the physical map corresponds to the impossibility that the Road Map initiative will be successful; and Bush's inability to use the physical map corresponds to the US's inability to deal adequately with the conflict. The fact that Bush holds the map as if he was still trying to read it may also suggest that he is incompetent and unaware of the reality of the situation, or that the administration is still pretending that the plan is viable when in fact it is not. The serious political message that is characteristic of Bell's cartoons is accompanied by potentially humorous effects, largely at the expense of Bush: the US President is not just unflatteringly represented as a monkey,[20] but also has a facial expression that may suggest puzzlement resulting from ignorance or incompetence.

The prominence of the Middle East Road Map in 2003 also prompted some metalinguistic reflections on the part of media commentators, mostly aimed at ridiculing the popularity of the metaphor and exposing its weaknesses. In an article entitled 'Politics at the cross-roads: No one can be without a roadmap now' (*Guardian Unlimited*, 2 June 2003), the expression 'road map' is described as 'the political term du jour', and as a reflection of 'the attraction geographical terms hold for politicians'. In another article, entitled 'A turn for the worse' (*Guardian Unlimited*, 30 April 2003), the author also describes 'road map' as a 'journalistic and diplomatic cliché', and humorously reflects on the different scenarios that the expression might evoke in British and American audiences. He points out that, for Americans, ' "road map" may evoke promise and excitement. It means Jack Kerouac and Highway 61 and Zen and the Art of Motorcycle Maintenance. In a big country, a road map takes you on a voyage of dauntless exploration to a shining destination.' In contrast, for British audiences,

> the metaphor is likelier to make us think of someone trying to work out if the B1137 really is going to be a good shortcut on the way from Chelmsford to Colchester . . . The irresistible image is of a couple arguing over the correct interpretations of the coloured lines and blobs on the pages in front of them. (*Guardian Unlimited*, 30 April 2003)

These different scenarios clearly disregard the influence of the context in which particular expressions are used, but they are also a useful reminder of the cross-linguistic and cross-cultural differences in the interpretation of metaphorical expressions. Chilton (1996), for example, discusses this issue in relation to Gorbachev's expressed wish, in the 1980s, that the Soviet Union be welcomed

[20] The representation of Bush as a monkey can also be seen as metaphorical, since a human being is represented as an animal. This kind of representation usually involves the mapping of characteristics that are stereotypically associated with the animal within a particular culture. In this case, the main relevant characteristics seem to be stupidity and clumsiness.

in the 'common European house': the Russian word used by Gorbachev, 'dom' normally refers to a 'collective apartment block' (Chilton 1996: 266). However, its translation into other European languages evoked private family homes, and therefore suggested intrusion rather than neighbourly cooperation. This, Chilton suggests, had an important influence on how Gorbachev's initiative was received in the West (see Musolff 2004: 115–40 for a discussion of later developments in the use of the EUROPEAN HOUSE metaphor).

In conclusion, this first case study has highlighted a number of important phenomena in the political use of metaphor. First, particular metaphors can be used both to 'name' and to 'frame' particular initiatives, with which they become inextricably associated. Second, once a particular metaphor occupies a prominent position in the public domain, it can be alluded to and exploited in different ways by different participants in political debates. Musolff (2004) describes this phenomenon as a 'virtual conversation' among debating parties that communicate primarily via the mass media rather than face-to-face. I have also shown how some extensions of the ROAD MAP metaphor were more creative than others. More importantly, some were consistent with the original formulation of the Quartet Group's plan, while others explicitly questioned its validity (see also Musolff's 2004 notion of 'metaphor negotiation'). In addition, the very prominence of the metaphor led to (humorous) metalinguistic reflections on its appropriateness and frequency of use. All of this results in a complex intertextual network, which can only be partly accounted for in terms of the three types of systematicity introduced by Cameron 1999 (local, discourse and global systematicity).

JOURNEY metaphors are of course globally systematic in English, and they are also discoursally systematic in politics, especially in relation to plans, policies, and the histories of nation states. In the period following the 2002 Quartet Group initiative, a specific ROAD MAP metaphor became systematic within international discourse on the Middle East. Its life-span was limited, however. As Musolff (2004: 155) has noted, 'some metaphorical formulations have a history of their own,' and may evolve in different ways within particular discourse communities at particular historical junctures. As I am writing this chapter a new peace initiative seems to be emerging (partly as a result of the death of the Palestinian President Yasser Arafat), but the Road Map is only infrequently and tentatively mentioned, probably because it has by now become associated with another failure (according to the original plan, the end of the conflict and the establishment of two separate states were supposed to occur in 2005). So, this kind of phenomenon leads to a particular kind of transient discourse systematicity, which is linked to a particular political initiative or event. Once the relevant initiative or event are no longer topical, the metaphorical systematicity also weakens.

3.7 Case study 2: an anti-immigration leaflet by the UK's British National Party

In this second case study, I will analyse in detail the use of metaphorical expressions in a single text: the front page of a leaflet by the UK's British National Party (BNP), which is reproduced in black and white as figure 3.2. The leaflet was put through the letter box of my house in Lancaster (in the North West of England) a few weeks before the European and local elections of 10 June 2004.

The BNP is a right-wing party which, in recent years, has had some electoral success at local level, especially in the North West of England. According to the party's official website (www.bnp.org.uk, Summer 2007), their mission is to 'secure a future for the indigenous peoples of these islands in the North Atlantic which have been our homeland for millennia.' The term 'indigenous' is used 'to describe the people whose ancestors were the earliest settlers here after the last great Ice Age and which have been complemented by the historic migrations from mainland Europe'. In practice, this mission results in an anti-immigration stance which is often described as racist and xenophobic by the media and by other political parties. The party's website calls for

> an immediate halt to all further immigration, the immediate deportation of criminal and illegal immigrants, and the introduction of a system of voluntary resettlement whereby those immigrants who are legally here will be afforded the opportunity to return to their lands of ethnic origin assisted by generous financial incentives.

In addition, the party pledges to 'clamp down on the flood of "asylum seekers", all of whom are either bogus or can find refuge much nearer their home countries'. Indeed, asylum is the only issue that is dealt with in the leaflet, and metaphor plays a crucial role in the anti-asylum arguments that are put forward on the front page.

Many studies have noted how metaphors can be employed to set out an opposition between 'in-groups' and 'out-groups', and to convey negative representations of members of minority groups, including economic migrants and asylum seekers (van Dijk 1987: 107, 2002; van Teeffelen 1994; El Refaie 2001; Wodak 2002; O'Brien 2003; Chilton 2004: 110–34). As I have already mentioned, some metaphorical source domains are conventionally used, in English as well as other languages, to describe the arrival of immigrants and its consequences (e.g. FLOOD, (NATURAL) DISASTERS, WAR/INVASION, DISEASE/PLAGUE, etc.). In the quotation from the BNP's website, the arrival of asylum seekers into Britain is referred to via the highly conventional metaphorical expression 'flood'. The same expression is used in the third paragraph of the BNP leaflet, while, in the second paragraph, illegal immigrants and asylum seekers are described as 'flooding in every week'. These expressions are

ELECTION COMMUNICATION ENGLAND NORTH WEST REGION JUNE 10
Printed & published by British National Party
PO Box 14, Welshpool, Powys SY21 0WE
ASYLUM IS MAKING BRITAIN EXPLODE
www.bnp.org.uk
TERRORIST TIME-BOMB: Asylum is allowing hundreds of 'asylum bombers' to plan their atrocities in Britain. The Madrid train bombings have been linked to Moroccan 'asylum-seekers' in London. The Security Services warn there are at least 4,000 extremists in Britain who have trained at al-Qaeda and Taliban terrorist camps. Letting in even more is madness.
ASYLUM TIME BOMB: There are around 2 million illegal immigrants and 'asylum seekers' in Britain pushing our services, benefits system and NHS to bursting point. Thousands more are flooding in every week.
EU TIME-BOMB: British membership of the European Union has blown away our borders and control over our own legal system. Since May 1st, 75 million potential migrants from eastern Europe can now walk into Britain and live here at our expense. 97% of all asylum applications are bogus yet the politicians do nothing to stop the flood and protect us.
FINANCIAL TIME-BOMB: Asylum is blowing a massive hole in our pockets. In 2003 asylum cost us £4,000 million (£4 billion). This year the figure will top £5 billion. That's £5 billion of taxpayer's money that is being stolen from our schools, hospitals, housing, public-transport and pensions.
HOUSING TIME-BOMB: Asylum is ripping apart our countryside. The government is already planning to build five giant new cities, each the size of Birmingham, over the next 30 years to house over 5 million new immigrants.
Ordinary people like you Voting British National Party ✓
it's about time! BNP

Figure 3.2 Front page of election leaflet by the British National Party

intertextually coherent with a wider pattern which, as I have argued in 3.3, is part of (anti-)immigration discourse generally. The main metaphorical chain in the leaflet, however, involves references to bombs, explosions and physical destruction. This pattern, I suggest, was strategically employed in order to reinforce and exploit the 'literal' connection between asylum seekers and terrorist activities that was becoming increasingly dominant at the time. In other words, the main choice of metaphor in the leaflet is both topic-triggered and consistent with the DISASTER metaphors that are characteristic of anti-immigration and anti-asylum discourses.

Throughout the text, the noun 'asylum' is used as the grammatical subject of verb phrases referring to (mostly destructive) activities that are normally caused by individual human agents (e.g. 'making (Britain) explode' in the title, and 'ripping apart' in the fifth paragraph; see also 'is allowing' in the first paragraph). In all such cases, 'asylum' can be said to be a metonymic reference to asylum seekers and/or current policy and those responsible for it. However, it is also possible to interpret these uses of 'asylum' as involving some degree of personification, whereby a complex set of processes involving many different people is presented as a single destructive agent (see 3.4.5 for the overlap between personification and metonymy). More specifically, in the title of the front page of the leaflet, 'asylum' is claimed to be 'making Britain explode'. In context, this reference to explosions can function both literally and metaphorically. I will explore the rest of the text before returning to the title.

The photograph that is placed immediately below the title (and that occupies about a third of the page) shows a group of young men burning a Union Jack in what looks like a street in an Arab country. This kind of scene is often shown in television reports of anti-West and anti-Britain demonstrations in the Arab world, and is therefore likely to be familiar to people in England. In fact, anti-American and anti-British demonstrations had been shown particularly frequently in the months prior to June 2004, as part of media reports on the wider consequences of the 2003 invasion of Iraq. A small image of Britain (i.e. without Northern Ireland) is placed on the right-hand side of the page just above (and in contact with) the part of the photograph containing the flames rising from the flag. This image is coloured in bright yellow and red, and has lines through it that make it look as if it is physically disintegrating. Visually, all this suggests that the 'real' flames that are burning the flag in the photograph have spread to the small image of Britain outside the photograph, and are also spreading to the words that make up the title (the word 'explode' is also in red and yellow, and the rest of the words look physically damaged). Since the image of Britain can stand metonymically for the country and its people, these visual representations may suggest that the violence and hatred which are rife in Arab countries are now directly affecting Britain and the British people. The headline (and the rest of the text) present asylum as the cause of this process. As with the reference to explosions in the title, the visual images of burning may be interpreted both literally (i.e. in relation to explosions caused by terrorists) and metaphorically (i.e. as a representation of the impact of the arrival of large numbers of people). This is due to the way in which asylum seekers are presented in the rest of the text.

The body of the front page of the leaflet is divided into five paragraphs, each accompanied by a small image of Britain 'burning'. Each paragraph opens with a short heading consisting of a noun phrase with a metaphorical head noun, 'time-bomb'. This expression (which literally refers to a bomb that has been programmed to go off at a particular time) is conventionally used metaphorically to refer to situations where processes already under way are about to cause serious and dramatic problems at an unspecified point in the near future. The repetition of 'time-bomb' also extends the 'explosion' scenario that is evoked by the title, and is consistent with the images of the flag and Britain burning. The different pre-modifiers for 'time-bomb' in the five paragraphs identify five different areas that, according to the BNP, are associated with serious problems caused by asylum.

The first paragraph ('Terrorist time-bomb'), establishes a connection that is central to the text as a whole, namely between asylum seekers and terrorist activities, which are prototypically represented by bomb explosions. The BNP could probably rely on the public's knowledge of how terrorists had entered the US under false pretences and spent time preparing and training for the attacks of 11 September 2001. Indeed, a reference is made to the possible presence in Britain of people who had been trained in the same camps that had been associated with the perpetrators of the 9/11 attacks. What is explicitly referred to in the first paragraph is the more recent train bombings in Madrid's central station (on 11 March 2004), which had been connected with the suspicious activities of groups of North-African origin in Britain. This possible real-world connection between a small number of asylum seekers and terrorist activities is then generalized to the whole group: in the first paragraph, the compound 'asylum bombers' is coined in order to refer to people who apply for asylum in order to plan and execute terrorist attacks; throughout the text, scare quotes are used for 'asylum seekers' to suggest deception (scare quotes are also used in the same way in the statement of the BNP's immigration policy quoted above). The tendency to generalize from the criminal activities of small groups of individuals to all members of minority groups (be they immigrants, members of ethnic minorities, or whatever) has been noted in other studies (e.g. van Dijk 1987: 198). Both in the first paragraph and in the rest of the leaflet, claims are also made about large numbers of people being involved ('hundreds of "asylum bombers" ', 'at least 4,000 extremists', '2 million illegal immigrants', 'Thousands more', '75 milion [sic] potential migrants', 'five giant new cities',

'5 million new immigrants'). However, little or no indication is given as to the sources and reliability of these figures.

After the establishment of a nonmetaphorical connection between asylum seekers and terrorism in the first paragraph, metaphorical expressions relating to explosions and physical destruction are used in the rest of the text to present the consequences of asylum (in addition to the repetition of 'time-bomb'). In the second paragraph, illegal immigrants and asylum seekers are described as 'pushing our services, benefit system and NHS to bursting point'. In the third paragraph, EU membership is presented as having 'blown away our borders and control over our own legal system'. In the fourth paragraph, the financial consequences of accommodating asylum seekers are presented as 'blowing a massive hole in our pockets'. And in the final paragraph, asylum is described as 'ripping apart our countryside'. In other words, the recurrence of expressions to do with bombs, explosions and physical destruction throughout the text helps to present the consequences of asylum in vivid and catastrophic terms, and to warn the public that the situation is about to become much worse.

The expressions I have mentioned are quite conventional in English, since the source domain of bombs/explosions is often used to represent (often somewhat hyperbolically) serious and sudden problems, especially if they are caused by large numbers of people or entities (e.g. 'One of Brazil's biggest industrial areas has become an environmental time-bomb which could explode at any time', from the BNC). However, in the leaflet this metaphorical pattern is particularly pervasive, and it reinforces (and is reinforced by) the visual images of burning: the literal burning of the flag turns into a literal/metaphorical 'burning' of the country itself (when bogus asylum seekers prepare for terrorist activities in Britain and cause serious problems for the local people, services and infrastructure). Cumulatively, therefore, these metaphorical expressions and images contribute to the overall intratextual coherence of this part of the leaflet (see Chilton and Schäffner 2002: 29), and to its persuasive intent: they are central to the representation of the current state of Britain as a potentially apocalyptic scenario, which is caused by current asylum policies and which can only be avoided if the BNP is voted into power. Other linguistic strategies are also employed in the leaflet, such as the pronoun 'we' referring implicitly to the white 'indigenous' population, the hyperbolic figures, and informal expressions such as 'walk into Britain' (third paragraph) to suggest metonymically that the citizens of new EU countries can now enter Britain with great ease. All of these strategies are part of the broader anti-immigration discourse that the leaflet reflects and contributes to.

The fact that the dominant source domain of explosions is topic-triggered, at least to some extent, also has important consequences. First, the choice of explosion metaphors may both reinforce the 'literal' association between terrorism and asylum seekers, and benefit from the previous existence of this association:

the various metaphorical expressions may be perceived by some readers as particularly apt and natural, reflecting a 'common-sense' view of asylum seekers (see also van Dijk 1987: 372–3; El Refaie 2001; O'Brien 2003 on the use of FLOOD and WATER metaphors where flooding or arrival on water were literally relevant). Second, the highly conventional metaphorical references that are used throughout (e.g. 'time-bomb', 'push to bursting point', etc.) are potentially revitalized, and may therefore have a greater impact than they would in a different context (see Goatly 1997: 276–80). In particular, the potential emotional associations of conventional expressions such as 'time-bomb' and 'ripping apart' (e.g. fear, anxiety) are more likely to be evoked, given the density of similar expressions and the literal references to recent bombings. Third, a potential for ambiguity is created: the title of the leaflet, for example, can be read both literally (as a reference to planned terrorist explosions) and metaphorically (as a reference to serious problems due to overcrowding and excessive demands on services). The same might well apply to other expressions, such as 'time-bomb'.

Overall, I have argued that a particular metaphorical pattern is strategically used in the leaflet in order to exploit an existing nonmetaphorical association between source and target domain, and to present a complex and controversial aspect of current affairs in simple, emotional and catastrophic terms. The leaflet both reflects and reinforces the anti-immigration discourse and ideology which the BNP aims to provide political representation for. Whether, or under what circumstances, the leaflet's persuasive effect might be successful is a different matter. There is some empirical evidence that metaphors can prevent the so-called 'boomerang effect' that occurs when highly charged language ends up alienating listeners or readers (Mio 1997). However, people tend to have strong opinions both on asylum and on the BNP's political stance, and are therefore unlikely to be dramatically affected by a single text. As a consequence, leaflets such as the one I have analysed tend to be targeted particularly at those members of the public who are already partly persuaded, such as (predominantly white) people who feel threatened by immigrants and asylum seekers, and who already hold prejudiced views against them (e.g. including the view that many, or most, asylum seekers engage in criminal or terrorist activities). The BNP's electoral strategy depended precisely on attracting this part of the electorate, who may normally vote for another party or not vote at all. In the event, the BNP gained no European seats on 10 June 2004, but won five more seats overall on local councils than in the previous (1999) elections.

3.8 Summary

In this chapter I have shown how metaphorical patterns are consistently used in politics to provide particular representations of issues, situations and events, and to achieve persuasive effects. This involves a wide variety of source and target domains, but some specific source domains (PATH/JOURNEY, CONTAINER, WAR, SPORTS and HUMAN BEINGS) are particularly dominant, especially in Anglo-American politics. Metaphors are particularly useful when it is necessary to simplify complex and abstract issues, and to present them in vivid and potentially emotional terms. They can contribute to the internal coherence of a particular text, and also function intertextually to link different texts dealing with similar issues. The most conventional linguistic patterns can be an important part of particular discourses, and can reflect and reinforce particular ideologies. Novel linguistic expressions, in contrast, tend to be used more deliberately to argue particular points in particular contexts. Indeed, the role of the specific context of use is crucial in order to understand the possible motivation for the choice of a particular metaphor, and its possible effects on listeners or readers. While there is mixed empirical evidence on the actual persuasive effects of individual uses, the rhetorical and ideological influence of metaphor is likely to result from the cumulative effects of related uses across many different utterances and texts.

4 Metaphor in science and education

4.1 A preliminary example: consciousness as 'fame in the brain'

The 2001 volume of the scientific journal *Cognition* included a series of articles on consciousness – a phenomenon which, over the last two decades, has been the subject of heated debate in philosophy and cognitive science (Leary 1990a; Searle 1997: 485). In the concluding article, entitled 'Are we explaining consciousness yet?', Daniel Dennett expresses what he sees as the scope of a 'theory of consciousness' as follows:

4.1 What a theory of consciousness needs to explain is how some relatively few contents become elevated to this political power, with all the ensuing aftermath, while most others evaporate into oblivion after doing their modest deeds in the ongoing projects of the brain. (Dennett 2001: 225)

If you find this decontextualized extract rather puzzling, it is partly because you are not yet familiar with the metaphor that underpins Dennett's account of consciousness in the article (and much of his recent work), namely that of consciousness as 'fame in the brain'. Let me now provide the context you need to make sense of Dennett's apparently bizarre statement.

In the article, Dennett is concerned with the following issue: how is it that much of what goes on in our brains remains unconscious, while some 'contents' of our brain activities become conscious at particular points in time? More specifically: what does it mean for some contents to become conscious?

An early and highly influential account of consciousness was proposed by the French philosopher René Descartes in the seventeenth century. According to Descartes, some of the information processed in the brain becomes conscious when it is projected onto a special location (the pineal gland, in his view), where it can be watched by a 'homunculus' (Latin for a 'little man'), who corresponds to the individual's soul. In his article, Dennett explicitly presents his own approach as alternative to Descartes's, which he describes as

4.2 the traditional, and still popular, Cartesian Theater Model, which supposes there is a place in the brain to which all the unconscious modules send their results for ultimate conscious appreciation by the Audience. (Dennett 2001: 222)

In contrast, there is growing consensus among contemporary scientists that there is no special location in the brain where conscious contents are projected and somehow perceived. Rather, consciousness is explained in terms of the particular status that some information achieves within the 'global neuronal workspace'. In a nutshell, the idea is that many networks of neurons process information in our brains at any given time; most of this information remains unconscious, i.e. is only accessible locally in the brain; some of this information, however, becomes simultaneously accessible to many different neural networks throughout the brain; this global accessibility is what it means for some brain contents to be conscious.

As with the Cartesian Theatre, the different versions of this view of consciousness involve metaphorical descriptions of the brain and its activities. For example, Dennett quotes a particular formulation of the emerging consensus in cognitive science according to which consciousness is achieved by a

4.3 distributed society of specialists that is equipped with a working memory, called a global workspace, whose contents can be broadcast to the system as a whole. (Baars 1988, quoted in Dennett 2001: 222)

Dennett also refers to the earlier 'pandemonium model' of consciousness, within which the brain is conceived of as a 'pandemonium – a collection of demons', so that

4.4 perhaps what is going on within the demons can be regarded as the unconscious part of thought, and what the demons are publicly shouting for each other to hear, as the conscious part of thought. (quoted in Dennett 2001: 224; see also Hoffman *et al.* 1990; McCarthy 1959: 147)

According to the metaphor identification procedure introduced in chapter 1 (see section 4.3.1), these extracts contain several metaphorical expressions, including for example: 'society', 'specialists', 'workspace', 'contents', 'broadcast' in extract 4.3, and 'demons', 'shouting' and 'hear' in extract 4.4. In Dennett's article, these expressions have contextual meanings that relate to processes in the brain. These contextual meanings contrast with the basic meanings of the various expressions, which are to do with the activities of human beings, or, in the case of demons, (human-like) supernatural entities. Crucially, these basic meanings are exploited in order to provide a model of how brain activity gives rise to consciousness. In terms of Cognitive Metaphor Theory (CMT) the target domain of consciousness is constructed in terms of scenarios drawn from source domains relating to human activities. The metaphoricity of this kind of expression, however, is gradually weakened if they are adopted as technical terms by the scientific community, and therefore acquire specialized meanings in expert genres and discourses. I will return to this issue in the course of the chapter.

Dennett's own earlier model of consciousness – the 'Multiple Drafts Model' – shared some of the assumptions of the pandemonium model, but, as Dennett puts it,

4.5 did not provide . . . a sufficiently vivid and imagination-friendly antidote to the Cartesian imagery we have all grown up with, so more recently I have proposed what I consider to be a more useful guiding metaphor: 'fame in the brain' or 'cerebral celebrity'. (Dennett 2001: 224)

Dennett goes on to explain that, in his view, the unconscious contents of brain activity do not have to move to a special location, or somehow switch to a different medium of representation, in order to become conscious. Rather,

4.6 heretofore unconscious contents, staying right where they are, can achieve something rather like fame in competition with other fame-seeking (or just potentially fame-*finding*) contents. And, according to this view, that is what consciousness is. (Dennett 2001: 224)

Here Dennett's 'guiding metaphor' is realized by means of a simile ('something rather like fame') and of metaphorical expressions such as 'fame-seeking' and 'fame-finding'. Dennett exploits the FAME source domain to elaborate his view that consciousness corresponds to global accessibility in the brain: in the same way as some individuals achieve fame by becoming known to many different people in many different places, some information in our brains achieves consciousness by becoming accessible to many different neural networks in different parts of the brain. Having introduced this metaphor, Dennett goes on to explicate it in more detail, particularly in order to prevent some potential mappings from the FAME source domain to the CONSCIOUSNESS target domain that he sees as inappropriate:

4.7 Of course consciousness couldn't be *fame*, exactly, in the brain, since to be famous is to be a shared intentional object *in the conscious minds* of many folk, and although the brain is usefully seen as composed of hordes of demons (or *homunculi*), if we were to imagine them to be *au courant* in the ways they would need to be to elevate some of their brethren to cerebral celebrity, we would be endowing these subhuman components with too much human psychology – and, of course, installing a patent infinite regress in the model as a theory of consciousness. The looming infinite regress can be stopped the way such threats are often happily stopped, not by abandoning the basic idea but by softening it. As long as your *homunculi* are more stupid and ignorant than the intelligent agent they compose, the nesting of homunculi within homunculi can be finite, bottoming out, eventually, with agents so unimpressive that they can be replaced by machines . . . So consciousness is not so much fame, then, as political influence – a good slang term is *clout*. When processes compete for ongoing control of the body, the one with the greatest clout dominates the scene until a process with even greater clout displaces it. In some oligarchies, perhaps, the only way to have clout is to

> be *known by the King*, dispenser of all powers and privileges. Our brains are more democratic, indeed somewhat anarchic. In the brain there is no King, no Official Viewer of the State Television Program, no Cartesian Theater, but there are still plenty of quite sharp differences in political clout exercised by contents over time. (Dennett 2001: 225)

In the first part of this extract, Dennett tries to deal with a problem, infinite regress, which different approaches to consciousness have not always managed to avoid. If consciousness is explained by postulating some kind of miniature entity in the brain which is itself somehow conscious (be it a homunculus, a demon, or whatever), the issue of defining consciousness is not addressed, but simply removed to a deeper level, where it still needs to be explained. The FAME metaphor can indeed suggest that the various parts of the brain are somehow conscious of particular items of information, in the same way as human beings are consciously aware of the existence of famous individuals. Dennett attempts to avoid infinite regress by making the 'demons' or 'homunculi' of his model progressively more 'stupid and ignorant' than whole human beings, so that the component parts of his model are not themselves conscious. In order to perform this rhetorical feat, he replaces 'fame' with 'political influence' or 'clout' as the expressions that most accurately evoke the source domain of his metaphor. This is presumably because an individual can have clout without others being consciously aware that this individual has some kind of influence over them. The notion of political influence or clout then leads to further political metaphors, whereby different theories of consciousness correspond to different political systems. In Dennett's view, the brain is best seen as democratic or anarchic, because there is no special location or module that is responsible for the conscious status of some contents rather than others.

It is at this point that Dennett makes the statement which I quoted at the beginning of this chapter (see extract 4.1): having proposed his account of consciousness, he goes on to consider the question of how it is that some contents of our brain activity become conscious and thereby often have a lasting influence (e.g. they are remembered), while others remain unconscious. I do not have the space here to discuss the rest of Dennett's argument and his continued use of a variety of metaphors, nor to do justice to Dennett's overall theory of consciousness in the context of current debates. I will only mention one particular extension of the FAME/CLOUT metaphor, which is used to express an important aspect of Dennett's theory, namely the idea that whether a particular content becomes conscious or not depends more on what else is going on in the brain at the same time than on the intrinsic properties of that particular item of information:

4.8 Consciousness, like fame, is not an *intrinsic* property, and not even just a *dispositional* property; it is a phenomenon that requires some actualization of

> the potential . . . Consider the following tale. Jim has written a remarkable first novel that has been enthusiastically read by some of the *cognoscenti*. His picture is all set to go on the cover of Time Magazine, and Oprah has lined him up for her television show. A national book tour is planned and Hollywood has already expressed interest in his book. That's all true on Tuesday. Wednesday morning San Francisco is destroyed in an earthquake, and the world's attention can hold nothing else for a month. Is Jim famous? He would have been, if it weren't for that darn earthquake. Maybe next month, if things return to normal, he'll *become* famous for deeds done earlier. But fame eluded him this week . . . All the *dispositional properties* normally sufficient for fame were in place, but their normal effects didn't get triggered, so no fame resulted. The same (I have held) is true of consciousness. The idea of some information being conscious for a few milliseconds, with none of the normal aftermath, is as covertly incoherent as the idea of somebody being famous for a few minutes, with none of the normal aftermath. Jim was potentially famous but didn't quite achieve fame . . . Real fame is not the *cause* of all the normal aftermath; it *is* the normal aftermath.
>
> The same point needs to be appreciated about consciousness. (Dennett 2001: 227; emphasis in original)

The final point is central to Dennett's theory: unlike other researchers on consciousness, Dennett claims that global accessibility *is* consciousness, and not a result of consciousness. In order to make this point, Dennett uses a strategy that can be described as a mini-allegory (see section 2.2.3 above, and note 12 in chapter 2): he outlines a hypothetical scenario in which someone narrowly misses out on becoming famous, and then explicitly signals that this scenario can be mapped onto the CONSCIOUSNESS target domain. Within the source scenario, it would not make sense to say that Jim was famous, since circumstances prevented him from actually becoming widely known; similarly, according to Dennett, it does not make sense to claim that some information has achieved consciousness unless it actually becomes globally accessible in the brain.

I chose to start this chapter with Dennett's article because the author's reliance on metaphor is so obvious and explicit as to require little argument on my part. In the rest of this chapter, I aim to show that Dennett's article is not an exception, but rather an example of the central role that metaphor plays in science, broadly conceived. I discuss examples from a range of different genres that discuss scientific issues for a range of different audiences, including specialist articles in scientific journals (such as Dennett's), popularizations of science in publications such as *The New Scientist*, and educational materials aimed at explaining scientific theories and concepts to students. While Dennett's article can be said to lie on the borderline between science and philosophy, many of my examples in the rest of the chapter are drawn from the natural sciences, and particularly genetics. I also consider the variety of functions that metaphor can perform in scientific practice and discourse. For example, it is fairly clear that Dennett uses the FAME metaphor for explanatory, persuasive and, to some extent, humorous purposes: he explicitly refers to it as a 'more useful guiding metaphor' than the one he used in his Multiple Drafts Model, which did not turn out to be a 'sufficiently vivid and imagination-friendly antidote' to the Cartesian Theatre model (Dennett 2001: 224). In this sense, scientific metaphors are not very different from the metaphors used in politics: they simplify complex issues, make invisible processes accessible, and help to provide convincing accounts of particular phenomena. Indeed, it is increasingly recognized that scientific knowledge 'like all knowledge – is achieved *through* and *by means of* symbolic activity, especially linguistic activity' (Leary 1990b: 20; see also Myers 1990). More controversially, however, it could be argued that the FAME metaphor is not simply a tool Dennett uses to express and support his (literal) theory of consciousness, but rather an essential part of the theory itself. The same could be said of the metaphors that underlie the other models of consciousness discussed by Dennett (there are in fact many more such examples in his article than I was able to discuss here). These are among the issues and phenomena that I discuss in this chapter.

4.2 Science and metaphor

'Science' is a difficult and controversial term to define. For the purposes of this chapter, I will define it generally as '[t]he observation, identification, description, experimental investigation, and theoretical explanation of phenomena' (*Encyclopaedia Britannica*, 1999). The role played by language in the activities listed in this definition is now well recognized (e.g. Myers 1990; e.g. Keller 1995), but it is nevertheless rather problematic to talk about the 'language', 'discourse' or 'register' of science:

> There is of course no single register of science: there are numerous scientific discourses, not only covering different disciplines and sub-disciplines but also, and more significantly, different participants in the processes of science: specialist articles (including abstracts), textbooks, science for lay readers and listeners and so on. These have in common the function that they are extending someone's knowledge in some technical domain: the audiences being addressed may be anywhere from high level professionals to complete novices, but the text is organized so as to tell them something that they don't already know, with 'telling' covering a range of interpersonal attitudes from a tentative suggestion to an aggressive attempt to persuade. (Halliday 2004: xv)

In this chapter, I occasionally use the term 'scientific discourse' when talking generally about ways of speaking and writing associated with scientific topics and activities across a range of disciplines and genres. I also distinguish among the more specific discourses associated with particular disciplines, subdisciplines or approaches (e.g. 'genetic discourse'). As suggested by Halliday, all these different discourses can be realized via texts belonging to different genres, such as scientific articles, popular science articles, textbooks and so on. My most general claim in this chapter is that metaphor plays an important role in all these discourses and genres. I also try to show *how* this is the case, with reference to a range of specific examples from several different disciplines.

According to a common, traditional view of science, scientists engage in the direct observation of phenomena, and use language to report their findings neutrally and objectively. This view has been shown to be inadequate in many studies which have pointed out that (a) the phenomena studied by scientists are often not directly accessible, and can be observed in more than one way (e.g. sub-atomic particles can only be observed via instruments whose output requires interpretation), and (b) scientific 'knowledge' or 'facts' are constructed via social (and linguistic) processes involving negotiation, argumentation, persuasion and compromise (e.g. the process of obtaining funding in order to carry out one's research programme, or the process of presenting one's findings in such a way that they will be accepted as valid by other scientists or by the general public). All this does not undermine the notion that scientific disciplines have rigorous and explicit methods for validating hypotheses and theories, but suggests that these activities also involve the linguistic construction of knowledge within particular genres and social practices (applying for grants, giving conference papers, writing academic articles, giving media interviews, etc.) (e.g. see Myers 1990).

Within the traditional view of science as a neutral and objective activity, metaphor tends to be regarded as at best irrelevant and at worst detrimental. Hobbes, for example, famously argued in his *Leviathan* that metaphors 'openly profess deceit' and should therefore be excluded from reasoning, demonstration and 'all rigorous search of truth' (1651, ch. 8) (e.g. see Leary 1990b: 8–9). This view has been progressively displaced by the recognition that the use of metaphor in science is both pervasive and essential. Indeed, many scientists have themselves written on the use of metaphor in their specific disciplines (e.g. see Leary 1990a for psychology; Keller 1995 for biology; Brown 2003 for chemistry).

If you are unconvinced by my opening example, you only need to think about some of the scientific phenomena that are frequently discussed in the media to appreciate the pervasiveness of metaphors in scientific vocabulary: phrases such as 'Big Bang', 'greenhouse effect', 'black holes' or 'genetic code' all contain metaphorical expressions conventionally used to talk about phenomena studied by scientists. You may also be used to thinking metaphorically about electricity in terms of waves or particles, about the atom as a miniature solar system, or about your heart as a pump.

Recent theories of metaphor, and particularly CMT, can explain why Hobbes's view of metaphor was mistaken. Scientists typically deal with phenomena that are not just poorly (or partially) understood, but also complex and often inaccessible to the senses. Their job is to understand and explain these phenomena and to persuade others that their understandings and explanations are valid. If metaphor enables us to think and talk about complex, abstract, inaccessible, poorly delineated areas of experience in terms of simpler, more concrete, more accessible and better delineated areas of experience, it is a crucial tool for scientists in particular. In addition, like metaphors generally, the metaphors used by scientists 'frame' the phenomena in question in particular ways, foregrounding some aspects and backgrounding others. This can significantly affect how particular phenomena are understood and, where relevant, dealt with.

While it is now widely recognized that metaphor plays an important role in science, there is less agreement on what exactly this role is. On the one hand, it can be argued that metaphor is an aid to scientific discoveries and scientific communication, but that it is ultimately possible, and desirable, to arrive at nonmetaphorical theories and explanations of phenomena (e.g. Black 1962). On the other hand, it can be argued that metaphors play an essential and permanent role in scientific theories, which is never (or never fully) supplanted by more advanced, nonmetaphorical accounts of phenomena (Leary 1990a; Sternberg 1990; Boyd 1993; Keller 1995; Brown 2003). What is generally accepted, in any case, is that metaphors have a crucial function in the development of models and theories, as well as in the presentation of scientific arguments within a variety of genres. In the rest of this chapter, I discuss the different ways in which metaphors are used in different scientific genres within a range of disciplines, both in terms of their textual realization, and in terms of the functions that can be attributed to them. I also attempt to point out both the potential and the limitations of the use of metaphors in science.

4.2.1 Metaphor and theory-making

In a classic paper on metaphor and theory change, Richard Boyd made an influential distinction between what he called 'exegetical' or 'pedagogical' metaphors on the one hand, and 'theory-constitutive' metaphors on the other. Pedagogical metaphors, he argued,

> play a role in the teaching or explication of theories, which already admit of entirely adequate nonmetaphorical (or, at any rate, less metaphorical) formulations. I have in mind, for example, talk about 'worm-holes' in general relativity, the description of the spatial localization of bound electrons in terms of an 'electron cloud,' or the description of atoms as 'miniature solar systems'. (Boyd 1993: 485–6)

According to Boyd, these metaphors can play an important part in theory change, but their essential characteristic is that they are dispensable, since scientists also have nonmetaphorical ways of describing and referring to the same phenomena.

In contrast, metaphors are defined as theory-constitutive if they 'play a role in the development and articulation of theories in relatively mature sciences' (Boyd 1993: 482):

> the cases of scientific metaphor which are most interesting from the point of view of the philosophy of science (and the philosophy of language generally) are those in which metaphorical expressions constitute, at least for a time, an irreplaceable part of the linguistic machinery of a scientific theory: cases in which there are metaphors which scientists use in expressing theoretical claims for which no adequate literal paraphrase is known. Such metaphors are *constitutive* of the theories they express, rather than merely exegetical. (Boyd 1993: 486, emphasis in original)

As this quotation shows, Boyd's distinction primarily hinges on the nature of the technical terminology associated with a theory: theory-constitutive metaphors provide vocabulary for phenomena for which scientists do not (or not yet) have any alternative terms. Boyd uses the term 'catachresis' to refer specifically to the phenomenon whereby metaphors 'are used to introduce theoretical terminology where none previously existed' (Boyd 1993: 482; see also Goatly 1997: 149 for metaphor's function of 'lexical gap filling').

As an example of a theory-constitutive metaphor, Boyd cites the use of COMPUTER metaphors in cognitive psychology. Expressions such as 'information-processing' and 'information-retrieval procedures', for example, are conventionally used by psychologists to talk about cognitive phenomena for which, Boyd argues, there is no alternative terminology. This, according to Boyd, suggests that the COMPUTER metaphor is theory-constitutive in the current stage of development of cognitive psychology. I will return to this particular metaphor below.

Boyd's distinction has been highly influential in the study of scientific metaphors, but, like many binary distinctions, has also proved rather problematic. A major issue is that scientific theories develop over time and the role of metaphors within theories also tends to change. For example, a metaphorical term might initially be introduced to indicate a poorly understood phenomenon (e.g. genetic 'code'), and then remain as a technical term even when scientists' knowledge of the target domain has increased, and reliance on the source domain has decreased. In such cases, metaphorical technical terms acquire new, specialized senses, and often tend to be perceived as nonmetaphorical, at least by experts. More crucially, metaphors may be initially introduced for theory-constitutive purposes and then be used for pedagogical purposes. Indeed, as I will show in the course of the chapter, similar metaphors are often exploited in specialist articles, popularizations for non-specialists and educational materials (see Knudsen 2003).

Boyd's distinction is therefore best seen not as capturing two different categories of metaphor, but rather two different functions that metaphors can perform when used in particular scientific texts and genres at particular points in the historical development of a theory (see also Knudsen 2003). It is of course possible for a metaphor to be used only for pedagogical purposes, or only for theory-constitutive purposes. However, it is often the case that the 'same' metaphor may have a primarily theory-constitutive function in one context and a primarily educational function in another, or may perform both functions at the same time. In addition, these two main functions of scientific metaphors can co-exist with other functions, such as argumentation, persuasion, vividness, humour and so on. I would argue, for example, that the FAME metaphor has a theory-constitutive function in Dennett's article, not just because it supplies some of the relevant terminology (e.g. 'fame-seeking'), but also because it provides the basic structure of his approach, and supports some of his most central claims (notably the claim that consciousness is the *realization* and not the cause of global accessibility). However, I would also argue that Dennett uses the metaphor in his article for the purposes of argumentation, persuasion and humour. As he explicitly points out, he developed this metaphor as an alternative to an earlier one that was not sufficiently 'vivid and imagination-friendly' (Dennett 2001: 224).

4.2.2 *More on the theory-constitutive use of metaphors*

When scientists attempt to explain poorly understood phenomena, or to develop alternative perspectives on previously studied phenomena, the initial selection of a suitable metaphor can be seen as a feat of intuition and imagination that can be likened to the process of artistic creation (e.g. Brown 2003). Indeed, there is evidence that scientists consciously use metaphors in creatively developing and organizing ideas (Gentner and Grudin 1985). However, unlike literary metaphors, scientific metaphors need to be explicitly and systematically explicated in order to be used in theory-making and to become established within a scientific community. Dennett clearly does this in his article in *Cognition*: after introducing the FAME metaphor, he explains in detail what aspects of the source domain apply to the target, and in order to do this he slightly modifies his use of metaphorical expressions (i.e. by switching from 'fame' to 'clout' as the main source metaphorical term). The usefulness of the metaphor, apart from its vividness, is that it frames the phenomenon of consciousness in a way that leads to the conclusion Dennett wishes to arrive at, namely that there is no separate property of consciousness apart from actual global accessibility, in the same way as one cannot be famous without actually becoming widely known.

Scientific metaphors tend to rely on explicit and systematic structural correlations across domains, and particularly on the mapping of relations from source to target domain. Consider, for example, Rutherford's metaphor of the atom as a miniature solar system. This metaphor involves the mapping of the relationship between the sun and the planets in the source domain to the relationship between the nucleus and the electrons in the target domain. The sun is larger than the planets and attracts them in such a way that they revolve around it. In the same way, the nucleus is larger than the electrons and attracts them in such a way that they revolve around it (but see Taber 2001 for the limitations of this analogy). Gentner and Jeziorski (1993) show that the use of metaphors based on systematic structural correlations has become established in the Western scientific tradition since the beginning of the seventeenth century. Previously, they argue, scientists tended to use metaphors in ways that were less constrained and systematic, and more based on surface similarities rather than on the mapping of relations between elements. In their view, this applies, for example, to the metaphors used by the alchemists to explain how all matter consisted of a combination of the primary elements: earth, air, fire and water.

The structural correlations that underlie the (modern) theory-constitutive use of metaphors can be exploited to model the target domain in a particular way, and, more specifically, to make predictions, provide explanations, formulate questions and hypotheses, and so on. Successful metaphors may contribute to the development of whole research programmes, and influence research paradigms for considerable periods of time. In this sense, scientific metaphors can play an important ideological role, since they can be central to the dominant ways in which particular phenomena are understood by influential groups of experts in particular cultural and historical contexts. For example, it is generally recognized that the dominant view of the human brain in cognitive psychology and cognitive science since the late 1970s has been a computational one: the brain is seen as a computing device and mental functioning as information processing, so that mental phenomena can be described using the kinds of algorithms used in computer programmes. In the extract below, for example, Kosslyn and Koenig (1992) use computational expressions such as 'processing', 'registering' and 'input' to refer to the workings of the brain, and explicitly recognize the role of language and concepts from the domain of computers in the explanation of mental phenomena:

4.9 The brain does something different from any other organ: It processes information. The brain registers input from the senses, interprets the input, and makes decisions about how to behave accordingly. Thus, we can characterize brain function in terms of how information is processed. . . . The language of information processing is derived from computers, so in order to specify how the brain works we must use key concepts from this language. (Kosslyn and Koenig 1992: 17–18)

Different variants and uses of the computer metaphor characterize the different models and theories that collectively form what is known as the 'Information Processing paradigm' (Lakoff 1987: 338–52; Leary 1990b; Sternberg 1990; Lakoff and Johnson 1999: 257–66). As Eysenck and Keane (2000) put it,

> [i]n spite of its diversity, cognitive psychology is unified by a common approach based on an analogy between the mind and the digital computer; this is the information processing approach. This approach is the dominant paradigm or theoretical orientation . . . within cognitive psychology, and has been for decades. (Eysenck and Keane 2000: 1)

In fact, the metaphorical relationship between the COMPUTER domain and the BRAIN domain goes both ways: computers were originally devised to do what human brains do, as suggested by the use of expressions such as 'memory' and 'artificial intelligence' in relation to computers (Hoffman *et al.* 1990). Subsequently, it was the brain that started to be modelled on computers, and new models have been proposed as increasingly complex computers have been developed (Kosslyn and Koenig 1992: 18–19).

The theory-constitutive use of the COMPUTER metaphor in the study of human cognition has led to important advances in cognitive psychology and cognitive science. However, the metaphor has also been criticized for the way in which, like all metaphors, it highlights some aspects of the target domain and downplays others. In particular, modelling human brains on computers has tended to direct attention towards particular human characteristics and processes (e.g. the ability to comprehend and remember information), and to background those aspects of human beings that affect cognitive processes but do not have a counterpart in the COMPUTER domain, such as bodily experience, emotions, goals, social relations, awareness of context and so on (Lakoff and Johnson 1980a; Sternberg 1990: 160–1; Lakoff and Johnson 1999: 265–6). In their critique of the COMPUTER metaphor, Lakoff and Johnson (1980a), in particular, stress that scientists should be more aware of the limitations of the main metaphors they use, and more willing to adopt others when the dominant ones are found wanting.[1]

Genetics is another field where the theory-constitutive use of a small set of metaphors has been highly productive in the understanding of central aspects of human beings (Keller 1995; Avise 2001; Nerlich and Dingwall 2003; Knudsen 2003). Keller (1995) argues that, in the early days of genetics at the beginning of the twentieth century, geneticists started to describe genes as autonomous

[1] Ironically, however, metaphor scholars themselves do not always reflect on the metaphors they use in their own theories. Technical terms such as 'source' and 'target' in relation to conceptual domains are metaphorical, for example, but their metaphorical basis is not normally discussed by the theorists who use them. In fact, this can be seen as a case of mixed metaphors (see section 1.2.3 above), since the basic meaning of 'source' is to do with the starting point of a flow of water, while that of 'target' is to do with objects that are aimed at in combat or sports.

agents, which were presented as solely responsible for the development of organisms. For example, in 1924, the geneticist R. A. Brink described genes as 'the primary internal agents controlling development' (quoted in Keller 1995: 7). The consistent personification of genes became characteristic of what Keller calls the 'discourse of gene action': this discourse contributed to establish a view of genes within which the cell's nucleus (which contains the genetic material) is all-important, while the role of the cytoplasm (the rest of the cell) is marginal. According to Keller, this contributed to the success of genetics in subsequent decades at the expense of embryology, for example, which is concerned with *how* a germ cell develops into a complex organism. In this respect, Keller stresses that dominant ways of talking about particular phenomena

> [t]hrough their influence on scientists, administrators, and funding agencies . . . provide powerful rationales for mobilizing resources, for identifying particular research agendas, for focusing our scientific energies and attention in particular areas. (Keller 1995: 21)

The influence of the 'discourse of gene action' was subsequently reinforced by the introduction of further metaphors that played a theory-constitutive role in the discourse of genetics, and particularly that of DNA as a 'code'. Erwin Schrödinger first used the term 'code-script' in 1944 to describe the role of chromosomes in individual development:

4.10 It is these chromosomes . . . that contain in some kind of code-script the entire pattern of the individual's future development and of its functioning in the mature state. Every complete set of chromosomes contains the full code . . . But the term code-script is, of course, too narrow. The chromosome structures are at the same time instrumental in bringing about the development they foreshadow. They are law-code and executive power – or, to use another simile, they are architect's plan and builder's craft – in one. (Schrödinger 1944: 22–3)

The metaphorical description of chromosomes as containing a complete 'code' for an individual's development suggests that development is fixed once and for all after fertilization, and does not depend on any other factors. Schrödinger then goes on to add that chromosomes do not simply 'contain' the code, but are also responsible for realizing the development described in the code. This point is made via two further pairs of metaphorical expressions: 'law-code and executive power' and 'architect's plan and builder's craft'.

Interestingly, the first metaphorical use of 'code-script' in the quotation above is signalled by the hedging expression 'some kind of'; similarly, the later pair of metaphorical expressions is accompanied by an explicit indication of their figurativeness (Schrödinger describes them as 'similes'). In time, however, the CODE metaphor became established not just within genetics, but also in public discourse about genes and heredity (Nerlich and Dingwall 2003; Knudsen 2003). According to Keller (1995), the success of this metaphor was sealed when, in 1953, Watson and Crick introduced the further metaphor of 'information' in talking about the newly discovered DNA:

4.11 In a long molecule, many different permutations are possible, and it therefore seems likely that the precise sequence of the bases is the code which carries the genetical information. (Watson and Crick 1953, quoted in Keller 1995: 17–18)

Keller comments that '[b]ecause DNA seemed to function as a linear code, using this notion of information for genetics appeared to be a natural' (Keller 1995: 19).

The general source domain of LANGUAGE/COMMUNICATION then started to be used more systematically to model the phenomena studied by geneticists, and further expressions from this domain have now become fully conventional, both in the discourse of experts and that of laypeople: the nucleotide bases of DNA are conventionally described as 'letters'; genes are sometimes described as 'sentences' consisting of sequences of these letters; cellular processes are described as 'translation' and 'transcription'; and expressions such as 'the language of genes' or 'the book of life' are commonly used in media reports on genetics.

According to Keller, the adoption of these metaphors rapidly gave geneticists authority and influence, even though the phenomena they were concerned with were initially poorly understood. The rise of genetics, she argues, culminated in 1990 with the launch of the international 'Human Genome Project', which was set up to find out the complete sequence of bases in human DNA. I will return to the metaphors used in presenting the results of this project in section 4.3.2 below.

Overall, it needs to be recognized that geneticists now have far greater and more detailed knowledge of their objects of study than when the CODE and INFORMATION metaphors were originally introduced. This means that terms such as 'code', 'letter' and 'translation' have acquired precise technical senses in expert discourse, which are less dependent on mappings from the source domain and more on knowledge of the target domain. On the other hand, metaphorical expressions from the LANGUAGE/COMMUNICATION source domain continue to be used systematically and, in some cases, explicitly and creatively. In addition, the dominant view of the role and functioning of genes is still structured in important ways by the CODE, INSTRUCTIONS and INFORMATION metaphors.

As shown in the quotations above, however, the version of the LANGUAGE/COMMUNICATION source domain that is used in genetics reflects a 'folk' theory of communication, whereby the existence of a code allows the straightforward transmission of messages from addresser to addressee. More specifically, DNA is described as a code consisting of letters and containing information about an organism's future development. This information is translated into messages that instruct enzymes to produce the proteins that ultimately result in the development and functioning of an organism. The theory-constitutive use of this metaphor can justify two important but controversial conclusions, namely: (a) that human beings are genetically determined (i.e. the whole of our development is fixed at the point of egg fertilization, and other factors, such as environment, lifestyle, make little or no difference), and (b) that, by mapping the whole human genome, scientists will have direct access to the essence of human beings and the future development of individuals.

One of the many critics of the dominant use of this metaphor has suggested that the same source domain could be used in a more adequate way to arrive at quite different conclusions about the progress of research:

> There is a notion, for example, that when we have mapped all the human genes . . . we will then be able 'to read the book of life': a piece of hype that comes not simply from the much maligned 'media' but from scientists themselves, as they jostle for funding. But the genome may be seen as an unknown language. To map the genes is merely to create a lexicon. How the genome works – its metaphorical syntax – is another matter again; and truly to understand the genome, we must come to terms with its literature – the ambiguities, the nuances, the subtexts. They are in there somewhere, and when the genome mapping is finished we will still be centuries from understanding them . . . The literature of the genome will take centuries to unfold. (Tudge 1999: 172–80; quoted in Nerlich and Dingwall 2003: 407)

Tudge exploits a more complex version of the LANGUAGE/COMMUNICATION source domain – one that is more compatible with the way in which language is viewed by linguists. He suggests that the genome should be seen as an unknown language and the goal of scientists as understanding the literature written in that language. This requires much more than knowing the vocabulary of the language, and inevitably involves subtleties and ambiguities. Tudge therefore concludes that finding out the complete sequence of human DNA is only a small step in understanding how human beings develop under the influence of multiple factors.

The potential oversimplifications that can arise from the conventional use of the CODE metaphor are particularly relevant when the metaphor is used in texts produced for non-specialists, who need to rely on source-domain knowledge more than the scientists themselves. In the next two sections, I consider the use of genetics metaphors in the media and in educational materials. Here I conclude this section with some final remarks on the theory-constitutive use of metaphor.

As I have shown, metaphors can be used in science for theory-constitutive purposes, i.e. to frame the subject of investigation in a particular way, so as to produce models, hypotheses, explanations and so on. Such metaphors also normally provide vocabulary resources that are applied to new phenomena, and that often continue to be used even when detailed knowledge about the target domain has been developed. Many of these technical terms (e.g. 'processing' in cognitive psychology, or 'code' in genetics) are often perceived as non-metaphorical, especially by scientists, but this does not mean that the relevant source domain has ceased to be involved in the structuring of the target. Indeed, scientists often refer explicitly to the metaphorical source domains they systematically exploit in their work, as is the case with Kosslyn and Koenig in extract 4.9 above, and further extensions and creative uses are always possible.

I have also shown how, like all metaphors, scientific metaphors frame target domains in particular ways, foregrounding some aspects and backgrounding others. This can affect what questions and hypotheses are investigated, what explanations are given and what conclusions are drawn. What Leary says below in relation to research on the nervous system applies generally to the use of metaphors across disciplines:

> It is important to realize that all these metaphors have had historically significant *directive* functions: They have directed the gaze – not to mention the theoretical and practical activities – of researchers toward different aspects of the nervous system. Indeed, it seems safe to say that, as a general rule, phenomena (such as the brain and its extensions) look somewhat different to – and tend to be conceptualized and treated somewhat differently by – possessors of different metaphorical frameworks. (Leary 1990b: 12)

Finally, theory-constitutive metaphors are typically fully explicated within a particular discipline, and rely on the mapping of structural relations from source to target domain. Unlike literary metaphors, which are valued for their uniqueness, scientific metaphors are 'made to be overused' (Gibbs 1994: 173; see also Boyd 1993). They are introduced in order to be adopted and developed by the relevant scientific community, and, if successful, become an essential part of the technical discourse of that community. In Cameron's (1999) terms, successful scientific metaphors become discoursally systematic among experts (see section 1.3 above). This process results in the progressive specification of the target domain-specific senses of metaphorical technical terms, which become conventionalized within particular scientific communities. As Knudsen puts it, expressions such as 'transcription' or 'translation process' in relation to DNA

> [f]ollowing years of clarification and application . . . have gradually settled to become unequivocal and 'closed' . . . within a particular context. But what happens if they are used in another context? (Knudsen 2003: 1253)

In the next sections I consider the use of metaphor in a range of non-specialist scientific genres.

4.3 Metaphor from expert discourse to science popularizations and the media

In this section I consider the relationship between the metaphors used in the specialized scientific publications discussed so far and those used in popular science publications and in general media reporting on scientific research. I show how, in some cases at least, the metaphorical expressions used in different genres can be traced back to the same underlying conceptual metaphors. There are often differences, however, in the specific ways in which metaphors are used, in terms of linguistic realization, textual function and use of material from the source domain (see Romaine 1996; Goatly 1997; Nelkin 2001; Knudsen 2003; Low 2005; Skorczynska and Deignan 2006).

4.3.1 Longevity and waste disposal in specialist and non-specialist science articles

As an example of these similarities and differences, in this section I compare some aspects of the use of metaphor in a scientific article on the mechanisms of ageing and in a popular science article on the same topic. The scientific article was written by two biologists based at University College London (David Gems and Joshua McElwee), and appeared in the journal *Mechanisms of Ageing and Development* in 2005 (Gems and McElwee 2005). The title is 'Broad spectrum detoxification: the major longevity assurance process regulated by insulin/IGF-1 signaling?' I cannot pretend that I fully understand all aspects of this work, but, for our purposes, suffice it to say the following. The authors studied a particular species of worm, *Caenorhabditis elegans*, and particularly a sub-group that lived significantly longer than average. They found that the long-living worms had a mutation in particular groups of genes, which, by acting in complex ways on other genes, protein and enzymes, ensured that the mechanisms whereby cells eliminate toxic materials remained active longer than they do in individuals without the mutation. They therefore suggest that ageing is primarily due to the fact that cells gradually stop preventing the accumulation of toxic materials. When, due to genetic mutations, these mechanisms remain active for longer, individuals age more slowly and have a longer life span. The fact that most individuals do not have this mutation is explained in evolutionary terms: keeping these mechanisms active is 'energetically costly', and is therefore not justified after an individual has performed its reproductory function.

In the abstract to their article, Gems and McElwee say that 'ageing results from molecular damage from highly diverse endobiotic toxins', which are 'by-products of diverse metabolic processes', and suggest that longevity requires:

> (a) energetically costly detoxification and excretion of molecular rubbish, and (b) conservation of existing proteins via molecular chaperones. Given the emphasis in this theory on investment in cellular waste disposal, and on protein conservation, we have dubbed it the green theory. (Gems and McElwee 2005: 381)

These short extracts contain several metaphorical technical terms that are commonly used in this particular area of research: the cellular materials that result from particular processes are referred to as 'products' or 'by-products', while those molecules that prevent the elimination of certain proteins are referred to as 'chaperones'. The characteristic metaphor of Gem and McElwee's particular line of research, however, is one where ageing is primarily caused by the accumulation of material in cells that is referred to as 'toxins' or 'rubbish', so that the prevention of ageing involves 'detoxification', 'waste disposal' or, in what could be interpreted as a variant metaphor, 'excretion'. As is common with scientific metaphors, micro-processes that are invisible to the naked eye are metaphorically constructed in terms of visible, concrete processes involving objects and human activities. Here I am going to focus particularly on the use of metaphorical expressions such as 'rubbish' and 'waste disposal' as metaphorical technical terms: the source domain of WASTE DISPOSAL is used, alongside other source domains, to model and explain processes at the cellular level whereby some materials accumulate in cells that have no specific uses, and that gradually cause damage to the cell if they are not eliminated.

After detailing their research methodology and specific findings, Gems and McElwee explicitly reflect on their use of what I have called the WASTE DISPOSAL source domain. They say that, according to the view they have proposed,

> 4.12 the cell is under constant threat from metabolic waste products and xenobiotics. We suggest that the smooth ER works as a cellular filter, deploying phase 1 and phase 2 metabolism to mobilise and excrete these mainly lipophilic toxins. This clears the cell of molecular rubbish, thereby preventing molecular damage, and ageing.
>
> The problems for the cell in terms of the theory proposed here have certain parallels with environmental problems arising from human industry. The principals [sic] of longevity assurance that it suggests – increased expenditure of energy on waste disposal to prevent damage to the cell, and the conservation of cellular constituents by the action of molecular chaperones – resemble the recommendations of green activists: to increase investment in clean waste disposal, to reduce pollution and to conserve resources (e.g. by recycling). For this reason we have nick-named the hypothesis presented here the green theory. (Gems and McElwee 2005: 383)

The first paragraph of this quotation contains several expressions that exploit the WASTE DISPOSAL source domain to express the authors' view of the cellular mechanisms that ensure longevity: 'waste products', 'filter' and 'molecular rubbish'. In the second paragraph, the authors make an explicit parallel between the processes they are concerned with and 'environmental problems arising from human industry'. More specifically, they explicitly set up correspondences between the financial cost of waste disposal and the extra effort involved in anti-ageing cellular processes, and between the activities of 'molecular chaperones' and those of green activists. They then exploit this more extended version of the metaphor to nickname their hypothesis 'the green theory'.

I would argue that the WASTE DISPOSAL metaphor is used for theory-constitutive purposes in Gems and McElwee's article: it provides a structured model for the view of ageing they propose, with specific cross-domain correspondences; it also provides a number of expressions that are used in a technical sense in the exposition of the authors' findings and resulting theory. In addition, the metaphor has an explanatory function (it provides a clear model for the processes under discussion), and contributes to the persuasiveness of the authors' argument. Importantly, it is also consistent with other metaphors in the area, as realized by expressions such as 'metabolic by-products', 'excretion' and so on.

Generally speaking, however, Gems and McElwee's article is not structured around the processes captured by the metaphor, but mostly follows the progress of the authors' research and spells out its relationship with previous studies in the same area. As Myers (1990) has suggested,

> professional articles create what I call a *narrative of science*; they follow the argument of the scientist, arrange time into a parallel series of simultaneous events all supporting their claim, and emphasize in their syntax and vocabulary the conceptual structure of the discipline. (Myers 1990: 142, italics in original)

At this point let me consider an article that appeared in *The New Scientist* in May 2005, shortly after the publication of Gems and McElwee's paper. *The New Scientist* is a general science magazine that primarily addresses an audience of non-specialists. The article in question is entitled 'Why humans grow old grungily' and is written by Jon Turney, who is described as 'course leader for Imperial College London's MSc in creative non-fiction writing'. The article begins as follows:

4.13 My attic is a sad sight, a jumble of frayed carpet offcuts, half-empty cans of congealed paint, broken videos, dead computers and inoperative exercise bikes. Just the thought of dragging it all to the dump tires me out.

Something similar is happening inside my body's cells – at least according to a new theory about why we age. The rubbish is piling up, and while I could clear it all out, that would take a lot of effort. So my metabolic cleaning systems are set to 'don't bother', and the result is that harmful garbage is accumulating.

Junk plays a central role in many theories of ageing. (Turney 2005: 44)

The author then goes on to compare existing theories of ageing based on the effect of 'free radicals' with more recent work on the effects of gene mutations, including particularly Gems and McElwee's (2005) article. In summarizing their argument, he explains that

4.14 cells need huge families of garbage-disposal enzymes to deal with all the junk they create. But the system carries a heavy overhead. It consumes lots of energy the organism could use elsewhere – particularly in reproduction . . . The end result is that evolution has favoured cells that opt out of the detox business and allow molecular detritus to pile up. (Turney 2005: 44)

The article ends with the following reflection:

4.15 And what of the prospects for using the green theory to combat the problem of human ageing? As it is more general than, say, free-radical theories of damage, you'd probably have to do lots of different things to keep the junk at bay. But the hope is that one or two of the genes involved in this system will turn out to have big effects all by themselves. Then, perhaps, we can learn to harness their effects, and live longer lives. Maybe I'd even find the time to clean out my attic. (Turney 2005: 44)

These quotations show how Turney takes Gems and McElwee's theory-constitutive metaphor and, in Knudsen's (2003) terms, 'opens it up': he uses it much more systematically and creatively in order to structure his article, explain the scientific issues and hypotheses clearly and vividly, and entertain his readers with some humorous phrasings and ambiguities.

The description of the author's attic in the first paragraph may appear to be entirely literal on a first reading, but the reader is then invited to project the 'attic' scenario onto processes that are occurring at the cellular level. This twist (which is not uncommon in this kind of article) introduces the topic of the article in a witty and engaging way. Throughout the rest of the article, the WASTE DISPOSAL metaphor is used in a way that is compatible with Gems and McElwee's use at a general level, but that is also freer both in terms of the range of linguistic expressions used (e.g. 'The rubbish is piling up', 'my metabolic cleaning systems are set to "don't bother" ', 'keep the junk at bay') and in terms of the exploitation of the potential of the source domain (e.g. the use of the junk-filled attic as a metaphor for toxin-full cells). Overall, the WASTE DISPOSAL metaphor is creatively employed to make the theory accessible in a way that is broadly faithful to the scientists' work but also vivid and humorous. The source domain is used more extensively but less rigorously, since *New Scientist* readers have less knowledge of the target domain than the readers of *Mechanisms of Ageing and Development*, but also wish to be informed in a clear and entertaining way. While, as we have seen, the authors of specialist articles tend to spell out the cross-domain mappings that they intend to evoke, non-specialist writers such as Turney do not equally attempt to constrain what material can be accurately projected from source to target domain. This may potentially result in some degree of imprecision (see also Low 2005).

In contrast with Gems and McElwee's paper, Turney's article also alternates between a narrative of science and what Myers calls 'narratives of nature', in which the phenomenon under investigation 'and not the scientific activity, is the subject, the narrative is chronological, and the syntax and vocabulary emphasize the externality of nature to scientific practices' (Myers 1990: 142).

This can be seen, for example, in the second paragraph of extract 4.13, where the author's narrative follows the processes that occur in the cell rather than the activities of the scientists who study these processes. In addition, the creative use of a particular metaphor to structure the author's argument, and to open and close the article, is a textual phenomenon that I also pointed out in relation to political reporting in chapter 3. In this sense, the use of metaphor in science popularizations resembles that of media reporting generally rather than that of specialized scientific genres (see also Skorczynska and Deignan 2006 for a study pointing out the differences in the use of metaphor between expert and non-expert publications in the area of economics).

4.3.2 Scientific debates in the media: more on genetics metaphors

As we have seen, the metaphors used by scientists to develop and explain their theories structure the subject of research in particular ways, and lead more naturally to some hypotheses and conclusions than to others. Metaphors also play an important role in public debates on scientific research and its wider social and political implications. In the move from specialized genres to scientific popularizations and the general media, however, the same metaphors may be used in a variety of ways for explanatory and persuasive purposes, not just by scientists, but also by journalists, politicians, representatives of various interest groups and so on (e.g. see Hamilton 2003). In these contexts, metaphors are not used to develop new understandings of phenomena but to explain scientific issues or advances in order to persuade audiences about the importance and future potential of particular types of research. As Brown puts it,

> [w]hen scientific issues are seen as public policy issues, the language and terms used in discussions of the science take on new roles. They become tools in persuasion and lose much of their connection with the scientific issues. (Brown 2003: 181)

When the relatively 'closed' metaphors used by scientists are 'opened up' in the public domain, there is also a danger that they will be used in ways that go beyond, or even against, the scientist's original intentions (Nerlich and Clarke 2000; Knudsen 2003; Weigman 2004).

I have already mentioned how some of the dominant metaphors for DNA, such as the CODE metaphor, can lend themselves to support biological determinism – the idea that the true essence of individuals resides in their genes, and their whole future development is fixed once and for all at conception (see Nelkin 2001; Nerlich and Dingwall 2003; Weigman 2004 for other common metaphors for DNA). This metaphor was exploited to support the eugenics movement in the USA in the 1920s and 1930s, when an individual's genetic material was seen as '"the master key to history", the "very soul" of the individual, and the source of social and moral order' (Nelkin 2001). This justified policies that favoured the 'purity' of races and the elimination of people with disabilities (see also Chew and Laubichler 2003).

Nowadays, there are fears that a strong interpretation of the metaphor of DNA as a 'code', an 'instruction manual' or a 'blueprint' could lead to discrimination if people's genetic details are disclosed to employers, insurance companies and so on. The two articles on ageing discussed in the previous sub-section, for example, suggest that certain genetic mutations significantly affect the life-spans of particular organisms. If we follow Schrödinger in seeing DNA as 'law-code and executive power', 'architect's plan and builder's craft' (see extract 4.10 above), we could simplistically conclude that the presence or absence of these mutations is all one needs to know in order to anticipate how long someone will live.

Not surprisingly, therefore, public debates on genetics research often involve a struggle over metaphors:

> Geneticists deploy a striking range of metaphors to promote their science, suggest its meanings and persuade the public of its value to health care and social policy. So too, critics use metaphorical constructs to express concerns about the problematic implications of the genetic revolution. And special interest groups mobilize images in their debates . . . These groups, including scientists, have become particularly skilled at pre-packaging images for the media. Journalists then amplify their messages in ways that are likely to have popular resonance. Through metaphors, genetics can seem to be a source of salvation or a means of exploitation and control. Are people simply the sum of their genes or are they a product of history? Is genetic engineering a 'boon' to health, or a way to 'tamper' with genes? Is the effort to understand the genome a quest for the 'holy grail' or are scientists 'playing God'? (Nelkin 2001: 556)

Brigitte Nerlich and her colleagues (Nerlich and Dingwall 2003; Nerlich *et al.* 2002) have studied the metaphors used by scientists and politicians (US President Bill Clinton and British Prime Minister Tony Blair) to announce the near-completion of the Human Genome project in June 2000, during a joint, satellite-linked press conference. While there were individual differences in the extent and creativity of metaphor use, all participants used metaphors to emphasize the magnitude of the achievement and simultaneously reassure the public that this research would only lead to positive outcomes (e.g. the treatment of currently incurable illnesses). President Clinton, for example, described the human genome as 'the most important, most wondrous map ever produced by humankind' (Nerlich and Dingwall 2003: 410). The scientists who participated in the press conference said that we can 'read our own instruction book' and 'have a revelation of the first draft of the book of human life' (Nerlich and Dingwall 2003: 416). These BOOK metaphors are closely related to the original CODE metaphor, which was used by a British scientist representing the Wellcome Trust: 'this code is the essence of mankind, and as long as human beings exist, this code is going to be important and will be used' (Nerlich and Dingwall 2003: 420).

Commenting on the same event, Weigman (2004) stated that the metaphors used by scientists and politicians can be confusing or misleading. She comments particularly on the exploitation of the conventional CODE metaphor for DNA to suggest that scientists are interpreting a divine language. At the White House event, scientist Francis Collins described the human genome as 'our own instruction book, previously known only to God' and President Clinton said that 'today we are learning the language in which God created life' (Weigman 2004: 117). Following Knudsen (2003), it could be argued that, in addressing the general public, scientists as well as politicians use the 'closed' metaphors of expert discourse as 'open' metaphors, in order to achieve their rhetorical goals.

The metaphors used to announce the near-completion of the Genome project contributed to sensationalize the event and reinforced the view that the information contained in the genome is central to who we are, and can easily be interpreted for the common good. Amongst other things, this can help to reassure the public and to ensure the centrality of genetic research as a funding priority. Nerlich *et al.* (2002) comment that the language used during the press conference was largely successful in influencing subsequent UK media reports, which often echoed the same positive metaphors. Some newspapers, however, used alternative metaphors to express their concerns. They raised the spectre of 'designer babies' and a 'genetic under-class', or went further in sketching future nightmare scenarios, as in this extract from the *Mirror*:

4.16 Genetic engineering. In theory babies could be genetically engineered. Their genetic material could be changed to make perfect babies. Impure genes and 'people' could be weeded out and destroyed and those whose genes are not perfect would not be allowed to have children. (quoted in Nerlich *et al.* 2002: 462–3)

The reassuring and euphoric metaphors of the official announcement are replaced here by more disquieting ones, where human beings are engineered like products or weeded out like unwanted plants.

As these examples show, the metaphors that are used in relation to scientific issues are not just relevant to the progress of research, but can also influence public and political opinion, and, potentially, public policy. Consequently, scientific metaphors need to be subjected to the same careful scrutiny as the political metaphors discussed in chapter 2, since they can be both enlightening and misleading:

Metaphors introduce a fundamental trade off between the generation of novel insights in science and the possibility of dangerous or even deadly misappropriation. (Chew and Laubichler 2003: 52)

4.4 Metaphor in educational materials

In section 4.2 above I introduced Boyd's (1993) notions of 'theory-constitutive' and 'pedagogical' metaphors and I suggested that this distinction is best seen as a way of capturing different *uses* rather than different *categories* of metaphors (see also Knudsen 2003). In this section I discuss the pedagogical use of metaphors in a variety of materials produced for the benefit of learners of different ages.

The potential use of metaphor as an educational tool is well recognized (Gentner and Gentner 1983; Petrie and Ortony 1993; Darian 2000; Taber 2001; e.g. see Cameron 2003). The fact that metaphor allows us to think and talk about one domain of experience in terms of another can be exploited in order to help students understand new, unfamiliar phenomena in terms of phenomena they are familiar with. Metaphors can therefore help to make topics clearer, more accessible, and easier to imagine and remember. This is particularly important when learners are introduced to phenomena that are not just new to them, but also complex and inaccessible to ordinary perception, such as electricity, atomic structure or the functions of DNA. In a number of different studies, the use of metaphor in educational materials has been shown to contribute to learners' ability to remember information, make inferences, answer questions and solve problems (e.g. Gentner and Gentner 1983; e.g. Mayer 1993; Petrie and Ortony 1993). There are also potential risks, however, as I will point out throughout this section (see also Green 1993).

The metaphorical use of a familiar scenario in introducing a particular scientific phenomenon can be seen in the short extract below, which is taken from the unit on electricity in the *Collins GCSE Physics Revision Guide:*[2]

4.17 A simple model of an electrical circuit

- The battery in an electrical circuit can be thought of as pushing electrical charge round the circuit to make a current. It also transfers energy to the electrical charge. The voltage of the battery is a measure of how much 'push' it can provide and how much energy it can transfer to the charge. (Bradley and Sunley 2005: 1)

The function of a battery in an electrical circuit cannot be directly observed, and can therefore be regarded as a relatively abstract concept. In the extract, the battery's function is described metaphorically in terms of the physical action of 'pushing', which is more concrete and familiar, as well as easier to visualize (other metaphorical expressions are used, such as 'transfer'). Once the metaphor has been introduced, it is used again to explain the notion of voltage, which is described as the amount of 'push' a battery is able to provide. In other

[2] GCSEs are the examinations that students in Britain take at sixteen years of age, at the end of the period of compulsory education.

words, an invisible, unfamiliar and relatively complex set of processes and characteristics is metaphorically presented in terms of a visible, familiar and relatively simple process. I would therefore argue that this metaphor has been chosen specifically for its pedagogic potential: it is not normally used for theory-constitutive purposes in other contexts, nor is it normally used by non-experts in relation to electricity. It is also interesting that both metaphorical uses of 'pushing' and 'push' in the extract are signalled in the extract: in the first sentence, the expression 'can be thought of as' explicitly marks the following expression as a metaphorical description of the relevant phenomenon; in the final sentence, 'push' is enclosed within scare quotes, which can suggest that the expression does not apply literally to the phenomena being described.

Cameron (2003) discusses a passage from a science textbook aimed at 10–11-year-old schoolchildren which includes a wider range of different metaphorical expressions. Below is part of the passage.

THE HEART
Blood is the body's transport system . . . At the centre of this system is your heart. It has four chambers with muscular walls. About once a second, the walls contract and squeeze blood out of the chambers into strong tubes, called arteries. The blood is pushed around your body. As the heart relaxes again, its chambers fill with more blood brought back to it by other tubes, the veins. This pumping, which we call a heart beat, happens every second of every day, for as long as you live . . . No man-made pump is as reliable as your heart. It can beat for 100 years or more without a rest. Also, the heart is adjustable. It can beat faster or slower, and change how much blood it pumps with each beat, depending on how active you are. (from S. Parker (1987), *The Body and How it Works*, quoted in Cameron 2003: 201)

Cameron (2003: 200–2) makes a distinction between three kinds of metaphorical expressions in the passage: 'sub-technical', 'technical' and 'technical + theory constitutive'. Sub-technical metaphors include, for example, the descriptions of the blood as 'the body's transport system', of the arteries as 'tubes' and of the heart as 'adjustable' (the metaphorical use of 'push' in extract 4.17 also falls within this category). These expressions are not conventionally used in scientific discussion of the functioning of the heart, and do not, therefore, have theory-constitutive uses in other contexts. Their use here is primarily due to their pedagogic potential: they appeal to knowledge that readers may already have (about transport, tubes and adjustable machines) in order to explain some aspects of the target domain (the TRANSPORT SYSTEM metaphor is used more systematically in the preceding section of the book). 'Technical' metaphors include expressions such as 'chambers' and 'wall', which are conventionally used to refer to the structure of the heart in scientific discussions, but which do not reflect the way in which the functioning of the heart is normally explained (i.e. the heart is not normally modelled on the concept of buildings). The use of the terms 'pumping' and 'pump', in contrast, are classified by Cameron as both technical and theory-constitutive: the functioning of the heart, she points out, has been primarily explained via the HEART IS A PUMP metaphor since the metaphor was introduced by William Harvey in the early seventeenth century (Cameron 2003: 204). In this context, however, it could be argued that this metaphor, and technical metaphors such as 'chambers' and 'wall', have a primarily pedagogic function, since they evoke source domains that are likely to be familiar to children from their everyday experience.

Cameron's work with a group of ten-year-old children, however, highlights the unpredictability of learners' interpretations of all three kinds of metaphors (Cameron 2003: 205–8). In particular, the participants in Cameron's study often treated the 'closed' technical metaphorical expressions in the 'Heart' passage as 'open' metaphors (Knudsen 2003), and applied insufficient and/or inappropriate source domain knowledge to their interpretation. For example, the use of 'walls' evoked the strength and protective function of physical walls; the use of 'chambers' evoked a storage space; and the use of 'pump' evoked a bicycle pump, so that, for example, the children concluded that the heart pumps air that pushes the blood round the body. As Cameron puts it, a 'problem for children, or other non-experts in a non-technical domain, is distinguishing between deliberate metaphors and technical terms that may be conventionalized metaphors' (Cameron 2003: 235).

The issue raised by Cameron is also relevant when particular theory-constitutive metaphors are used in a more systematic way in educational materials to provide a coherent but potentially simplistic introduction to the target domain. The extracts I am going to discuss are taken from an interactive tutorial available on the website of 'The Genetic Science Learning Center' at the University of Utah (http://gslc.genetics. utah.edu, 2007), which is described as 'an outreach education program located in the midst of bioscience research at the University of Utah' whose 'mission is to help people understand how genetics affects their lives and society'.

The Centre's homepage includes, amongst others, a link labelled 'The Basics and Beyond'. This link leads to another page where one can take a 'Tour of the Basics', which is intended for those who are 'a little confused by all the talk about DNA and genes' (http://gslc.genetics.utah.edu/units/ basics/index.cfm). Importantly, the Tour of the Basics can also be accessed from the homepage via the 'Teacher resources and lesson plans' link. Here the Tour is presented as an activity suitable for ages 11 to 18 (US grades 7–12), and is described as an 'interactive introduction to DNA and genetics presenting basic information and explanations of DNA, genes, chromosomes, inheritance and mitosis/meiosis'. No prior knowledge is said to be required on the part of students, although 'basic knowledge of cell structure may be helpful' (http://gslc.genetics.utah.edu/ teachers/tindex/overview.cfm?id=101).

I do not have the space here to do justice to the visual aspects of the tour (but readers are strongly advised to take the tour themselves: http://gslc.genetics.utah.edu/units/basics/tour/). I will focus primarily on the explanatory text that accompanies the visuals in the first of the six sections of the tour, entitled 'What is DNA?' This section begins by introducing the cells of the inner ear, and raises the question of how 'these cells "know" that their role is to support hearing instead of something else'. The answer to this question is given as follows (NB: extracts 4.18–20 below appear on consecutive pages in the section on DNA):

4.18 Instructions providing all of the information necessary for a living organism to grow and live reside in the nucleus of every cell. These instructions tell the cell what role it will play in the body. What do these instructions look like?

4.19 The instructions come in the form of a molecule called DNA. DNA encodes a detailed set of plans, like a blueprint for building different parts of the cell. How can a molecule hold information?

4.20 The DNA molecule comes in the form of a twisted ladder shape scientists call a 'double helix'. The ladder's rungs are built with the four-letter DNA alphabet: A, C, T and G. These alphabet pieces join together according to special rules. A always pairs with T, and C always pairs with G. How can only four letters tell the cell what to do?

4.21 The DNA strand is made of letters: ATGCTCGAATAAATGTCAATTTGA
The letters make words:
ATG CTC GAA TAA ATG TCA ATT TGA
The words make sentences:
<ATG CTC GAA TAA> <ATG TCA ATT TGA>
These 'sentences' are called genes. Genes tell the cell to make other molecules called proteins. Proteins enable a cell to perform special functions, such as working with other groups of cells to make hearing possible.

In these extracts, DNA is systematically described by means of an INSTRUCTIONS metaphor: the noun 'instructions' is used four times in the first two extracts and 'information' occurs in the first extract; in addition, in the following section of the Tour (entitled 'What is a gene?'), genes are described as 'instruction manuals for our bodies'. This metaphor can be seen as part of the general LANGUAGE/COMMUNICATION metaphor for DNA which, as I have shown earlier, has been used for theory-constitutive purposes since the early days of genetics. In extract 4.19, further similar metaphors are introduced to explain the function of DNA: the verb 'encodes' exploits the well-established CODE metaphor, while the expression 'a detailed set of plans' and the simile 'like a blueprint for building' can be seen as further, more specific, linguistic realizations of the INSTRUCTIONS metaphor. In this context, the convention of labelling the nucleotide bases of DNA via four letters of the alphabet reinforces and extends the notion that DNA is a set of instructions. In extract 4.21, the letters of DNA are described as forming words and sentences, with the latter corresponding to genes. This description is reinforced by a visual realization of the metaphor, since the background to extract 4.21 looks like the page of a note pad or copybook. Keller's (1995) 'discourse of gene action' is also evident in the use of personification: '[g]enes tell the cell'.

As we have seen, these metaphors have a long history in genetic discourse: they started to be used for theory-constitutive purposes when genes and DNA were discovered, and are commonly used in non-expert genres and the media for explanatory and persuasive purposes. We have also seen, however, how these metaphors have been questioned for the way in which they suggest that an individual's entire development is determined exclusively by his or her genes, and that scientists can straightforwardly 'read' the essence and future development of human beings by mapping their DNA. The pedagogical use of these metaphors, therefore, could be regarded as potentially problematic, especially in cases where a single overarching metaphor of DNA/genes as instructions structures the whole of an educational text (the only other metaphor in the DNA part of the Tour is that of the 'ladder', but this relates to the visual appearance of the DNA molecule rather than to its function). In addition, as Cameron (2003) has noted, learners often cannot distinguish between metaphorical technical terms and non-technical metaphors, and may therefore exploit the source domains in unpredictable ways. The Tour not only fails to provide any alternative metaphors, but also does not signal that many expressions are metaphorical technical terms (the only instance of signalling is the use of quotation marks for "sentences"). Rather, the authors of the website combine technical metaphorical expressions (e.g. 'encodes', 'instructions') with non-technical expressions from the same source domain (e.g. 'a detailed set of plans', 'alphabet pieces') in order to produce a coherent and accessible, but inevitably partial, introduction to DNA.

What is particularly missing from the DNA section of the Tour (and from the other sections too) is any sense that the relevant phenomena are being modelled metaphorically in a particular way for explanatory purposes, and that any metaphorical model has limitations and possible alternatives (especially considering that the target age range is 11–18). Taber (2001) stresses that, when metaphors are used for educational purposes, students should be encouraged to reflect in detail on the differences as well as the similarities between source and target domains. Spiro *et al.* (1989) suggest that learners should be provided with *alternative* metaphors for the same phenomena, since reliance on single metaphors can eventually prevent students from reaching more advanced levels of understanding (see also Cameron 2003: 39).

One possible alternative metaphor is provided by Miller (1988), who is concerned with explaining to university students the concept that the development of organisms involves a complex interaction between genes and experience. Miller reports that, in order to explain the metaphor to his students, he takes four different food items (i.e., developmental outcomes) that use flour as a base (i.e., genetic factors), but that also have other ingredients that will interact with flour in unique ways (i.e., yielding different developmental trajectories). Also, different cooking methods (i.e., experiential factors) influence these developmental trajectories and yield different developmental outcomes. (Miller 1988: 148)

He then shows his students how a combination of flour, salt and water leads to a tortilla if fried, and a 'matzo' if baked. If yeast is added and the mixture is baked, the result is bread. Miller uses this metaphor to explain how the 'developmental outcome is a complex transaction involving the flour (genes), other ingredients, and the nature of the developmental process (cooking method)' (Miller 1988: 148). This metaphor is arguably even more accessible[3] than the CODE or INSTRUCTIONS metaphor for DNA, but structures the target domain quite differently: in the LANGUAGE/COMMUNICATION metaphors, genes are the main (or even only) factor in development, while in the COOKING metaphor they are only one amongst many factors. Miller's metaphor also accounts for the fact that different developmental factors interact in complex and inextricable ways. As he puts it, it 'would be entirely arbitrary to quantify the degree to which bread is a function of flour (i.e., heritability) as opposed to baking (i.e., environment)' (Miller 1988: 148).

One could argue, of course, that Miller's metaphor reflects a very different view of genes from that of early geneticists such as Schrödinger (see extract 4.10 above). However, nowadays the contribution of environmental factors is generally recognized in genetics, so that the COOKING metaphor arguably reflects current views better than the INSTRUCTIONS metaphor used in the 'Tour of the Basics' on the website of 'The Genetic Science Learning Center'. The crucial point here is that learners should ideally be equipped with more than one metaphorical model of the phenomena they study, in order to reduce the possibility of mistaken or partial understandings.

4.5 Source domains in scientific metaphors

The examples I have discussed in the previous sections show that there are considerable similarities and overlaps between the domains that function as metaphorical sources in scientific discourse generally and those that we have seen in other areas, such as politics. By and large, the source domains exploited by scientists correspond to relatively concrete, well-structured, familiar and accessible areas of experience. This is the case, for example, with the Cartesian theatre metaphor in the study of consciousness, the WASTE DISPOSAL metaphor in studies of longevity or the CODE/INSTRUCTIONS metaphors

[3] Miller's ingredients and food items are obviously culture-specific, but his cooking metaphor could easily be adapted to other cultural contexts.

in genetics. Personification is also commonly used, as in the Pandemonium model of consciousness and in what Keller (1995) calls 'the discourse of gene action'. As I have said before, metaphorical source domains provide models of the phenomena under investigation, and '[t]o be useful, models have to be simplified representations of something more complex' (Taber 2001: 222). In Miller's (1988) COOKING metaphor for development, for example, the source domain is clearly simpler, more accessible, concrete and familiar than the target domain, while in the case of CODE metaphors in genetics a rather simplistic view of language and communication is employed as source domain.

I have also shown that there is no neat separation between the metaphors used for theory-constitutive purposes in expert genres and those that are used for explanatory, pedagogical and persuasive purposes in non-expert genres. We have seen how theory-constitutive metaphors are developed and extended in science popularizations, educational materials and media debates. On the other hand, it has been argued that scientists often exploit the same metaphorical resources that are conventionally used in everyday language (see Brown 2003). Lakoff and Johnson (1980a), for example, see the COMPUTER metaphors used by psychologists and neuroscientists as extensions and elaborations of some of the metaphors that are commonly used in relation to the mind, such as THE MIND IS A MACHINE (e.g. 'I'm a little rusty today' or 'We've been working on this problem all day and now we are running out of steam') (Lakoff and Johnson 1980b: 27–8). They argue that

> [w]hen the basic metaphors of a scientific theory are extensions of basic metaphors in our everyday conceptual system, then we feel that such a theory is 'intuitive' or 'natural'. (Lakoff and Johnson 1980a: 207)

In the course of the chapter, however, I have also shown how the theory-constitutive use of metaphor on the part of scientists often involves greater explicitness and rigour in the specification of cross-domain correspondences (and lack of correspondences) than is the case in other areas, such as literature and politics. When particular metaphors are adopted within a scientific community, they tend to evolve towards greater and greater clarification of what aspects of the source domain apply to the target; in time, the meanings of technical metaphorical expressions tend to rely more on increasing knowledge of the target domain and less on projections from the source domains. As Knudsen (2003) puts it, these metaphors become 'closed'. In non-expert genres, however, these metaphors may be 'opened up' and used in ways that may go beyond the specific mappings exploited by experts, in order to maximize the explanatory and persuasive potential of source domains.

The exploitation of familiar and accessible areas of experience is particularly obvious when metaphors are devised primarily for pedagogical purposes, as in the case of Miller's cooking metaphor and the 'pushing' metaphors for electricity in extract 4.17 above. However, the choice of source domains in scientific discourse also crucially depends on the scientist's current understanding of particular phenomena and on his or her attempt to present and support their intuitions or findings about the nature of these phenomena. Source domains may not therefore always be quite as simple, concrete and accessible as those exploited by politicians or journalists. In Dennett's CONSCIOUSNESS IS FAME/POLITICAL CLOUT metaphor, for example, the source domain is certainly more familiar and accessible than the target domain, but is itself rather complex and abstract. Its choice inevitably involves a trade-off between accessibility and vividness on the one hand, and the constraints imposed by the specific view of phenomena that Dennett wishes to propose on the other. The same can be said of Rutherford's metaphor of the atom as a miniature solar system. At the time of the introduction of the metaphor, the solar system was better known and understood than atomic structure, but its characteristics are neither simple nor accessible to direct observation. Indeed, Taber (2001) has found that today's students may not be sufficiently familiar with astronomy to benefit from the metaphor in their understanding of atomic structure.

In fact, scientists may sometimes go well beyond familiar experiences in order to provide metaphorical models of particular phenomena. A striking example of this is Kosslyn and Koenig's OCTOPUS metaphor for neural networks (Kosslyn and Koenig 1992: 19–24). Kosslyn and Koenig point out that early computers functioned in ways that are rather unlike what is known about the human brain. However, more recently, a form of computation with 'brain-like features' has been developed. This form of computation is known as 'neural networks' computation, as well as 'parallel distributed processing' or 'connectionism'. It involves 'sets of interconnected units that work together to perform a specific type of information processing'. In order to explain the central features of this kind of computation, Kosslyn and Koenig begin 'with some fictional marine zoology' (Kosslyn and Koenig 1992: 19):

> Professor Jack Costlow was forced to work on a low budget. Having no money to fund deep sea explorations, he explored the mysteries of tidal pools. His rise to fame began with an accidental discovery of a form of recreation practiced by octopi . . . The octopi lined up in three rows. The octopi in the first row intertwined tentacles with the octopi in the second row, who in turn intertwined tentacles with the octopi in the third row. Professor Costlow noticed that whenever anything brushed one of the free tentacles of an octopus in the first row, that octopus would squeeze tentacles with all the octopi in the middle row. Those octopi in turn would squeeze tentacles with the octopi in the third row. What caught the Professor's attention, however, was what happened when something brushed against several of the octopi in the first row, leading all of them to squeeze the octopi in the middle row. Now some of the octopi in the middle row squeezed the octopi in the third row harder! Depending on how they squeezed, a different octopus in the third row waved its free tentacles out of the water. (Kosslyn and Koenig 1992: 19)

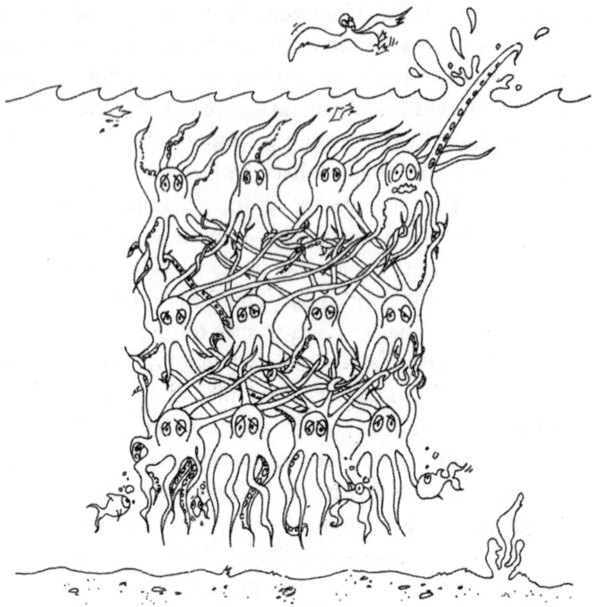

Figure 4.1 Kosslyn and Koenig's (1992) octopus network

Kosslyn and Koenig's representation of the octopus network is reproduced in figure 4.1.

Kosslyn and Koenig go on to explain that Professor Costlow initially thought that he had accidentally discovered 'a coven of sadistic octopi'. However, he then realized that '[d]epending on how many octopi were brushed in the first row, different octopi in the third row waved their tentacles out of the water' (Kosslyn and Koenig 1992: 19). He therefore concluded that the octopi were in fact unknowingly reporting the density of fish in the sea to seagulls flying above them.

Having introduced this fictional scenario, Kosslyn and Koenig (1992: 20–4) go on to explain in detail how the characteristics of their imaginary octopus network match the characteristics of new, parallel computational networks, and how these, in turn, can be seen as models of the functioning of neurons in the brain.[4] I do not have the space here to do justice to Kosslyn and Koenig's detailed explication of the octopus network metaphor. What this example aims to show is how, in some cases, source domains may be invented for the purposes of

[4] Kosslyn and Koenig's use of the octopus scenario is similar to Dennett's use of the story in which a novelist narrowly missed becoming famous (see 4.1 above): a hypothetical scenario is first introduced and then metaphorically projected onto a target scenario, as a kind of mini-allegory.

modelling particular phenomena, rather than selected from familiar 'real' experiences. It is still the case, of course, that the octopus network is much simpler, vivid and entertaining than the networks in the target domains (i.e. computers and human brains). Nevertheless, it is clearly the case that the exploitation of familiar areas of experience is not a necessary requirement for metaphors to be used successfully for modelling and explanation. In such cases, the source domain is constructed precisely to fit the basic characteristics of the phenomena it is designed to model (for another example, see John Searle's (1997) famous 'Chinese room thought experiment'). This kind of phenomenon is particularly characteristic of scientific discourse, due to the challenges involved in attempting to understand and explain precisely phenomena with particularly complex structures and relations.

4.6 Case study 1: 'regulatory T cells' in specialist scientific articles

In the two case studies I present in the rest of this chapter I continue to discuss the differences and similarities between the metaphors used by experts to communicate amongst themselves and the metaphors used for the benefit of learners. Both case studies are concerned with metaphors for the workings of the human immune system, but each focuses on a different genre. In this section, I analyse a series of articles included in a special issue of the scientific journal *Nature Immunology*; in the second case study, I discuss a section from the BBC's website that provides revision material for students preparing for the GCSE examination in Biology.

The fourth issue of the 2005 volume of *Nature Immunology* (see www.nature.com/ni/focus/regulatory_tcells/index.html) was entirely devoted to 'regulatory T cells' (T_{reg} cells) – a sub-group of lymphocytes produced by the thymus (hence the name 'T' cells), which have the crucial function of maintaining 'immunological self-tolerance': they prevent the body's immune system from reacting against the body's own healthy cells, while reacting against harmful external agents. Failure in the functioning of T_{reg} cells results in a variety of autoimmune diseases, and scientists hope that a better understanding of these cells may lead to new treatments for allergies, cancer and other conditions. The special issue includes an editorial and five specially commissioned articles: a 'perspective' paper (Schwartz 2005) and four 'review' papers (Belkaid and Rouse 2005; Fontenot and Rudensky 2005; Sakaguchi 2005; von Boehmer 2005).

In order to provide an initial overview of the nature and variety of the metaphorical expressions used in the special issue, I begin by discussing some extracts from the editorial (entitled 'Essence of Harmony'), which introduces the special issue as a whole (*Nature Immunology*, 2005, p. 325). Extract 4.22

below is the opening of the editorial; extract 4.23 is taken from one of the middle paragraphs; and extract 4.24 includes the final four sentences:

4.22 The human body, with its multitude of complexities, requires harmonious interactions among all its constituents for the maintenance of homeostasis. Because every member of this intricate community has its own 'agenda', a peaceful and productive existence is not trivial. Fortunately, the body has several means for avoiding potential and detrimental conflicts between immune responses to self versus non-self. A fundamental strategy is ensuring that the immune cell repertoire is sufficiently devoid of those that could cause harm to self while maintaining a wide selection of those that are adept at taking appropriate action against foreign invaders and stressed cells. Another level of control is provided by the active regulation of immune responses through cellular interactions and soluble mediators. These checks and balances are the essence of harmony that maintains the status quo.

This issue of *Nature Immunology* examines how such harmony may be achieved by a subset of T lymphocytes called regulatory T cells (T_{reg} cells).

4.23 Why the preoccupation with the biology of T_{reg} cells? The answer lies in their far-reaching effect on our health. T_{reg} cells may influence the outcome of infection, autoimmunity, transplantation, cancer and even allergy. However, the T_{reg} cell is very much a 'double-edged sword', creating a 'yin' for every 'yang' and vice versa, leading to an outcome that is context dependent.

4.24 The existence of T_{reg} cells with such profound effect on myriad conditions underscores the complexity of the immune system and the need for multiple layers of oversight. This control system is not a static barrier but instead is a process of dynamic interaction with its microenvironment. The ultimate aim is to achieve the balance and harmony required for the well-being of the body, either naturally or through artificial intervention. Present wisdom suggests that T_{reg} cells are at the center of this equilibrium.

In these extracts, the ideal state of stability for the organism ('homeostasis') is described via metaphorical expressions drawn from the source domains of MUSIC ('harmony', 'harmonious') and BALANCE ('balance'; note also the etymology of 'equilibrium'). The cellular processes involved in maintaining, or failing to maintain, this ideal state are described via metaphorical expressions drawn from a wide variety of domains, including: WAR/PHYSICAL CONFLICT (e.g. 'conflict', 'foreign invaders', 'strategy'; note also 'peaceful' in extract 4.22); COMMUNICATION (e.g. 'interaction', 'responses', 'mediator'); HUMAN BEINGS AND THEIR CHARACTERISTICS/ACTIVITIES (e.g. 'community', 'taking appropriate action'); MACHINES (e.g. 'control', 'control system', 'regulation', 'regulatory') and BUSINESS ('agenda', 'productive').

Some of these expressions have conventional metaphorical senses in general language use: 'balance', for example, is conventionally used to describe situations in which different entities/phenomena exist or apply in equal proportions (e.g. 'His text preserves a careful balance between deference, quotation and his own selective critical comment,' from the BNC); similarly, 'conflict' is conventionally used to describe disagreements, or situations in which it is difficult for different entities to co-exist (e.g. 'The two tunes underline the conflict between good and evil,' from the BNC). In the context of the specialized discourse of immunology, however, many of the metaphorical expressions I have pointed out are 'technical' metaphors (Cameron 2003): they have acquired conventional senses that are specific to the target domain and that are familiar to experts in the relevant disciplines. This applies to 'conflict', 'responses', 'control', 'foreign invaders' and so on.

More specifically, I argue that the expressions that I have related to the source domains of BALANCE, WAR/PHYSICAL CONFLICT, COMMUNICATION, HUMAN BEINGS and MACHINES have a theory-constitutive function in the editorial and in immunology discourse more generally: they are a central and indispensable part of expert vocabulary in immunology, and the relevant source domains structure different aspects of the current understanding of the function and working of the immune system. The expressions that I have listed above under the source domains of MUSIC and BUSINESS, on the other hand, are not conventionally used in immunology discourse and cannot therefore be regarded as technical terms. Rather, their conventional metaphorical senses in everyday language can be applied to the phenomena discussed in the editorial, as in the case of 'harmony' for homeostasis or of different 'agendas' for the different needs and functions of different parts of an organism.

Overall, we can begin to see how the molecular processes that characterize the functioning of the immune system are consistently described in terms of a set of well-structured and accessible source domains that relate to familiar human activities. These source domains are used in ways that are broadly compatible with each other, but each source domain captures particular aspects of the target domain. The different source domains also differ in terms of the role they play in the current understanding of the functioning of the immune system, and therefore in the extent to which they provide metaphorical technical terms.

The extracts quoted above also include examples of more creative and informal non-technical metaphors, some of which are explicitly signalled via the use of quotation marks: 'agenda', 'double-edged sword' and 'a "yin" for every "yang" '. The same signalling device is also used in the editorial, and in the five articles, to mark the first occurrence of metaphorical technical terms which are then repeatedly used without quotation marks. This is the case with 'regulate' and 'suppressor cells' in the extract below:

4.25 Although all cells 'regulate' other cells in some way, T_{reg} cells are exceptional because their main role seems to be suppression of the function of other cells, hence they are also called 'suppressor cells'. (*Nature Immunology*, 2005, p. 25)

I now explore the main metaphorical patterns in the five articles included in the special issue of *Nature Immunology*, which contain a total of 22,439 words. The discussion is based on a combination of traditional 'manual' analysis with the results of an automatic analysis of the lexis of the articles via the 'Wordlist' and 'Concord' facilities of the software package *WordSmith Tools* (Scott 1999).

Dominant metaphorical source domains in the five 'T_{reg} cells' articles

It is well known that the functioning of the immune system is conventionally explained in terms of metaphors from the source domain of WAR, or PHYSICAL CONFLICT/AGGRESSION more generally: entities such as viruses and bacteria are conventionally described as external agents that attack the body, while the immune system defends the body by attempting to eliminate any harmful invasion from outside (e.g. Goatly 1997: 49–51; e.g. Darian 2003). This use of metaphor is consistent with a more general tendency to construct illnesses as enemies to be fought by the body, the sick person or the doctors (see 5.3 below for more discussion). In the five articles from *Nature Immunology*, external bodies are described as 'foreign antigens' (8 instances) that 'invade' (2 instances) the body. The workings of the immune system in relation to these antigens are described via metaphorical expressions such as the following: 'protection', 'protective' and 'protect' (10 instances in total); 'defense', 'defensive, 'defend' (6 instances in total); 'blockade' and 'block' (13 instances in total). The role of T_{reg} cells in preventing the immune system from reacting against the body itself (the 'host') is described via the expressions 'suppression', 'suppress', 'suppressive', 'suppressor' (286 instances in total). The result is a scenario with different metaphorical wars going on, including particularly: a war between the immune system and harmful external agents, and a war between the T_{reg} cells and the potential excesses of the immune system itself. The mutual actions of different types of cells on each other are systematically described via expressions to do with physical aggression and war: 'destructive' and 'destruction' (5 instances in total); 'elimination' and 'eliminate' (7 instances in total); 'kill' and 'killer' (7 instances in total); 'damage' (11 instances); 'strategies' (5 instances); 'targeting' and 'targets' (23 instances in total); and 'aggressive' (2 instances). The possibility that T_{reg} cells may accidentally block the operation of other cells that are not actually potentially harmful to the host is described as 'collateral tissue damage' (2 instances) or as 'bystander' suppression (10 instances).

It is also well recognized that molecular processes are conventionally explained in terms of metaphorical expressions drawing from the source domain of LANGUAGE/COMMUNICATION. In the five articles, the activation of different parts of the immune system to prevent different types of damage is systematically described in terms of 'responses' or 'responding' (123 instances in total) and 'interaction' or 'interacting' (53 instances in total). Particular molecular processes are referred to as 'transcription' (15 instances), 'signalling' or producing 'signals' (47 instances in total), 'mediating' (67 instances), and 'expressing' or the 'expression' or particular substances or behaviours (113 instances). There are also a few instances of expressions that construct the processes whereby some cells acquire particular functions in terms of 'tutoring' or 'instruction' on the part of other cells (2 instances in total). These expressions are less common, however, and are used within quotation marks, which may function as an explicit signal of metaphoricity.

Another dominant metaphorical pattern in the five articles draws from the source domain of MACHINERY. A range of different processes are described as 'mechanisms' (64 instances in total), and the ways in which some cells affect other cells are described in terms of 'control' (47 instances) and 'regulation' or having a 'regulatory' function (61 instances in total). As is common with other scientific disciplines, MACHINERY metaphors often involve the use of vocabulary to do with computers in particular. A particular cellular process is conventionally described as 'deletion' (15 instances), and there are two references to cells being 'programmed'. Less conventional uses of computer metaphors are explicitly signalled via quotation marks, as in the case of a particular 'mechanism' that is described as 'hard-wired'.

The patterns I have described so far often involve the personification of cells as invaders, killers, defenders, communicators and so on. The five articles also contain several other patterns of personification, which draw from different aspects of the general source domain of HUMAN BEINGS. Groups of cells are described as 'populations' (30 instances), and the developmental relationships within groups of cells are captured by terms such as 'family' (5 instances) and 'lineage' (31 instances). Some central processes within the immune system are systematically described in terms of human processes and characteristics such as 'tolerance' (71 instances), 'inhibition' or 'inhibiting' (11 instances in total) and 'recognition' or 'recognizing' (30 instances in total), and 'avidity' (14 instances). Similarly, cells are systematically described by means of adjectives or nouns that typically apply to human beings, including 'dominant' (25 instances), competitive (4 instances), naïve (23 instances) and 'helper' (4 instances). As we have seen before, less conventional instances of personification are signalled via the use of quotation marks, as in the case of 'a "rational" molecular marker', or 'natural T_{reg} cells and their "cousins" '.

The repetition and recurrence of metaphorical expressions are therefore exploited throughout the five articles in order to convey a particular view of the phenomenon under consideration. Cumulatively, the expressions I have explicitly mentioned in this section account for 1,259 words, which represent approximately 5.5 per cent of the words included in the five articles (in terms of tokens, I have mentioned 397 metaphorically used words from the WAR/PHYSICAL CONFLICT domain, 420 from the LANGUAGE/COMMUNICATION DOMAIN, 190 from the MACHINES domain, and 252 from the general HUMAN BEINGS DOMAIN). More importantly, the vast majority of these expressions are 'technical' metaphors, and cumulatively account for most of the technical terminology in the articles. In Boyd's (1993) terms, these metaphors have a theory-constitutive function because there are, in most cases, no nonmetaphorical alternatives for expressing particular concepts. For example, the function of the particular type of T cells under investigation is described via two alternative technical metaphors, i.e. 'regulation' or 'suppression', but no equivalent nonmetaphorical term is used in the articles. Similarly, there is no obvious nonmetaphorical alternative for central immunological terms such as '(self-)tolerance' and 'response'. More importantly, it can be argued that some of the concepts provided by the four source domains I have mentioned structure the particular model of the immune system that is assumed in the five articles: this applies to notions such as attack, defence, response, self-tolerance, control, regulation and so on (metaphorical 'balance' between different aspects of the immune system may also be included here, even though the term only occurs five times in the articles). Although many of the expressions I have mentioned are used in the articles in specialized, technical senses, it is interesting that most of the main source domains are also exploited to produce more novel metaphorical expressions, such as 'hard-wired' mechanism or cellular 'cousins'. This suggests that they are still active as metaphorical source domains in spite of the fact that many of the expressions they provide have highly conventionalized technical senses.

Interestingly, the recent proposal of an alternative view of the immune system involves the very explicit adoption of alternative metaphors for its functioning. In a book entitled *The Web of Life*, Capra (1996) states that

> [a]ccording to traditional immunology, the lymphocytes identify an intruding agent, the antibodies attach themselves to it, and, by doing so, neutralize it . . . Recent research has shown that under normal conditions the antibodies circulating in the body bind to many (if not all) types of cells, including themselves. The entire system looks more like a network, more like people talking to each other, than soldiers out looking for an enemy. (Capra 1996: 272; see also Goatly 1997: 51)

Within this view, antibodies do not need to distinguish between foreign agents and the body's own cells in order to destroy the former and tolerate the latter. Rather, antibodies bind with all types of cells and 'regulate' their numbers and activities in order to ensure that there is no damage to the host. External agents are therefore normally incorporated into the body rather than destroyed. Destruction only occurs when external agents enter the body in such quantities that they cannot be easily kept under control. While Capra uses many of the metaphors of mainstream immunology discourse (notably that of 'regulation') the view of the immune system as a 'cognitive, self-organizing and self-regulating network' eliminates the 'puzzle of the self/non-self distinction' which lies at the heart of the 'T_{reg} cells' articles: '[t]he immune system simply does not and need not distinguish between body cells and foreign agents, because both are subjected to the same regulatory processes' (Capra 1996: 273). This alternative view has different practical consequences for medical practice, for example with respect to the use of antibiotics as an appropriate way of helping the body deal with infection (see Goatly 1997: 49–51).

I now turn to a description of the mainstream view of the immune system in a sample of educational materials.

4.7 Case study 2: the immune system in an educational text

In this second case study I consider the way in which the immune system is described in the educational material provided by the BBC for the benefit of British schoolchildren. As part of its educational services, the BBC provides, on its website, 'Bitesize revision' in a range of subjects for students preparing for GCSEs (www.bbc.co.uk/schools/gcsebitesize/, 2007). The metaphorical use of 'bitesize' in the title of the webpages is extended in the slogan: 'Revision that's easier to digest'. Both metaphorical expressions ('bitesize' and 'digest') are part of a conventional pattern whereby we talk about understanding new or difficult ideas in terms of digestion (see Lakoff and Johnson 1999: 241). In this context, these expressions are used to emphasize that the website provides to-be-learned information in short sections that are easy for students to understand and remember rapidly and, presumably, without excessive effort.

The Biology section of the 'Bitesize revision' site includes a subsection on 'Maintaining Health' (www.bbc.co.uk/schools/gcsebitesize/biology/humansasorganisms/maintaininghealthrev1.shtml). I am going to consider three consecutive pages within this sub-section, entitled respectively: 'Immune system: passive immunity', 'Immune system: active immunity' and 'More about white blood cells'. These pages contain 1,283 words in total, and provide an overview of the functioning of the immune system. I will show how these pages exploit some of the metaphors that I have discussed in the previous case study, but in a rather different way. More specifically, a small subset of the source domains used in the *Nature Immunology* articles are here exploited in a more systematic and less technical way to enhance the comprehensibility and memorability of the information that readers need to learn.

The extracts below are the opening paragraphs of the sections on passive and active immunity respectively (bold type is used in the original):

4.26 Most pathogens have to get inside our body to spread infection. Once they are inside, the body provides ideal living conditions – plenty of food, water and warmth. Standing in their way is our body's **immune system** – a collective name for the body's co-ordinated response to the invading pathogens.

4.27 When pathogens get past the first line of defence and enter the system, the body's **acquired** or **active immune system** takes over. Active immunity is triggered by a specific attack by a specific pathogen. The detection of any 'foreign' cells or substances is called an **immune response**.

These two extracts contain metaphorical expressions that can be related to the main source domains I discussed in my analysis of the *Nature Immunology* articles in the previous section: WAR/PHYSICAL CONFLICT (e.g. 'attack'), COMMUNICATION ('response') and HUMAN/LIVING BEINGS (e.g. 'ideal living conditions'). However, there are important differences between the two sets of data, both in terms of the kinds of metaphorical expressions that are used and in terms of their frequency and use.

Some of the metaphorical expressions used in extracts 4.26 and 4.27 correspond to the technical metaphors that I have identified in expert discourse, such as 'attack' and 'response'. However, the extracts also contain several metaphorical expressions that draw from the same source domains but that are not commonly used as technical terms. This applies particularly to the expressions 'standing in their way' and 'line of defence' for the WAR/PHYSICAL CONFLICT source domain, and to the systematic use of personifying expressions. External pathogens are presented as agents of the actions denoted by the expressions 'get inside', 'are inside' and 'enter', as well as 'get past the first line of defence'. In addition to being described as 'invading' and 'foreign', they are presented as requiring 'ideal living conditions' that prototypically apply to animate organisms: 'plenty of food, water and warmth'. The body itself is potentially personified as the provider of these conditions, while the use of the informal expression 'standing in their way' in extract 4.26 personifies the immune system much more explicitly than technical terms such as 'response'. The use of these particular personifying expressions also results in the systematic construction of the body as a container, which can be 'entered' by external pathogens if they manage to get past the 'line of defence' set up by the immune system.

The phenomena I have observed in the two short extracts quoted above are typical of the rest of the text devoted to the immune system on the BBC's revision website. An analysis of the three sub-sections also reveals some interesting differences in the extent to which different metaphorical source domains are exploited. The use of the COMMUNICATION source domain is limited to the expressions 'respond/response' (6 instances in total), 'markers' (4 instances), 'signals' (1 instance) and 'send out messages' (1 instance). In contrast, the WAR/PHYSICAL CONFLICT source domain and the HUMAN BEINGS source domain are consistently exploited throughout, both via the use of technical and non-technical metaphorical expressions.

The various components of the immune system are presented not just as a '(line of) defence' (6 instances in total), but also as 'barriers' (4 instances) and a 'fighting force' (1 instance). Their role is described as 'protecting' the body (2 instances) and enabling it to 'resist' external attacks (1 instance), while their activities in relation to external pathogens are described as being 'on the lookout' (1 instance), 'killing' (8 instances), 'engulfing' (5 instances), 'neutralizing' (6 instances), 'destroying' (4 instances) and 'making (toxins) safe' (1 instance). On three occasions, various parts of the immune system are also presented as 'trapping' external agents, which may evoke the related source domain of HUNTING. External pathogens are presented as 'hostile' (1 instance), 'foreign' (7 instances), 'invaders/invading' (9 instances in total), 'attacking' or mounting an 'attack' (5 instances in total), 'triggering' a response (5 instances), causing 'damage' (2 instances) and, as we have already seen, as 'getting past' the body's lines of defence. In total, I have identified 71 metaphorically used words that can be related to the WAR/PHYSICAL CONFLICT source domain. This amounts to 5.5 per cent of the words included in the data from the BBC's website (1,283 words in total). In contrast, according to my analysis, WAR/PHYSICAL CONFLICT expressions amount to 1.7 per cent of the words in the five articles from *Nature Immunology*.

In addition to the personifying effects of many WAR/PHYSICAL CONFLICT expressions, the BBC webpages also include many other expressions that attribute human behaviour and characteristics to the components of the immune system and to external pathogens. I have already mentioned several instances of personification in my analysis of extracts 4.26 and 4.27. In addition, various part of the immune system are described as '(key) players' (2 instances), that 'recognise' (2 instances), 'detect' (2 instances) harmful pathogens, 'carry' particular antibodies, and 'carry' harmful agents 'away' (3 instances in total). Further, non-technical instances of personification include: the immune system 'considering' some cells as not its own (1 instance), lymphocytes 'trying out' different types of antibodies (1 instance), antibodies having 'a kind of memory' and emitting signals 'which bring nearby phagocytes to the scene' (1 instance) and some bacteria being described as 'friendly' (2 instances). What is interesting about these expressions is not so much their overall frequency, but the fact that they are mostly informal expressions, that are conventionally used metaphorically in language generally, but that are not normally part of technical discourse.

The webpages also include some expressions that exploit different source domains in order to explain particular concepts. In the extract below, for example, the idea that different antibodies may be employed to fight a particular infection is metaphorically presented via the notion that antibodies vary in 'shape', like the different keys a burglar may try to use in order to open a lock:

4.28 the lymphocytes respond by 'trying out' a range of antibody 'shapes', until they find the right one – like a burglar using skeleton keys, trying each key in turn until one fits the lock.

Overall, both the expert data and the educational data on the immune system include metaphorical patterns that present cellular processes in terms of human activities, including particularly physical conflict and communication. The *Nature Immunology* articles, however, rely in roughly equal measure on four main source domains, and mostly employ technical metaphorical expressions. Where novel metaphorical expressions are used, signalling tends to occur, particularly via the insertion of quotation marks. The BBC materials, in contrast, make a particularly systematic use of the WAR/PHYSICAL CONFLICT source domain, and combine technical and non-technical metaphorical expressions. The result is the systematic construction of the workings of the immune system in terms of a physical scenario in which different parts of the body fight against the invasion of foreign agents. The description of the function of white blood cells below is typical of how the BBC's materials are written:

4.29 The key players in the active immune system are the white blood cells. They identify invading pathogens and either
- engulf them and destroy them
- produce antibodies which kill them, or
- produce antitoxins which neutralise toxins made by the invaders

Clearly, the source domains of WAR/PHYSICAL CONFLICT, and that of HUMAN BEINGS more generally, are used for pedagogical purposes in order to provide a comprehensible and memorable account of the phenomena that students are supposed to study in preparation for their exams. Readers' knowledge of familiar scenarios, and of familiar metaphorical expressions, is exploited in order to introduce an unfamiliar topic clearly and concisely. Among other things, the various metaphorical scenarios are used to present the complex phenomena under discussion in terms of mini-narratives, including agents, goals and actions, as, for example, in the case of the burglar in the simile in extract 4.28. On the other hand, however, the discussion is rather elementary, and does not provide readers with clear distinctions between technical metaphorical expressions and non-technical metaphors. Quotation marks are mostly used for the most informal metaphorical expressions, such as 'trying out' and 'shapes' in extract 4.28, but no other signalling device is employed systematically to distinguish between technical and non-technical metaphors. This could potentially lead to the kinds of confusion discussed by Cameron (2003) (see section 4.4 above).

4.8 Summary

In this chapter, I have shown that metaphor plays a central role in science. I have discussed the use of metaphor on the part of experts to develop and explicate their theories, as well as the use of metaphor in non-expert genres such as popular scientific publications and educational materials. I have pointed out that media and educational texts often draw from the same source domains as expert publications, but I have also discussed some important differences in how these source domains are exploited in different genres aimed at different audiences. This can potentially result in mystification and oversimplification, especially in cases where learners, for example, are not provided with alternative metaphors for the same phenomena. I have shown that the metaphors used in expert scientific genres tend to be spelt out more rigorously and explicitly than those used in politics or literature, but I have suggested that scientists also use metaphors for rhetorical effects, and that dominant scientific metaphors can play an important ideological role.

5 Metaphor in other genres and discourses: two further case studies

5.1 Introduction

Metaphor plays an important role in a wide range of human activities and types of communication – many more than can be discussed in this book. For example, as I write, I use my computer to work with 'files' and 'folders' that are part of my 'desktop', and I do things such as 'opening' and 'closing' documents, sending them to the 'trash' and so on. In other words, the computer interface most of us use is partly modelled on a metaphor where the source domain is the traditional office, with desks, filing cabinets and so on (see also Fauconnier and Turner 2002: 22–4). Similarly, medical and military metaphors underlie the use of software to 'defend' our computers from the threats represented by entities known as 'viruses', 'bugs' and so on. The use of metaphor has indeed been studied in relation to a wide variety of spheres of activity, genres and discourses, ranging from the discourse of trade (e.g. Eubanks 2000) to foreign language learning (e.g. Littlemore and Low 2006), and from psychotherapy (e.g. Combs and Freedman 1990) to religion (e.g. Charteris-Black 2004).

In this chapter, I broaden the scope of the discussion to consider the use of metaphor in two further domains of activity: a particularly pervasive genre, namely advertising, and a particularly sensitive discourse, namely the discourse of illness. The chapter is therefore divided into two parts, each containing a general introduction and a case study.

5.2 Metaphor and advertising

Metaphor is generally regarded as a frequent and central characteristic of advertisements,[1] involving both the use of language and images (see Leech 1966; Barthes 1981; Myers 1994; Forceville 1996; Cook 2001). This can be explained with reference to two main functions that metaphors can perform in advertisements, or 'ads'. First, metaphors can be used as attention-grabbing devices,

[1] The term 'advertise' itself is an etymological metaphor, since it derives from the Latin 'advertere', which means 'turn towards' (see also Goddard 1998: 11).

especially when they are relatively novel and salient, and when they involve visual images. Second, metaphors can be used in order to present what is being advertised in terms of other entities that have the characteristics which the advertisers want us to associate with the product.

For example, for a number of years Boddingtons beer was advertised in the UK via a metaphorical association of its foam and texture with cream. Print advertisements included the slogan 'Boddingtons. The cream of Manchester' and showed pictures such as a pint of beer shaped as a slice of cake, placed on top of a cake-serving utensil and with foam/cream falling down one side (see Myers 1994: 122–3). Pictures such as this were very eye-catching, due to the oddity of the hybrid objects they involved, as well as to the use of a black background to contrast with the orange and white colours of the image in the foreground. The slogan, on the other hand, was printed in black at the bottom of the page against an orange background, and explicitly spelt out the metaphorical association between beer and cream suggested by the picture. The expression 'the cream of' is conventionally used to suggest that something is the best part of something else, in the same way as cream is (conventionally taken to be) the best part of milk. In the Boddingtons case, therefore, it was suggested that this particular type of beer is the best thing about the English city of Manchester.

In the Boddingtons ads, the same metaphorical association of cream and beer was expressed both visually and verbally. In other cases, the use of a particular metaphor for the product may be limited only to the picture, or only to the verbal part of the ad (see Forceville 1996). The latter option is less frequent, however, due to the centrality and flexibility of images in advertising involving a visual component (e.g. in the press, on billboards, on television, on the World Wide Web). Apart from their attention-grabbing potential, pictures also allow the conflation of source and target concepts into a single hybrid entity. For example, the ad I have just described features an object that is the combination of two normally separate entities: a slice of cake topped with cream, which functions as the source concept of the metaphor, and a pint of beer topped with foam, which functions as the target concept (see also Forceville 1996: 163).[2] This kind of conflation is less easy to achieve by means of language, since individual expressions can normally only mention either the source (e.g. 'cream' in 'The cream of Manchester'), or the target of the metaphor (e.g. 'Boddingtons'). As Forceville (1996) has shown, there are also cases where source and target concepts are included in the picture as separate entities, or where only the object functioning as source is visually present. In the latter kind

[2] Objects of this kind can be see as visual 'blends', in the terms used by Fauconnier and Turner (2002).

of case, the verbal component of the ad normally spells out the metaphorical relationship between the represented object and the product.

For example, a mailshot I received from Barclays Bank in January 2007 included a leaflet showing, on successive pages, the following objects: an apple, a segment of orange, a bunch of grapes, a tray of blueberries, and a glass of clear water. The relevance of these objects to the services provided by the bank is not at all obvious, but was spelt out by the verbal parts of the leaflet, and by the letter included in the mailshot. The letter explained that the bank was offering a new type of loan that customers could use to bring together all their debts, and pay them off at a rate of interest that was presented as competitive. This loan was offered at a time (the beginning of the year) when the recipients of the letter were particularly likely to be in debt, as a result of excessive spending over the Christmas and New Year period. The letter went on to set up a parallel between the financial consequences of overspending and the health consequences of the excessive eating and drinking associated with the same period of the year. Both the letter and the leaflet described the bank as catering for the 'financial health' of its customers by offering a 'debt detox' which would enable customers to 'cleanse' their repayments and achieve a 'healthier debt situation'. These metaphorical expressions present financial concepts and activities in terms of health and healthy living. This helps to explain the significance of the images I have described. Fruit and water are regarded as good for people's health, and are the kind of food and drink associated with fashionable 'detoxification' regimes. Consequently, in the light of the verbal components of the mailshot, the various types of fruit and the glass of water stand metaphorically for the loan services provided by Barclays, so that the positive health associations of these objects are mapped onto the financial services offered by the bank. The suggestion is that, in the same way as people will eat more healthily to counterbalance the effects of the recent holiday season, they will also take up the bank's offer to remedy the spending excesses they have indulged in. The bank itself is therefore implicitly presented as acting out of concern and good will rather than for financial profit. In other words, the choice of visual and verbal metaphors highlights the positive characteristics that the bank wants to be associated with (e.g. caring for its customers), and plays down those that it does not want to be associated with (e.g. trying to make as much profit as possible). In cases such as this, the function of the verbal components of the mailshot in relation to the pictures can be captured by Roland Barthes's (1981) notion of 'anchorage': the text spells out and constrains the significance of the pictures, and thereby facilitates the inferences desired by the advertisers. Whether readers actually draw these inferences is a different matter, of course, but it is important to bear in mind that, by and large, advertising works, in spite of the indifference and cynicism with which it is often received (e.g. see Goddard 1998: 2).

Figure 5.1 Lucozade advertisement

5.2.1 *Case study 1: an advertisement for Lucozade*

In this section I discuss the use of metaphor in an advertisement for the soft drink Lucozade, which is reproduced in black and white in figure 5.1.

I came across this ad in several service stations along one of England's main motorways in spring 2007. It was placed on small billboards located near the entrance of the main building of each service station, where motorists go to find shops, restaurants, fast food outlets, and so on. I then discovered that the ad was part of a 5-million-pound multimedia advertising campaign devised by brand communications agency Billington Cartmell to advertise the drink Lucozade Energy. According to the agency's website (www.bcl.co.uk/, 2007), the campaign reached over 2 million people in 68 cities, and had a high level of recall amongst the age group that Lucozade wished to target (people aged between 16 and 34): apparently, 79 per cent of interviewees within this age group claimed to have viewed the advertising campaign 29 times. The campaign (called 'Energising Britain') aimed to target potential consumers in the two kinds of situations where, according to Billington Cartmell, 'Lucozade Energy is needed most to provide an everyday boost – at work and in the car.'

The ad in figure 5.1 was obviously aimed at people travelling by car, who stop at service stations to take a break, go to the lavatory, have a snack and, if necessary, refuel their vehicle. It is relatively simple, as is appropriate for ads that are seen by people on the move (in this particular case, walking from the car park to the main building of the service station). It includes two lines of text at the top and one at the bottom, for a total of seven words. Much of the space is occupied by the picture in the middle of the ad, which includes a Lucozade bottle placed horizontally above the 'Energising Britain' slogan. The main colour of the letters and picture is bright orange. This makes them stand out from the black background and connects them to the Lucozade bottle itself, which includes orange alongside red, yellow and black.

The ad relies primarily on a REFUELLING metaphor: the function of the Lucozade Energy drink for viewers of the ad is presented in terms of the function of fuel for cars. This metaphor is realized both verbally and visually. The two lines of text at the top of the ad display the kind of graphological, grammatical and lexical parallelism that is a well-known characteristic of advertisements (as well as of poetry, political oratory, etc.) (see Leech 1966, Myers 1994, Goddard 1998, Cook 2001). The two lines are printed on top of each other in the same font and colour. Each line contains an imperative clause consisting of the same verb ('refuel') followed by a noun phrase functioning as direct object. Both direct objects contain the morpheme 'your', which occurs as a separate determiner in the first line and as part of the word 'yourself' in the second. Parallel structures of this kind are typically associated with foregrounding effects (see Leech 1969): they tend to make texts (or portions of texts) particularly noticeable, memorable, aesthetically pleasing and so on. In addition, they may also draw attention to the parts of each parallel structure that are *different*, and invite readers to find relationships of similarity or contrast between them (see Short 1996). In the case of the top two lines of the ad, there is a contrast in the meaning of the two noun phrases that function as direct objects of 'refuel' ('this car' and 'yourself'), and this contrast affects the interpretation of the verb. In the first line, 'refuel' is used in its basic meaning of 'putting fuel inside a vehicle so that it can function'. In the second line, the same verb is used in relation to the viewer of the ad, who is addressed directly via the use of second-person pronouns. This second occurrence of 'refuel' is clearly metaphorical: in the terms used in chapter 1 (section 1.2.1), the basic meaning of the verb (the process of filling cars with fuel) contrasts with the contextual meaning, which can be paraphrased as the process of ingesting something that will make us feel better and stronger, so that we can continue being active. In this particular case, the most relevant type of activity is that of being able to continue to drive the car until one's destination. In other words, the parallelism is used to construct the addressee of the ad as a vehicle, and to suggest that, like a vehicle, he or she needs refuelling.

The picture exploits the same metaphor to present Lucozade Energy as the product that the viewer needs to buy in order to do for themselves what they do for their car by refuelling it. Going from top to bottom, we see an object in the shape of a fuel pump consisting of small bubbles that have squirted out of the Lucozade bottle lying horizontally below. This entity is the kind of hybrid object that I have already mentioned: it is connected to the target domain (the product) via its make-up, colour and origin, but its shape relates to the source domain that is also evoked by the use of 'refuel' above (cars and refuelling). The incongruity of a fuel-pump shape made up of orange bubbles spurting out of a bottle is both eye-catching and potentially amusing, but also poses an interpretative puzzle. This puzzle can be resolved via a non-literal interpretation of the entity whose shape we are presented with. The fuel pump is metonymically related to fuel (i.e. fuel pumps and fuel are contiguous in our knowledge of the world), and the concept of fuel is used to construct metaphorically the liquid that comes out of the Lucozade bottle. The verbal and visual components of the ad therefore interact to provide the same metaphorical construction of the product. The text explicitly evokes a metaphorical mapping between people and cars, and between refuelling and doing something for oneself. The picture provides the main advertising message by relating fuel to Lucozade Energy via the picture of the fuel pump. In other words, here the words do not anchor the picture as in the Barclays mailshot I described earlier; rather, words and picture are mutually reinforcing and complementary.

The vertical structuring of the ad is also significant. Kress and van Leeuwen (2006: 186–93) have noted that the top–bottom opposition can be used in pictures to contrast the 'ideal' with the 'real'. In the case of advertisements, this contrast involves the 'promise of the product' on the one hand with the product itself on the other. In the Lucozade ad, the REFUELLING metaphor occupies the top part of the ad, including both the metaphorical use of 'refuel' in the text, and the fuel-pump shape. Verbal and visual metaphors are exploited to present a particular, idealized image of the product, namely that of a liquid that is as essential to people as fuel (which is also liquid) is to cars. The bottom part of the picture then presents the product itself, in sufficient detail so that viewers will be able to recognize it on the drink shelves of the service station shops, or any other shop they might visit.

The particular choice of metaphor in the ad is not novel, of course. The use of 'refuel' in relation to human beings and their activities is fairly conventional, and is often included in dictionaries. In the following extract from the BNC, the verb is used metaphorically in the same way as in the ad, to refer to the effect of certain types of drink on the body: 'High carbohydrate drinks will help refuel your muscles and will come in handy in the hour or so after the race if you are not able to eat anything.' This use of 'refuel' can be seen as a part of a conventional metaphorical construction of people as machines, which includes a mapping between fuel and food/drink. This same mapping is also realized by conventional expressions such as 'I am running out of steam', where a different kind of machine and fuel function as metaphorical sources.

The exploitation of conventional metaphors is fairly common in ads, since, normally, the goal of advertisers is not to challenge people's world-views, but rather to rely on their existing knowledge in order to affect their behaviour as consumers (see Cook 1994, 2001). In the case of the Lucozade drink, the metaphor serves the advertisers' goals of emphasizing the desirable aspects of the product and hiding the less desirable ones. In the metaphorical source scenario, fuel is essential for the functioning of the car, and refuelling is therefore a necessary activity (albeit intermittently) at service stations. The choice of metaphorical source is clearly aimed to suggest that Lucozade is equally essential for human beings, and particularly for drivers on long motorway journeys, who need to keep fresh and alert. Conversely, the metaphor 'hides' the less positive aspects of the product, such as the fact that a high-calorie drink may not be the best option for someone who is engaged in a sedentary activity (as a driver, and even more as a passenger).

The ad also contains some elements of creativity. The visual realization of the metaphor is relatively novel (even though the underlying conceptual mapping is not), and there is some degree of originality in the interaction between the verbal and visual components of the ad. In addition, the choice of source domain is clearly situationally triggered here, i.e. it is inspired by the setting in which the ad was meant to be placed (see section 3.4.7 above). Service stations are places where one can buy both fuel for one's vehicle and food/drink for oneself. The connection between the location and the chosen metaphorical source scenario may therefore add an element of wit and humour to the ad (see also the newspaper headlines discussed in 1.2.3 above), as well as contribute to the overall advertising message: since refuelling is strongly associated with service stations, the metaphorical construction of Lucozade as fuel may help to establish a similar association between the drink and service stations. Finally, the REFUELLING metaphor is coherent with the name of the product (Lucozade Energy) and the slogan printed at the bottom of the page (Energising Britain[3]): both 'energy' and 'energising' can be used in relation to the vigour and strength of human beings on the one hand and, on the other hand, to the ability of machines to operate thanks to the power derived from fuels of various kinds. Other ads in the same campaign exploit the different meanings of 'energy' and 'energising' in similar ways.

Overall, metaphor is used strategically in the Lucozade ad to achieve a number of goals that are typical of contemporary advertising. The ad is a typical 'product

[3] Here 'Britain' can be seen as a metonymy for the people who live in Britain, and who are the target of the advertising campaign.

advertisement', i.e. its main goal is to persuade viewers to buy a particular product (as opposed to ads for political parties, charities, etc.) (see Cook 2001: 15). As I have explained, the metaphorical construction of Lucozade as fuel exploits the association between the setting of the ad and refuelling, and suggests that the consumption of the drink is just as essential to the continuation of one's journey as filling up one's car. As Cook (2001: 219–21) has suggested, however, contemporary advertising as a genre cannot simply be defined in terms of the goal of altering consumers' behaviour, but also by a range of further characteristics. These include, amongst others, the multi-modal combination of language and pictures, the use of parallelism and metaphor, the exploitation of indeterminate meanings, and 'an attempt to give pleasure' (Cook 2001: 221). Indeed, the use of metaphor is central to the soft-sell technique used in the ad, which involves both some degree of indeterminacy and, potentially, humour. Although imperatives are used in the top two lines of text, the advertisers have not opted for the hard-sell technique of telling us directly and explicitly to purchase the product (e.g. as in the hypothetical line 'Buy Lucozade Energy'). The top line of text tells us to buy fuel, but fuel is not the product that is being advertised. The imperative in the second line of text *is* relevant to the product, but we have to work out this relevance for ourselves by interpreting 'refuel' metaphorically, and by inferring from the use of metonymy and metaphor in the picture that Lucozade Energy is the kind of fuel we need. The use of the metaphor, in other words, enables the advertisers to appeal to viewers to buy the product without any direct references to purchase (or even drinking), and without any explicit statements of praise for the product. In addition, some degree of humour may result from the situational relevance of the source domain (i.e. the real-world connection between service stations and refuelling), and from the incongruity of a fuel-pump shape squirting out from a bottle. Ultimately, of course, both the indirectness and humour might make it more likely that viewers will find the ad appealing, and respond to it by buying the product.

In the next section I turn to the other main topic of this chapter, namely the use of metaphor in discourses of illness.

5.3 Metaphor and illness

Metaphor is relevant to the linguistic and conceptual construction of illness in more than one way. As a physical or mental condition to be understood and treated, illness can be modelled metaphorically by experts like any other phenomenon that is the subject of scientific investigation. Indeed, some of the metaphors I discussed in chapter 4 (notably those relating to genes and to the immune system) have direct implications for how illness is understood and approached in science and medicine. However, illness is also an individual, personal state of being, which is normally associated with physical discomfort or pain, and with feelings of anxiety, fear, isolation and, potentially, shame. As such, it belongs to the kind of complex, subjective and poorly delineated experiences that tend to be conventionally verbalized and conceptualized through metaphor. Crucially, however, sufferers and experts need to interact and cooperate in the process of treatment, and metaphor may be used more or less successfully, sensitively and harmoniously within these interactions. More broadly, metaphor often plays a part in the representation of illness in the media, particularly in the case of high-profile diseases such as cancer, or of epidemics such as SARS and avian influenza (e.g. Nerlich and Halliday 2007). These media representations may also affect the individual experience of sufferers, as well as public perceptions more generally.

Susan Sontag famously exposed the potentially damaging role of metaphor in discourses surrounding illness, particularly in relation to cancer (Sontag 1979) and AIDS (Sontag 1988). In *Metaphor and Illness* (Sontag 1979), she emphasized the negative consequences of the prominence of WAR metaphors in the construction of disease generally, and cancer in particular. She showed how cancer is conventionally described via warfare scenarios, where the disease is an enemy and a killer, patients are victims of invasion, and treatment is counter-attack. Within this metaphor, cancer drugs, for example, are conventionally described as 'aggressive' and their use as involving the 'bombardment' of the patient's body. This, Sontag argues, is one of the dominant metaphors that contribute to the demonization of the illness, and to an unnecessary increase in patients' feelings of fear, helplessness and isolation. Sontag's proposed solution to the damaging effects of metaphor is radical: she argues for the elimination of metaphor from the discourses surrounding illness, and looks forward to a time when medical advances will make metaphor unnecessary.

While Sontag's contribution remains highly illuminating and influential, her view of a metaphor-free future for illness has since been dismissed as both unrealistic and undesirable. This is not just the view of metaphor scholars like myself, but also of medical experts, who recognize the unavoidable role metaphors play in the construction of illness, and who increasingly focus on how this role can be exploited for beneficial effects. More specifically, a number of studies by medical professionals have described metaphor both as a useful resource and as a potential danger in the linguistic construction of illness. Metaphor is seen as a resource insofar as it enables sufferers to express and share their experiences, and professionals to clarify various aspects of diseases and treatments. It is a danger when, as Sontag showed, it contributes to representations of illness that are demoralizing and confusing for sufferers and those close to them. This is particularly important in the light of potential evidence that, in the case of illnesses such as cancer, patients' attitudes and states of mind influence the length of their survival periods (e.g. Greer 1991). What tends to be advocated, therefore, is not the elimination of metaphor, but a more conscious, sensitive and effective use of metaphor, especially on the part of professionals interacting with sufferers (e.g. Canter 1988; Czechmeister 1994; Skott 2002; Reisfield 2004).

Reisfield (2004), for example, states that metaphors 'can have a powerful influence on the practice of medicine and the experience of illness' (Reisfield 2004: 4024), and goes on to examine the main metaphorical source domains that are conventionally applied to cancer, namely WAR and JOURNEYS. He comments on the dominance of military metaphors in the ways cancer is conventionally talked about, not just by medical practitioners, but also by patients and pharmaceutical companies. For example, he points out how the manufacturers of a particular cancer drug declare that their website was 'developed to help you FIGHT HARD and FIGHT BACK in your battle against advanced breast cancer' (www.femara.com/home-metastatic.jsp?m=1). He also discusses a patient support website called 'cancerbattleplan.com', which is centred around the message: 'you must fight to win this battle' (www.cancerbattleplan.com/). Reisfield traces the origin of this metaphor to the discovery of bacteria in the late nineteenth century (see also Sontag 1979), and explains its dominance in terms of two different phenomena. On the one hand, the WAR source domain is generally pervasive, or, in Kövecses's (2002) terms, has a wide metaphorical scope. On the other hand, it is relatively easy and apparently 'natural' to view cancer as a dangerous enemy, health practitioners as an army, doctors as commanders, patients as soldiers, drugs and weaponry, and so on. Like Sontag, Reisfield also points out the limitations and disadvantages of this metaphor (e.g. its masculine bias, the possibility of defeat, the potential view of the patient's body as a battlefield), and reflects on the different view afforded by JOURNEY metaphors for cancer. Within the JOURNEY source domain, the patient is a traveller, the doctor a guide, and different routes and directions may always be chosen. Crucially, there is no such thing as defeat, and 'the journey continues through cancer treatment and beyond' (Reisfield 2004: 4026). Unlike Sontag, however, Reisfield argues that no metaphor is inherently harmful. Rather, different metaphors may be appropriate for different individuals, so that doctors have to be sensitive to patients' needs and assist them in exploiting the metaphors that are most beneficial for them as individuals.

For example, Reisfield describes the experience of a World War 2 historian for whom military metaphors were particularly 'enabling' as a cancer patient, even in the terminal phase of the disease (see also Skott 2002). While recovering from surgery, this particular cancer sufferer wrote in a letter to a friend:

> [t]he attack was successful, although I am expecting a counterattack any moment from all sides, if any more of those nodes are malignant. Notwithstanding, I have surrounded myself by barbed wire, land mines, and several squads of infantry, and we are ready to take on all comers. (quoted in Reisfield 2004: 4025)

Other patients, however, may find WAR metaphors inappropriate and disheartening, and may feel more comfortable with other conventional metaphors for illness, or may indeed creatively invent their own metaphors, often drawing from their personal experiences. For example, in the quotation below a journalist suffering from cancer explicitly questions the appropriateness of the WAR metaphor for cancer and presents a JOURNEY metaphor as more appropriate to her own relationship with the illness:

> I read obituaries and always look at the date of birth. Those of my vintage have often died 'after a long battle with cancer' . . . Why should people with cancer be expected to take up arms? It is better to see cancer as a journey. Everyone says that being positive helps you to come through, and being positive during a journey seems easier to me than being positive during a war in which the enemy is all around you. (*Observer Weekend Magazine*, 22 January 2005)

This leads to similar observations to those that I made in chapter 5 in relation to education. By and large, metaphors are not intrinsically harmful or beneficial, especially at the level of the individual: what matters is how a metaphor is used, and the extent to which individuals are free and able to select the metaphors that work best for them.

5.3.1 Case study 2: metaphor and depression in a radio phone-in programme

In this section I discuss the use of metaphor in a radio phone-in programme on clinical depression. The programme was aired on 1 June 2005 on BBC Radio 4, as part of a regular, long-running slot entitled *Woman's Hour*. It followed an earlier discussion of depression which was broadcast in the same slot on 31 May 2005. The presenter, Jenni Murray, opened the programme by reporting that, according to recent research, depression had replaced back pain as the most frequent reason for taking time off work in the UK. This, she added, raised the question of 'what makes a person brave enough to come clean'. Murray then invited listeners to phone in if they had experienced depression themselves or if they had come into close contact with sufferers. Two statements recorded during the previous programme were aired, one from a sufferer and one from a psychologist. The sufferer challenged the general perception of depressives as people who do not make a contribution to society, while the psychologist pointed out that people who are in close contact with sufferers tend to feel angry and frustrated when their efforts to help do not seem to make a difference.

The rest of the programme includes contributions from fourteen callers. Of these, nine claimed to have suffered or be suffering from depression themselves; two were professionals in relevant fields (a doctor and an employment solicitor); two were parents who had cared for grown-up children suffering from depression; and one was a woman of Asian origin who rang to point out that depression was still a taboo in her community. Only two of the callers were male: the employment solicitor and a man suffering from bipolar disorder.[4] A consultant psychiatrist, Dr Natasha Bijlani, was in the studio and was frequently invited by Murray to provide her professional opinion on the issues raised by the callers. Overall, the programme lasted for 50 minutes, and, when transcribed, consisted of just under 8,000 words (including hesitations, fillers, repetitions, etc.).

A variety of issues were mentioned by callers. Sufferers and ex-sufferers mentioned the difficulty they experienced in having their condition recognised and accepted by others, particularly due to the fact that they did not *look* ill. They also talked about the guilt and anxiety that result from not knowing whether they really had a medical condition, and reported both positive and negative experiences with treatment and with employers' reactions. Carers emphasized the difficulties they experienced in looking after their children and in relating to medical professionals. Dr Bijlani (who was addressed by Murray throughout by her first name, Natasha) covered a variety of issues including different 'triggers' for depression and different types of treatment. Other topics included the stigma that is associated with depression, cultural differences in attitudes towards it, and the lack of adequate resources for the treatment of depression sufferers in the UK National Health System.

My interest in the programme lay in the fact that, like other types of mental illness, depression poses particularly acute problems for understanding and communication. Since it does not have obvious physical consequences, it is often hard to relate to and talk about, both for sufferers and for those around them. It is also associated with intense mental and emotional experiences, and, like mental illness generally, carries a considerable amount of social stigma. I therefore wanted to investigate how both sufferers and non-sufferers, and lay people and experts, talk about depression in the context of a phone-in programme, and how they use metaphor in their contributions.

Overall, my analysis of the programme revealed that, according to the identification procedure described in chapter 1 (section 1.2.1), approximately 13 per cent of the words produced by participants in the discussion are used metaphorically. This corresponds to a metaphor density of 130 per 1,000 words, which is higher than that recorded by Cameron in classroom interaction (27 per 1,000 words) and in conciliation talk (between 98 and 107 per 1,000 words) (Cameron and Stelma 2004: 20). These figures seem to suggest that the topic of depression is particularly conducive to the use of metaphorical expressions, arguably due to the subjectivity, complexity and sensitiveness of the disease. Here I do not

[4] The programme is primarily targeted at women, but also has a substantial male audience (*The Independent*, 6 October 1996).

attempt to consider *all* uses of metaphor in the data, but I focus only on those metaphorical expressions that concern the experience of depression (on the part of sufferers or carers), as well as the causes, treatment and consequences of the disease.

In the rest of this section I show how a wide variety of metaphors are used by callers in relation to depression, its causes and its consequences. Not surprisingly, the metaphors used by non-sufferers show a different perspective on the disease from those used by sufferers, and the metaphors used by Dr Bijlani differ considerably from those used by the other callers.

Metaphors used by sufferers I will begin by quoting part of the contribution by one of the callers, Virginia. This will give you a flavour of the data, as well as introduce some of the metaphors used by sufferers to talk about their experience of depression. As with other callers, Virginia was first introduced by Murray and then asked 'What did you want to say?' (NB: in the extract below, 'P' indicates turns by the presenter and 'V' indicates turns by Virginia):[5]

5.1 V: Um, essentially I just wanted to um say how difficult depression is because it's so intangible and that makes it very difficult to accept both for the person who is suffering depression and for those around them and it gives it an added dimension of uncertainty and guilt and anxiety and you have to walk around this because it is not clearly defined um because people can't pinpoint it uum, and I think that's part of the stigma attached to it really that because it's / it's not a sort of concrete visible, um tangible illness um people don't know how to, respond to it and you yourself feel uum guilty about it anxious about it you ask yourself whether it's real whether it's imagined whether perhaps you could shake it off, uum for th / to the reason that it isn't concrete

P: What have you done about it Virginia?

V: Uum, well essentially um I went through a phase of depression after university about three years ago and, um I was put on quite mild antidepressants and that helped a lot with the sort of anxiety because it / it calmed me down and it helped me to cope on an everyday level, um but I still have that sort of unresolved feeling in my mind, of of/ of not quite being sure exactly what it was what it is, uum and I think people around me feel the same I mean essentially, um I would have loved to have had a broken leg with a huge plaster cast on or, and this is going to sound absolutely dreadful but almost something like cancer and have my hair fall out just something that people could, identify and know and put it in a category in a box and I can just relax and say I am ill and I need to get better and and there's something wrong with me rather than having this sort of thing inside, that / that I don't know what to do with and other people don't know what to do with, uum so although um, I've more or less come

[5] The conventions used in the transcription of the programme were as follows:

/	self-repair	//	interruption
[ ]	overlap	(. . .)	unintelligible talk
,	short pause (1–2 seconds)	text::	extension of syllable

> out of it now uum, I still have you know feelings in / in my mind of / the the difficulty of of both having dealt with and dealing with it personally and also how society deals with it um, because it's / it's something that it isn't I think often taken as a serious illness in a way we can understand that because it's not as visible as other illnesses but it's just as debilitating and just as serious //

Depression as a physical entity Like other callers who had suffered from depression, Virginia emphasizes the lack of concreteness and visibility of the disease, which makes it difficult for patients to feel legitimately ill, and for others to sympathize fully. Nonetheless, in order to convey her experiences, Virginia uses a number of metaphorical expressions that construct depression as a physical entity, such as the underlined expressions in the examples below:

5.2 whether perhaps you could shake it off

5.3 something that people could, identify and know and put it in a category in a box

5.4 rather than having this sort of thing inside, that/ that I don't know what to do with and other people don't know what to do with

The expression 'shake it off' in extract 5.2 is not, strictly speaking, consistent with the previous emphasis on lack of visibility, since it presents depression as something that is placed on top of the sufferer. However, the expression is used to suggest the possibility that a sufferer may get better easily, and without any help or treatment. In contrast, the description of depression as a 'thing' that is 'inside' the sufferer, in extract 5.4, more clearly emphasizes the lack of visibility of the condition, while also reflecting a general tendency to present the body as the container of emotions (Kövecses 2000: 37). More specifically, Virginia describes a mental and emotional experience as a physical object, and conveys the invisibility of the condition by describing it as being 'inside'. This contrasts with other medical problems that have clear external manifestations (a leg in plaster, hair loss resulting from cancer treatment). Virginia's claim that she and others do not know what to 'do with' this 'thing' presents the ability to deal successfully with depression in terms of the successful use or manipulation of physical objects. This can be related to a general metaphorical tendency whereby the ability to manipulate concrete entities is mapped onto the more abstract notions of control and success, as in the following example from the BNC: 'Take my situation; you'd never be able to handle that, would you?'

In extract 5.3 Virginia uses another concretizing metaphor (see Leech 1969) in order to express her wish that others were able to understand her illness. She does not just present her depression as a physical entity, but also describes understanding and categorization as the process of putting something in a container. This metaphorical view of categorization is conventional, of course, but it is made particularly noticeable, in my view, by Virginia's substitution of the nonmetaphorical 'category' with the metaphorical 'box'. Overall, therefore, in the two turns quoted above Virginia makes use of at least three separate metaphorical scenarios in which depression is a physical entity: one where it is an object that can be shaken off; one where she wishes it to be an entity that can be put in a category/box; and one where it is a thing inside her that she and others do not know what to do with.

No other caller uses as many concretizing metaphors as Virginia. However, depression is described by one sufferer as 'part' of her, and the metaphors used by several other callers implicitly construct depression as a physical entity. This applies particularly to the highly conventional metaphorical used of the verb 'have' in the expression 'have depression', in which suffering from the disease is implicitly presented in terms of possession of an object. The same tendency has been observed for all kinds of emotional states (Kövecses 2000: 36), as well as for mental or physical states more generally (e.g. 'to have doubts', 'to have a headache'). In addition, two sufferers describe themselves or their depression via the conventional metaphorical expression 'burden', which presents the condition as a weight that limits one's own and others' freedom of action.

Depression as a journey The most pervasive metaphorical pattern in the data, involving both repetition and recurrence, involved the construction of the experience of depression as a journey. In extract 5.1 above, Virginia says that she 'went through a phase of depression after university', and that she has 'more or less come out of it now'. Three other callers (two sufferers and one carer) use the expression 'coming out of (depression)', and Murray uses both this expression and the alternative 'coming through'. In addition, one sufferer, Monica, talks about being still 'in the midst of' her depression, and mentions that, at a particular point in the past, she 'wasn't in a place where [a particular therapy] could be of benefit'.

These metaphorical expressions are different from the instances of JOURNEY metaphors that I have discussed in previous chapters, and that are normally considered within CMT. Here the relevant source scenario does not involve movement along a path from a starting point to a destination. Rather, it involves entering an area or enclosed space and then coming out of it. Kövecses (2000: 36) has noted that the existence of emotions generally is conventionally constructed as being in a bounded space (e.g. 'She was in ecstasy'). In the case of depression, however, this bounded space is implicitly constructed as unpleasant, and as difficult to get out of, so that, as Monica puts it, you can spend a long time 'in the midst' of it. Interestingly, sufferers in my data seem to use this particular kind of JOURNEY metaphors rather than the DOWN metaphors for negative emotional states that are normally discussed in relation to depression and negative emotions generally (e.g. 'I'm feeling down', 'He's really low these days'; Lakoff and Johnson 1980b: 15; McCullen and Conway 2002).[6]

The data also contains instances of other JOURNEY metaphors, which are used by specific individuals. In extract 5.1 above, Virginia talks about the 'uncertainty, guilt and anxiety' associated with depression as an obstacle one has to 'walk around'. In the example below, another sufferer, Gill, talks about the importance of feeling comfortable with therapists in order to benefit from counselling or other types of psychological therapy (metaphorical expressions are underlined):

5.5 sometimes there is things that you have to explore which you, feel um very unsafe these are places that you just can't go to a:nd if the person that you're with is nót someone you like and trust, you can't go there it's just not safe to go there,

Here the problems experienced by sufferers are presented as concrete entities ('things') and the process of discussing them as exploration ('explore'). This is then developed into a fuller metaphorical scenario in which difficult topics and issues are unsafe 'places' the sufferer cannot 'go to' unless they have a positive and trusting relationship with the therapist. In other words, the experience of depression is presented as a situation in which some places (i.e. issues) cannot be safely reached (i.e. thought/talked about) without a trusted fellow traveller (the therapist).

In spite of their differences, all JOURNEY metaphors used by sufferers involve scenarios in which movement is difficult, unpleasant and/or unsafe. This helps to convey the extent of the mental and emotional difficulties they experience.

Other metaphors used by sufferers A variety of other metaphorical expressions are used by sufferers in relation to their experiences of depression, drawing from a range of different source domains.

Two sufferers use the highly conventional metaphorical expression 'breakdown' in relation to their depression, which constructs mental illness in terms of the malfunctioning of machinery. The data contains a few further expressions in which the sufferer is presented as a machine that is not working properly. These expressions are in fact mostly used by Dr Bijlani, but one sufferer does say that 'symptoms have disabled' her. Another sufferer, Alison, talks about the time when she had 'literally shut down', thereby presenting herself as a physical entity (e.g. a shop) which is no longer open and therefore no longer

6 As I mentioned in chapter 2 (note 8), the term 'depression' itself derives from the Latin verb 'de-premere', which indicates downward pressure.

performs its normal functions. The expression 'shut down' is also conventionally used metaphorically in relation to machines not working, and this sense may actually be relevant to the choice and interpretation of this expression in Alison's utterance. I would also note that the occurrence of the prepositional adverb 'down' in both 'breakdown' and 'shut down' is consistent with the conventional metaphorical association of negative emotional states with being 'down' or 'low', even though different metaphorical scenarios are involved in each case.

There are also at least two cases in the data where a downward direction of movement stands metaphorically for a *positive* change, and particularly for a decrease in the anxiety experienced by depression sufferers. In extract 5.1 Virginia uses the highly conventional expression 'calmed me down' to refer to the fact that antidepressants made her feel less anxious. A less conventional use of a similar expression can be seen in the extract below, where a sufferer, Gill, talks about the benefit she obtained from Cognitive Behavioural Therapy (the *relevant* metaphorical expressions are underlined):

5.6 It taught me that, um anxiety is something which you actually can control up to a point but you can control it you can bring it down from the extreme point of being you know unable to breathe um to:: the point where you can actually think about it and once you can start to think about it you can start to examine it and once you can start to examine it you can see that it's actually not based on anything

Here the experience of anxiety is described in terms of a metaphorical scenario where something rises beyond a safe level, and has to be brought down to an appropriate position. This expresses the fear and helplessness associated with anxiety, and the difficulty involved in trying to control it.

Overall, sufferers used a variety of metaphors in which their experiences are presented in terms of different concrete, physical scenarios. The various metaphors are quite different from one other, but, interestingly, they are never used to explain the causes of depression, or to relate the disease to some characteristic of the sufferer. Indeed, it has been noted in other studies that depression sufferers tend to explain the disease as a consequence of circumstances beyond their control (e.g. childhood traumas, stress, misfortune), and to suggest that anybody in the same circumstances would have developed depression (Kangas 2001). Not all participants in the *Woman's Hour* discussion do this, but, not surprisingly, none attribute the depression to their own approach to life. In the next section, I show that the situation is different with the contributions of non-sufferers to the discussion.

Metaphors used by carers and an expert The person who makes the largest contribution to the discussion in the *Woman's Hour* programme is

Dr Bijlani, the consultant psychiatrist who has been invited to the studio in order to act as the 'expert' on the topic of depression. Throughout, she is asked by the show's presenter to provide her opinion on the issues raised by callers, and has 18 full conversational turns, for a total of just over 1,600 words (corresponding to just over 20 per cent of the talk in the programme as a whole). In her contributions, Dr Bijlani deals with a variety of topics, including the causes of and treatments for depression, common reactions in the workplace, and the lack of resources in the National Health Service. Given the extent of her contributions, it is not surprising that she also produces the largest number and variety of metaphors for depression in the programme. However, she also produces several extended metaphors that, I suggest, may well be part of her expert repertoire of explanations of various aspects of depression. In this session, I focus particularly on Dr Bijlani's metaphors, and show how these overlap more with those used by carers than with those used by sufferers.

Depression as problems with vision The most striking contrast between sufferers' and non-sufferers' accounts of depression is that, in some cases, the latter attribute the disease to the sufferers' approach to life. This is expressed metaphorically by Dr Bijlani and one of the mothers in terms of visual problems and colour contrasts (in the examples below, B indicates turns by Dr Bijlani and M indicates turns by Margaret, whose daughter suffered from depression; only the *relevant* metaphorical expressions are underlined):

5.7 B: . . . classically in in people who get depressed can think/ start thinking in very black and white terms things around them seem very very black and everybody else is having a very white rosy time, they magnify anything awful that happens to them and and and just see the doom and gloom side of life, in cognitive behaviour therapy you kind of meet the therapist every single week you get homework and the therapist gradually s/ takes you through a talking way of trying to understand, that life isn't all black and white but there's a grey/ grey area that can be saw/ that can be, you know very really applied to you and so it's, making you think more positively//

5.8 B: Yes and no, obviously if you're someone who's going to be pessimistic and take a negative outlook of life,

5.9 M: . . . she has always been/ she's now forty one and she has always been a person who has looked on the black side of things brought things on top of her

In extract 5.7, Dr Bijlani uses an extended metaphor to describe the approach to life that 'classically' leads to depression, and to explain how Cognitive Behavioural Therapy can help. She exploits some conventional metaphorical contrasts between different colours, as well as the conventional conceptualization of thought and comprehension in terms of vision (Lakoff and Johnson 1999: 238–40). The expression 'black and white' is conventionally used to suggest the perception of a clear-cut contrast, which is often presented as overly simplistic. At the beginning of extract 5.7, this expression begins to suggest that depression sufferers tend to exaggerate the contrast between their own negative experiences and others' positive experiences. Subsequently, the metaphorical opposition between things that seem 'very very black' and 'a very white rosy time' suggests a further contrast between negativity and sadness ('black') and positivity and happiness ('white, 'rosy') (e.g. Kövecses 2000: 25; see also McMullen and Conway 2002). This contrast is presented as the result of the sufferer's inability to 'see' things properly. This is also expressed via the conventional use of the verb 'magnify', which suggests exaggerated attention to negative aspects of their lives. The therapist's contribution is then described as an attempt to appreciate the applicability of a 'grey' area to the person's life. Normally, the use of 'grey' in 'grey area' suggests lack of clarity, and has rather negative connotations, as in 'there was a grey area of uncertainty surrounding these problems', from the BNC (see Deignan 1995: 185–90 for conventional colour metaphors). Here, however, the ability to note the greyness of life is evaluated positively in contrast with a black-and-white perception, since it stands for a recognition that everybody's life has both positive and negative aspects.

The relatively elaborate nature of the use of metaphor in extract 5.7 suggests that this may be one of the ways in which Dr Bijlani normally explains a possible cause of depression to non-expert audiences. In extract 5.8 the same metaphor recurs in the conventional metaphorical use of the noun 'outlook', which has a basic meaning to do with vision, but which can be used to indicate someone's attitude to something. In extract 5.9 Margaret also uses a metaphor to do with vision in order to convey the personal characteristics that she associates with her daughter's depressive tendencies. She describes her daughter's attitude to life in terms of excessive visual attention ('looked on') for negative aspects of life, which are metaphorically referred to as 'the black side of things'.

Margaret's use of metaphor may well be an echo of the metaphors used by Dr Bijlani (although extract 5.9 occurs 4,500 words after extract 5.7). It is nonetheless interesting that both an expert and a non-expert use a metaphor that presents depression as the result of the sufferer's own attitude to life, rather than of actual adversity. As a consultant psychiatrist, Dr Bijlani steers well clear of any suggestion of blame. In contrast, Margaret's words do indicate some degree of frustration with her daughter's approach to life. Indeed, in extract 5.9, the 'black and white' metaphor is followed by the expression 'brought things on top of her'. This expression metaphorically presents negative experiences in terms of concrete objects falling onto someone, but the verb 'brought' suggests that this is actively caused by the person in question.

Depression as the snapping of an elastic band Another fairly elaborate extended metaphor is used by Dr Bijlani in response to a question concerning whether people can, metaphorically, 'thrive' on stress in the workplace (the *relevant* metaphorical expressions are underlined; dotted underlining is used for similes):

5.10 B: Again I think it is an ignorant attitude and it's a misperception nobody can thrive on stress, stress is fine up to a certain point but if it's going to be continuing stress the body can only take so much it's rather like an elastic band if you take the analogy of an elastic band the more you stretch it it will stretch but it comes a point where everything has a limit and it will snap, human beings in a way their mind is like an elastic band you can stretch it and it'll work effectively up to a certain point but if you put undue stress on it it will snap and you will get depressive symptoms as a result//

In order to describe the negative effects of continued stress, Dr Bijlani begins with a simile ('it's like an elastic band') and explicitly mentions that she is using an analogy. She then points out that elastic bands snap if they are stretched excessively, and then repeats the simile in relation to the minds of human beings. The simile is then explicated via metaphorical expressions that construct stress in terms of stretching, and depressive symptoms in terms of the snapping of an elastic band. The combination of simile and metaphorical expressions (see also extract 1.8 in chapter 1) evokes a highly concrete and visual scenario, which is used to convey a particular kind of mental experience.

This metaphorisation of stress is of course not entirely novel: the term 'stress' itself is a highly conventional metaphorical expression that works in a similar way, since 'stress' has a basic meaning to do with physical pressure. Nonetheless, the gradual and explicit way in which the metaphorical scenario is introduced seems to suggest that this is also one of Dr Bijlani's habitual ways of explaining to laypeople the relationships between stress and depression. The way in which the source–target correspondences are introduced is in fact reminiscent of some of the examples I discussed earlier in the chapter on science and education (chapter 4).

Extract 5.10 also shows that Dr Bijlani uses different metaphors to present different scenarios in which people may become depressed. While in extracts 5.7 and 5.8 depression was described as resulting, in part at least, from the sufferer's characteristics, in extract 5.10 it is presented as the result of circumstances beyond the sufferer's control.

Other metaphors used primarily by non-sufferers A number of other metaphors are used by non-sufferers in the course of the programme. Both Dr Bijlani and one of the carers exploit the highly conventional metaphor HAPPY IS UP/SAD IS DOWN (Lakoff and Johnson 1980b: 15). Dr Bijlani, for example, talks about people who are 'in the depth of very very severe depression'. A related and equally conventional set of metaphorical expressions presents the provision of help to sufferers in terms of physical support. Various participants talk about 'support' for sufferers, and one carer describes her attempt to 'bolster' them. The latter expression is more specific than 'support', since, in its most basic meaning, the noun 'bolster' indicates a particular type of long, firm pillow. However, both expressions can be seen as instantiations of the very general conceptual metaphor HELP/ASSISTANCE IS SUPPORT, which can be applied to a wide variety of specific target domains (see Grady 1997a, Semino 2005).

As I mentioned earlier, Dr Bijlani uses a wider variety of metaphorical expressions than other participants. The metaphorical scenarios suggested by these expressions vary, amongst other things, in terms of the role that is attributed to depression sufferers in the onset and development of the disease, and consequently in terms of the degree of sympathy that they express towards their plight. While the visual metaphors I discussed earlier suggest that depression may result from the sufferers' own approach to life, Dr Bijlani also uses several metaphors in which depression is constructed as an external attacker. For example, she explains that depression 'can strike anybody', and describes sufferers as 'victims'. These expressions convey greater sympathy for sufferers, and suggest that the disease is nothing to do with their own attitudes or actions. Although, as I mentioned earlier, the conceptualization of illness as an enemy is highly conventional, it is used by only one of the sufferers in my data, who describes herself as still 'battling' with depression.

Finally, one of Dr Bijlani's contributions includes a comment on the origin of an etymological metaphor that is repeatedly used by participants, namely that of the 'stigma' associated with depression:

5.11 society perceives people who have mental illness as being different and stigma, um the Oxford English Dictionary ide/ defines it as a mark of disgrace or infamy so anything that makes people stand out from the rest of society particularly in a negative way, causes stigma to be applied to that person

Indeed, 'stigma' has a (largely archaic) basic meaning that is to do with physical marks made on the skin of people who had committed particular crimes.[7] This kind of metalinguistic comment contributes to asserting Dr Bijlani's role as expert, but also suggests her perception that people need to be aware of the (metaphorical) origin of words associated with depression, and of how they have acquired their current meanings and connotations.[8]

[7] The plural 'stigmata' is also used to refer to the wounds on the body of the crucified Christ, which are sometimes believed to appear on the bodies of saints or particularly pious individuals.

[8] Interestingly, McCullen and Conway (2002) have noted that, historically, depression has been positively evaluated in the case of some groups of male sufferers (e.g. artists suffering from melancholia), but never in the case of female sufferers.

Concluding remarks Overall, my analysis has shown that participants in the *Woman's Hour* phone-in programme used a variety of metaphors to convey their experience or understanding of a variety of aspects of depression. This applies particularly to the many aspects of depression that are highly subjective, abstract and complex, such as the ways in which depression may begin or the sensation of being depressed. Broadly speaking, the data displays a phenomenon Goatly (1997: 259–61) calls 'diversification', namely the use of different source domains or scenarios in relation to the same broad target domain. In textual terms, I have shown how the different source domains/scenarios are exploited via repetition (e.g. 'support' for patients), recurrence (e.g. use of different expressions to do with movement) and extension (e.g. the 'elastic band' example). The instances of repetition and recurrence across speakers can be seen as evidence that participants echo each other's uses of metaphor, at least to some extent. However, most of the expressions involved are highly conventional, so it is difficult to make definite claims about mutual influences in metaphor use.

Several of the examples I have discussed can be seen as metaphorical clusters, since their metaphorical density is higher than the average for the programme as a whole. Clustering tends to correspond to moments in which participants attempt to express particularly salient experiences or to propose particular explanations. In extract 5.5 above, for example, Gill uses an extended JOURNEY metaphor (e.g. 'there are places that you just can't go to') to convey the fact that some topics are impossible to discuss unless the patient totally trusts the therapist. According to my analysis, the 50-word extract I quoted above contains 12 metaphorically used words (see underlining in extract 5.5). This corresponds to 240 metaphorically words per 1,000 words, which is higher than the average for the programme as a whole (130 per 1,000 words).

I have also shown how the choice of source domain or scenario affects the way in which depression is presented, and particularly the way in which the role of sufferers is viewed. Interestingly, sufferers and non-sufferers use different metaphors in the course of the programme, particularly in relation to the onset of depression. This seems to reflect different perspectives on the disease: although they tend to experience guilt, sufferers do not present themselves as in any way responsible for the illness, while non-sufferers see depression as a possible result of the sufferers' own characteristics. Sufferers also do not seem to use metaphors that provide a clear role for them in the process of recovery, except in terms of a scenario where someone tries to get out of an unpleasant area or container. Finally, I have shown how the expert who is the main contributor to the discussion uses a wider variety of metaphors than other participants, and extends some of them in ways that appear to be pre-packaged, at least to some extent. These expert metaphors provide different conceptualizations of patients and of the diseases, and are used to explain different phenomena in accessible terms, to provide different perspectives on particular issues (e.g. the onset of depression), and to express sympathy and understanding (e.g. the 'victims' metaphor).

5.4 Summary

In this chapter I have considered the role of metaphor in a particularly pervasive genre (advertising) and a highly sensitive discourse (the discourse of illness). In the first case, which involved a billboard advertisement for the soft drink Lucozade, I showed how metaphor is exploited to attract the attention of viewers, as well as to project positive properties onto the product. I discussed the interaction between verbal and visual metaphor, and I noted how the choice of source domain is inspired by the setting in which the ad is meant to be seen. The second case study was concerned with a phone-in radio programme on the topic of depression. I showed how a variety of metaphors are used by participants to talk about different aspects of the disease, and I noted some important differences between the metaphors used by sufferers and non-sufferers, and by a consultant psychiatrist as opposed to non-experts. Overall, this chapter aimed to demonstrate that the centrality of metaphor in communication and thought goes well beyond the areas and genres considered in chapters 2, 3 and 4.

6 Corpora and metaphor

6.1 A preliminary example: the metaphorical uses of the adjective 'rich'

In the preceding chapters, I have repeatedly used evidence from electronic language corpora in order to make or support particular points about conventional patterns in metaphor use. In this chapter I explore more systematically the contribution of corpus linguistics to the study of metaphor. Corpus-based metaphor study is a relatively new area, but some significant results have already been achieved and there is considerable potential for further advances in the future. In this section I begin, as usual, with a preliminary example.

Lakoff (1993) argues that, in English, there is a close relationship between two main conventional conceptual metaphors for life: LIFE IS A JOURNEY and A PURPOSEFUL LIFE IS A BUSINESS. This relationship (which Lakoff calls 'duality') is based on the different ways in which purposes are constructed within the two metaphors, namely as destinations in LIFE IS A JOURNEY, and as desired objects to be acquired in A PURPOSEFUL LIFE IS A BUSINESS.[1] Here I am not concerned with Lakoff's claim that duality is a common and important phenomenon, but rather with the linguistic evidence provided by Lakoff in support of the conventional metaphor A PURPOSEFUL LIFE IS A BUSINESS, which is given below:

A PURPOSEFUL LIFE IS A BUSINESS
He has a rich life. It's an enriching experience. I want to get a lot out of life. He's going about the business of everyday life. It's time to take stock of my life. (Lakoff 1993: 227)

Two of the five examples of linguistic realizations of the conceptual metaphor contain metaphorical expressions that fairly clearly evoke the source domain of BUSINESS, i.e. the word 'business' itself and the expression 'take stock of'. The sentence 'I want to get a lot out of life' contains much more generic

[1] According to Lakoff (1993), some metaphors form pairs (or 'duals') within which the same concept is constructed either as an object or as a location. The term 'duality' is used to capture this phenomenon.

vocabulary, which could probably be explained in terms of the more general CONTAINER image schema. In the first two examples, however, the lexical items that are supposed to relate to the BUSINESS source domain are 'rich' and 'enriching'. At first sight, this may seem plausible, given that, in the contemporary world, there is a strong association between wealth and business. Indeed, Lakoff makes a reference to 'this culture' (i.e. presumably North American culture) when he says that the main activity via which one acquires desired objects is business. Nonetheless, the inclusion of 'rich' and 'enriching' under A PURPOSEFUL LIFE IS A BUSINESS still seems problematic to me, as conventional metaphorical expressions often reflect earlier states of particular societies and cultures, and are therefore not necessarily best explained in contemporary terms (see Deignan 2003; McArthur 2005). More generally, my concerns about these examples raise the issue of what counts as adequate evidence for the existence of particular conceptual metaphors. Here I consider the adjective 'rich' in particular, and show what a corpus-based analysis can contribute to an understanding of how it functions metaphorically.

I used the software program *WordSmith Tools* (Scott 1999) to search for the word 'rich' as a string of letters in the BNC Sampler – a 2-million word sub-corpus of the 100-million word BNC. The BNC Sampler is divided roughly equally between spoken and written data, and the written part includes genres such as fiction, news reports and academic writing (for more detail, see www.comp.lancs.ac.uk/ucrel/bnc2sampler/sampler.htm). My search for instances of 'rich' in the Sampler resulted in a concordance containing 139 citations. This is a list of the 139 examples of 'rich' contained in the corpus (used either as a noun or as an adjective), with the words that immediately precede and follow 'rich' in each case. A sample from the concordance is reproduced in figure 6.1. *WordSmith Tools* also allowed me to expand the amount of co-text I could see if I wanted to examine particular examples in more detail. Ideally, this kind of concordance-based analysis should be carried out on larger numbers of citations of particular expressions, especially when they are relatively common, as in the case of 'rich'. However, here I want to show what insights can be achieved by exploiting a relatively small corpus and a highly manageable number of citations.

Out of my 139 examples of 'rich', 7 were irrelevant to my analysis, either because 'rich' was used as a proper name (both first name and surname), or because the word itself was being mentioned, rather than used, by participants in a game of Scrabble. Of the remaining 132 examples, I analysed 61 as non-metaphorical. These were cases where 'rich' was used in what I regarded as its basic meaning (see 1.2.1 above), i.e. to indicate financial wealth or value, primarily in relation to people, groups, countries and so on. Two representative examples are given below:

RICH: 139 entries (sort: File,File)

N	Concordance	Set	File
1	mment cannot and should not do everything. In Britain we have a rich reserve of good will, energy, commitment in our voluntary se		\cg\jng.txt
2	ls being encouraged, it's to lower wages and condition and give rich financial benefits to the few. There is a rule for a central rese		cg\hlw.txt
3	, but I've been very happy you know, ups and downs. Never very rich. And n no great heights and no great depths either. D d		g\hem.txt
4	f a million people, in operations large and small. Few will ever get rich, but between them they've produced, in recent years, nearly f		g\he4.txt
5	e production of base load electricity. It's a market that despite our rich coal reserves, is fixed in such a way that it ensures that befor		cg\hdt.txt
6	get changed the basic rules which ensure that a country which is rich in coal resources ensures that it makes the most of the use o		cg\hdt.txt
7	dad what politics were about and he said, well Tories are for the rich and Labour's for the poor. The only thing the Tories can't tax		cg\hdt.txt
8	eds a balanced energy policy, which ensures that our varied and rich reserves are utilized in the most efficient way. The qualificati		cg\hdt.txt
9	teract with our systems though an interactive self teaching sentry rich environment. So we can get rid of all of those different costly		g\hdg.txt
10	storically, poor countries were introduced to international trade by rich ones like ours, because they were introduced as colonies. T		g\g3u.txt
11	ed. The poorest countries still produce the raw materials. But the rich countries, ourselves, do the rest. They provide the shipping, t		g\g3u.txt
12	he the reason this has occurred is because of a poverty amongst rich countries rich people which is causing poverty amongst poor		g\g3u.txt
13	this has occurred is because of a poverty amongst rich countries rich people which is causing poverty amongst poor people which		g\g3u.txt
14	using poverty amongst poor people which is material. Maybe this rich people's poverty is, is a moral poverty. When we think of love		g\g3u.txt
15	And Jose in fact talked er in terms of the poor evangelizing the rich. That was how he put it in his theological terms. And that wa		g\g3u.txt
16	unning short of cash. Well they, they better start with perhaps the rich? And er, by the way, pensions, pensions are er, are taxed!		cg\fx5.txt
17	re's no good leaving nothing to the spouse, unless that spouse is rich in his or her own right Rich in comparative terms, then there		cg\fms.txt
18	g to the spouse, unless that spouse is rich in his or her own right Rich in comparative terms, then there may be good reasons not t		cg\fms.txt
19	you know the grace of our lord Jesus Christ, that though he was rich for your sakes he became poor, so that you through his pove		\cg\flu.txt
20	sakes he became poor, so that you through his poverty might be rich, god, he's purpose follows his people, he's not that we've ad		\cg\flu.txt
21	mothy in his first letter in chapter six it is command those who are rich in this present world not to be arrogant or to put their hope in		\cg\flu.txt
22	I feel like to eat my Mars bar now. me, rich. I was gonna say me and rich, no I dont think so no that's j		g\kpg.txt
23	me, rich. I was gonna say me and rich, no I don't think so no that's just where they 'll be a flush. Do		g\kpg.txt
24	ple have money if the people have money Well they do, look, the rich people can buy a house any time they want Mm, mm		g\kdu.txt
25	can buy a house any time they want Mm, mm and the rich will buy a house in this area, like you have Embassy people		g\kdu.txt
26	asily got Oh my God. Well I remember a doctor and a rich man saying to me, I'm gonna get out of this place, it's just lik		g\kdu.txt
27	Yeah, I mean she wants to get out and She wants a rich good looking chap then, she		g\kdm.txt
28	oh who've you been on the phone to tonight? Mat and Rich, but, but Mat last are you seeing Katie this week?		g\kd6.txt
29	Wealth. Ingots. Rich. Ingots. He got Wealth, Ingots. Rich. Ingots. He got him, he got		g\kd0.txt
30	got it? What was it? Rich. Sounds like ditch. Oh blim		g\kd0.txt
31	in the afternoon, so I don't know. God! Rich bastard. But I says how can they make money now, how ca		og\kca.txt
32	ing girls right, but they've both married, they're both involved with rich farmers. Liz married a farmer from when they got married, ju		og\kca.txt
33	thing to say but I don't necessarily mind people robbing from the rich but when it's poor people robbing from the poor, it's a really		og\kc7.txt

Figure 6.1 Sample concordance of 'rich' in the British National Corpus

6.1 he said, well Tories are for the rich and Labour's for the poor.

6.2 poor countries were introduced to international trade by rich ones like ours

The remaining 71 examples (i.e. approximately 50 per cent of all occurrences in the BNC Sampler) were analysed as metaphorical, since 'rich' was used not to indicate financial wealth but rather other qualities, which could be said to be metaphorically constructed via the notion of wealth. A number of more specific patterns could be identified within the metaphorical examples. Consider the examples below:

6.3 It's a market that despite our rich coal reserves, is fixed in such a way that

6.4 Gemsbok national park is also rich in wildlife

6.5 which, in moist, rich soil, grows huge basal leaves,

6.6 festivals and exhibitions which add to the rich culture of its architectural, artistic and musical heritage.

6.7 In Britain we have a rich reserve of good will, energy, commitment in our voluntary sector

In all five examples, I would argue, the contextual meaning of 'rich' is to do with the abundance of something that is positively evaluated. However, each example differs from the others in terms of the kind of abundance that is being suggested and the general target domain that is involved. In extract 6.3, 'rich' is used to indicate the abundant availability of a valuable physical resource, which has strong financial consequences. In examples such as extract 6.4, 'rich' indicates the abundance of a particular form of life in a particular area, which is presented as positive, but which does not have direct financial implications. Extract 6.5 exemplifies a more specific use of 'rich' in relation to the high quality, and particularly the fertility, of land. Extracts 6.6 and 6.7 involve more abstract qualities: in extract 6.6 'rich' suggests the abundance, variety and prestige of a place's cultural resources and activities; in extract 6.7 it indicates the abundance of particular positive characteristics in the inhabitants of a specific country (here the noun 'reserve' is also used metaphorically).

My concordance contains between six and eight further instances of each of the uses of 'rich' exemplified above, which cumulatively account for approximately half of the examples I analysed as metaphorical. These also include two instances of the fixed expression 'rich pickings', which is conventionally used metaphorically to indicate the possibility of easily acquiring money or other valuable objects. The majority of the remaining metaphorical uses of 'rich' in my concordance are to do with qualities of objects that can be perceived via the senses:

6.8 to produce silk-like fabrics that are soft, drape well, and have a rich, lustrous appearance.

6.9 Both provide sensational autumn leaf colour in rich reds and purples.

6.10 a voice high in pitch but rich in timbre.

6.11 in the air around us, deep and rich with the scent of wild herbs.

In extract 6.8, 'rich' may suggest that the fabrics being described look expensive, but it also indicates their beauty and the intensity of their visual effect. I would argue that the notions of intensity and pleasurable effects are also what brings together the following three examples, even though they relate, respectively, to vision, sound and smell. In my concordance, examples such as extracts 6.8 and 6.9 largely outnumber the cases that involve senses other than vision. I also have a couple of examples that can be related to taste, such as 'Rich Chocolate Cake'. Here 'rich' seems to suggest both the abundance of ingredients that lend flavour and intensity to food, and the experience of eating such food.

Since my concordance included a relatively small number of citations, I also extracted the top 50 collocates of 'rich' from the whole of the BNC, which, as I have already mentioned, contains 90 million words of written British English and 10 million words of spoken British English from the late twentieth century. More precisely, I accessed the online version of the BNC and used a facility that allowed me to obtain a list of the lexical items that tend to co-occur with 'rich' (see http://escorp.unizh.ch/).[2] An analysis of the collocates broadly

[2] Collocations were calculated in terms of mutual information and with a window span of five words to the left and five to the right of 'rich'.

confirmed the observations I had derived from the concordance. In addition, it also brought to my attention the use of 'rich' to describe food that is excessively heavy and fattening, which was not properly represented in the 'taste' group in my concordance (e.g. 'Doctors may be closer to solving the mystery of why Frenchmen who eat rich, fatty food, take little exercise and smoke heavily manage to escape the consequences of heart disease').

What conclusions can be drawn from this kind of analysis? More specifically, what are the implications of my corpus-based analysis for the validity of Lakoff's claim that expressions such as 'He has a rich life' provide evidence for the existence of the conceptual metaphor A PURPOSEFUL LIFE IS A BUSINESS?

My analysis cannot of course challenge the claim that some metaphorical patterns in the English language provide evidence for the existence of the conceptual metaphor A PURPOSEFUL LIFE IS A BUSINESS. What my analysis does question is the claim that the expression 'rich life' is part of a pattern that is best captured via this particular conceptual metaphor. In fact, 'life' is not one of the top fifty collocates of 'rich', and the whole of the BNC only contains four instances of 'rich' premodifying 'life', one of which is the name of a company. What the corpus data seems to suggest is that 'rich' is conventionally used metaphorically in relation to elements and qualities from a set of target domains, including particularly natural resources, land, culture, food and the senses. The properties that appear to be conventionally mapped from the concept evoked by 'rich' are primarily abundance, and, in some cases, variety (e.g. extract 6.6) and intensity (e.g. extract 6.9). In the vast majority of cases, 'rich' suggests a positive evaluation, namely that whatever is presented as abundant is valuable and has a positive effect. All this can be explained in terms of the fact that, in its most basic meaning, 'rich' indicates the abundance of money and/or possessions, which is normally regarded as positive. However, where there is abundance of something that can also be negatively evaluated (notably fatty ingredients in food), rich can also suggest a negative evaluation, as I have shown.[3]

Going back to Lakoff's claims, I would argue that the expression 'rich life' (which is infrequent in British English) is not part of a pattern whereby the source domain of BUSINESS is mapped onto the target domain of LIFE. Rather, it is part of a pattern where the abundance (as well as variety and intensity) of something (usually) positive in a range of target domains is constructed in terms

[3] 'Rich' is also used negatively in the idiomatic expression 'That's (a bit) rich', which is normally used when someone criticizes someone else for something they themselves do. It is not obvious to me how this particular sense of the adjective has developed from the basic meaning of the adjective. One possibility is that the expression derives from the use of 'rich' to indicate something that is hard to digest. In this case, it would be related to expressions such as 'The traditionalist camp has had to swallow some bitter pills,' from the BNC. Grady (1997a: 294) sees such expressions as realizations of the primary metaphor ACQUIESCING IS SWALLOWING.

of wealth. What seems to be mapped, however, is not the process of 'acquiring' money or properties, but the quality of 'possessing' them. After all, wealth has only come to be associated with business activities relatively recently, and the history of 'rich' as a word started in times when wealth was primarily inherited (the first citation of 'rich' in the Oxford English Dictionary is dated at the year 900). This particular mapping of wealth onto abundance, intensity and variety can satisfactorily explain why the expression 'He has a rich life' suggests that the person's life involves many different, intense and positive experiences. If there is such a conceptual metaphor as A PURPOSEFUL LIFE IS A BUSINESS, the evidence needs to be found elsewhere.[4]

In the rest of this chapter, I show how corpus-based methods have been used to question and refine the claims made within CMT, and to advance the study of metaphor more generally. Corpora have also been exploited to investigate the use of metaphor in particular genres, and to compare the metaphors used in different language and cultures. Since I have already demonstrated the applicability of a corpus methodology throughout the book, this chapter includes a single case study.

6.2 Choosing corpora and finding metaphorical expressions

As should have become clear by now, I use the term 'corpus' (plural: 'corpora') to refer to a collection of texts which is stored in electronic form and is searchable by means of appropriate software. Corpora vary, however, in terms of size, the language and language samples they contain, and any additional information that may be added to them.

Some corpora aim to provide a representative picture of a particular language as used in a particular part of the world at a particular time in history. These corpora tend to be large, although what counts as 'large' keeps changing as the power of computers increases. The corpus I normally refer to in this book, the British National Corpus (BNC), contains, as I have already mentioned, 100 million words of late twentieth-century British English. Of these, 10 million words are transcriptions of spoken interactions, including both informal conversations and more specific activity types, such as business meetings and lectures. The 90 million words of written English are equally divided among texts drawn from genres that are subsumed under nine different 'domains', including imaginative writing, world affairs, natural and pure sciences, and so on. The whole of

[4] It could be pointed out that simply consulting a dictionary would have led to similar observations to those I arrived at by consulting the corpus. This is true, in part, especially in the case of corpus-based dictionaries such as the *Macmillan English Dictionary* and the *Collins Cobuild English Language Dictionary*. In such cases, lexicographers wrote their entries on the basis of the kind of concordance-based analysis I have just demonstrated. However, a dictionary would not have provided information such as the frequency of metaphorical uses of 'rich' and the frequency of the specific expression 'rich life'.

the corpus has been annotated for parts-of-speech information. In other words, specially designed software has been used to add, to each word in the corpus, a 'tag' that indicates whether it is a noun, an adjective and so on (as well as what type of noun, adjective, etc.). Some sub-parts of the corpus have also received further types of annotation (for more detail, see www.natcorp.ox.ac.uk/).

Using the BNC as a convenient (if arbitrary) benchmark, I will now provide a brief overview of other types of corpora (see Biber *et al.* 1998; McEnery and Wilson 2001 for more detail on types of corpora and corpus linguistics generally). The Bank of English corpus, for example, differs from the BNC in a number of ways (see www.titania.bham.ac.uk/docs/about.htm): it contains whole texts, while some sections of the BNC contain text samples; it includes spoken and written data from international varieties of English, rather than just British English; it is constantly being added to, rather than being fixed in size (the 2002 edition included 450 million words, but the corpus is continuing to grow); it is not balanced in terms of the genres and domains that texts are drawn from; it has not been pre-annotated for part-of-speech information, although it does include a 'tagger' that would allow me, for example, to use it to search for 'rich' as a noun, as I could do with the BNC.

Other corpora differ from these because they capture different varieties of English (e.g. the Brown corpus of American English), different historical periods in the development of English (e.g. the Helsinki corpus of Old, Middle and Early Modern English), or, indeed, different languages, as well as more than one language. In addition, some corpora do not aim to reflect the state of a whole language, but are more specialized, i.e. they contain texts from specific genres or registers. These corpora tend to be smaller than general-purpose corpora, and are usually constructed in order to investigate very specific phenomena. For example, metaphor scholars have constructed and analysed corpora containing classroom discourse (Cameron 2003), political manifestos (Charteris-Black 2004), business articles in the press (Koller 2004b) and so on. Some studies have also involved corpora containing comparable texts in different languages, such as newspaper articles on European issues in British English and, respectively, Italian (Semino 2002b) and German (Musolff 2004).

Having selected a suitable corpus, however, one is faced with the task of exploiting it for metaphor analysis. Some attempts have been made to produce software for the automatic identification of metaphorical expressions (e.g. Mason 2004), and further work is currently in progress, including by myself and my colleagues at Lancaster University (Hardie *et al.* 2007). However, there is not, as yet, a well-established and reliable automatic method for identifying metaphorical expressions in large datasets. Similarly, there are at the moment no widely available corpora that have been annotated for metaphor, although this situation should soon change thanks to work currently in progress at the Free University in Amsterdam (Steen *et al.* forthcoming). There are, however, a number of ways in which corpora can facilitate the study of metaphorical patterns on a large scale (see also Musolff 2004: 63–82; Stefanowitsch and Gries 2006).

As I have already shown, it is possible to generate concordances of particular expressions in a corpus, which results in lists of occurrences with the immediately preceding and following co-text. One can then 'manually' analyse (part of) these concordances in order to distinguish between metaphorical and nonmetaphorical uses of the relevant expressions, and to investigate patterns of metaphoricity. This methodology, which I used for my analysis of 'rich' in section 6.1, is best demonstrated in Alice Deignan's work (1999; 2005). It is also possible to use suitable software to investigate the collocates of particular metaphorical expressions in a corpus, namely to find out what words tend to co-occur with the expression under analysis. In addition, the software package *WordSmith Tools* (Scott 1999) has a facility that allows the investigation of 'key words', namely words which occur unusually frequently in a particular dataset as compared with a larger reference corpus. It is therefore possible to check for the presence of metaphorical expressions among the key words in one's data.

One may also exploit corpora in order to search for vocabulary associated with specific source domains, which researchers expect to be dominant or significant in their data. For example, one may search for WAR metaphors in a corpus of business reporting by generating a list of expressions from the lexical field of war (with the help of dictionaries and thesauri), and then concordance these expressions in the corpus (see Koller 2004b for this kind of approach). A frequently used variant of this technique involves exploiting a 'smaller' corpus alongside a 'larger' corpus. The smaller corpus is analysed manually in order to identify the most frequent and relevant metaphorical expressions, which Charteris-Black (2004) calls 'metaphor keys'.[5] Then the larger corpus is searched automatically in order to find further instances of these expressions (see, for example, Semino 2002b; Cameron and Deignan 2003; Charteris-Black 2004; Musolff 2004). Koller (2004b) uses both thesauri and the 'small corpus' approach in order to produce a list of metaphorical expressions to be searched in her corpus of business print media. A recent pilot study has suggested that this method can be partly automated by semantically annotating one's data, i.e. using software such as the Wmatrix tool (http://ucrel.lancs.ac.uk/wmatrix/) to allocate each word or expression to one or more semantic fields. This makes it possible, for example, to generate a list of expressions that have been annotated

[5] Metaphor keys are metaphorical expressions that the researcher finds to be interesting and frequent in a manual analysis of a particular set of data, so that they are subsequently concordanced in a larger corpus. They should not be confused with 'key words' in *WordSmith Tools*, which are words whose frequency in a particular dataset is found by the software to be higher than in a reference corpus in terms of statistical significance.

for the 'war' semantic field, which can then be analysed for the presence of metaphorical expressions (see Hardie *et al.* 2007). A different kind of approach involves searching for vocabulary that relates to the target domain (e.g. expressions to do with emotions) and then looking in the surrounding co-text for relevant metaphorical expressions (see Stefanowitsch 2006). I demonstrate a variant of this method in my case study below. Finally, it is also possible to search for metaphorical 'signals' or 'tuning devices' in a corpus (Goatly 1997; Cameron and Deignan 2003), namely expressions that are sometimes used in close proximity to linguistic metaphors, such as 'as it were' or 'literally' (see 1.2.3 above). Clearly, different methods can also be combined, but the suitability of each method crucially depends on the goals of each particular study.

6.3 Corpus-based approaches to metaphor

It is possible to distinguish three main types of corpus-based studies of metaphor. The first type typically involves the use of general-purpose corpora in order to investigate systematic patterns of metaphoricity in a language generally, and to consider the implications of the observed patterns for potential underlying conceptual metaphors. These studies often aim to test the validity of claims that have previously been made within CMT. The second type of study is typically concerned with the investigation of metaphorical patterns in smaller corpora representing particular genres at particular points in history. This leads to the discovery of differences and similarities in metaphor use across different genres, and to reflections on the rhetorical and ideological dimensions of metaphor use. In Cameron's (1999) terms, these two types of studies focus, respectively, on globally systematic and discoursally systematic metaphorical patterns (see 1.3 above). The third type of study involves the analysis of comparable corpora in different languages, in order to investigate similarities and differences in metaphor use across language and cultures. In the next sub-sections, I consider each of these types of study in turn.

6.3.1 Corpora and general metaphorical patterns

Corpus-based methods are ideally suited to investigate the use of conventional metaphorical expressions, and particularly their frequencies, distribution, collocations and so on. Several prominent studies have aimed more specifically to test the validity of the claims made within CMT. As I have already mentioned, a major weakness of CMT is that it has been largely developed on the basis of relatively small sets of examples that were either constructed by the researcher, or collected in a relatively random fashion. The adoption of a corpus methodology has the potential to put metaphor theory on a sounder empirical footing, especially with respect to the extrapolation of hypotheses about conceptual metaphors from linguistic evidence. If the existence of particular conceptual metaphors is primarily reflected in the presence of conventional and pervasive patterns of metaphorical expressions in language use, a corpus-based methodology is eminently appropriate for CMT, since it makes it possible to retrieve and analyse large numbers of naturally occurring instances of particular expressions.

By and large, corpus-based studies of metaphorical patterns in English have partly confirmed and partly challenged the claims made within CMT. In addition, they have led to further insights and raised further issues to be investigated. This is particularly evident in Deignan's pioneering work on the Bank of English corpus (1999, 2005). In a number of studies based on the analysis of concordance data, Deignan has found further evidence for the existence of systematic patterns in the use of conventional metaphorical expressions, but has also shown that these patterns are both more 'dynamic' and more 'fixed' than suggested by CMT. Deignan has found a high degree of unpredictability in terms of which lexical items associated with a particular source domain are conventionally used in relation to a particular target domain (or set of related target domains). In addition, she has found that the characteristics and behaviour of conventional metaphorical expressions do not appear to be predictable from their basic, non-metaphorical uses. I will briefly illustrate both of these general phenomena with reference to some of Deignan's case studies.

Deignan (2005: 174–83) considers, for example, the conceptual metaphor COMPLEX ABSTRACT SYSTEMS ARE PLANTS. According to Kövecses (2002: 98–101), this conceptual metaphor captures the way in which a variety of different types of 'abstract systems' (including companies, economic and political systems, sets of ideas, people, etc.) are conventionally constructed in terms of the characteristics and life cycle of plants. This metaphor is linguistically realized by expressions such as 'Please turn to the local branch of the organization' (Kövecses 2002: 99).[6] Deignan concordanced, in the Bank of English, over 20 lexical items from the domain of PLANTS, such as 'plant', 'budding', 'seed', 'harvest' and so on. She found evidence that, indeed, some aspects of the PLANT source domain are systematically mapped onto a variety of target domains that involve some kind of development. In addition, she noticed that this applies particularly to a set of sub-domains of the more general COMPLEX ABSTRACT SYSTEMS domains, notably BUSINESS, RELATIONSHIPS, IDEAS and PEOPLE. Importantly, the corpus data also suggested that some metaphorical expressions drawing from the PLANT source domain are strongly associated with one of these target sub-domains in particular, and are seldom used in relation to the others. For example, people and businesses

[6] This very general conceptual metaphor subsumes Lakoff and Johnson's IDEAS ARE PLANTS (e.g. *The seeds of his great ideas were planted in his youth*; Lakoff and Johnson 1980b: 47).

are often presented as 'blossoming' and 'flourishing', but not as 'withering', while 'flower' tends to be used metaphorically in relation to creative projects. In addition, Deignan points out how the metaphorical uses of some words to do with plants only occur within a limited number of fixed expressions: the word 'bud', for example, only occurred in the data in the expression 'nip in the bud'. Finally, Deignan noted that the metaphorical senses of some expressions did not easily fit into the general pattern whereby the characteristics and life cycle of plants are mapped onto the characteristics and development of other entities. This applies, for example, to the metaphorical use of 'grapevine' in the sense 'informal network', which, Deignan points out, 'is not an obvious realization of a conceptual metaphor of growth and development' (Deignan 2005: 176).

Deignan's corpus analyses have also revealed some interesting differences between metaphorical and nonmetaphorical uses of the same (or related) expressions, which have not yet been adequately considered and accounted for in metaphor theory. For example, many animal metaphors are realized by verbs which only have metaphorical meanings (e.g. 'to squirrel', 'to dog', 'to parrot'), whereas the relevant literal terms tend to be nouns (e.g. 'squirrel', 'dog', 'parrot'). This may be due to the fact that (literal) animals are entities, and are therefore typically referred to by nouns. However, animal metaphors tend to capture particular behaviours, and these are typically referred to by verbs (see Deignan 2005: 152–5; see also Goatly 1997: 92 on metaphor and derivational processes in word formation). There are also cases where different inflections of the same word have different conventional metaphorical uses. Consider, for example, the noun 'rock' (Deignan 2005: 157–9). Deignan has found that, when it is used in the singular, the noun normally carries a positive evaluation, as in: 'the sanctity of human life – the rock on which our society is built' (Deignan 2005: 158). In contrast, the plural 'rocks' tends to be used as part of a more general JOURNEY metaphor to indicate problems and difficulties, as in 'The marriage has been on the rocks for a while' (Deignan 2005: 158). Another interesting contrast is shown by the conventional metaphorical uses of words that are normally considered as antonyms, such as 'light' and 'dark' (Deignan 2005: 183–91). When used metaphorically, 'light' is most frequently used in relation to knowledge, as in 'Lyn's seen the light' (Deignan 2005: 186). In contrast, the most frequent metaphorical uses of 'dark' relate to negative emotional states, as in 'He recalls those dark days when he was beset by disillusionment' (Deignan 2005: 188). All in all, Deignan's corpus-based studies highlight the importance of investigating in detail the uses and patterning of metaphorical expressions in real language use, and show how this often raises issues that have not yet been adequately considered and explained within metaphor theory.

Similar results have been obtained by using corpora to search for expressions that relate to particular target domains. For example, Stefanowitsch (2006) concordanced a series of emotion words in the BNC (e.g. 'anger', 'joy', 'fear', 'happiness'), and explored the co-text in each case in order to identify metaphorical expressions that are typically used in relation to the relevant emotion concept. He showed how this method enabled him to arrive at a possible set of conventional conceptual metaphors for emotions that is more reliable and precise than that proposed by Kövecses via what Stefanowitsch calls the 'introspective method'. In a similar study, I exploited a quarter-of-a-million word corpus of written British English narratives that had been previously annotated for instances of references to speaking and writing (e.g. 'She had pleaded, cajoled and quarreled violently') (see Semino 2005). Thanks to this pre-existing annotation, I was able to produce concordances of expressions relating to the target domain of COMMUNICATION and explore the ways in which various aspects of this broad domain are metaphorized in the corpus. My findings confirm, in part, the claims that had previously been made in this area (Reddy 1993; Grady 1998), but also provide a more comprehensive picture of how communication is metaphorically constructed in English. More specifically, I was able to show that communication is conventionally constructed metaphorically via a set of source domains that relate to physical activities (e.g. MOTION, SUPPORT, PHYSICAL AGGRESSION), and that each of these source domains captures specific components and aspects of communication. For example, agreement is conventionally constructed in terms of physical support, as in expressions such as 'he supported the very same regime in a letter to a fellow MP', while disagreement and criticism are conventionally constructed in terms of physical aggression, as in 'Delors attacked Balladur's idea of a "Europe of circles".' I will return to this study in section 6.4 below.

6.3.2 Corpora and genre-specific metaphorical patterns

As I mentioned in 2.2 above, Goatly (1997: 293–327) assembled a corpus of English including six different genres: conversation, national news reports, popular science, magazine advertising, modern novels, modern English poetry. He then conducted a manual analysis that resulted in a quantitative overview of a variety of aspects of metaphor use in the different sections of the corpus. For example, he found that poetry has the highest percentage of novel metaphorical expressions out of all linguistic metaphors (56 per cent), followed by magazine advertising (31 per cent), modern novels (28 per cent) and popular science (18 per cent). Interestingly, he also noticed that novel metaphors are more likely to be textually signalled (via expressions such as 'in a way' and 'metaphorically speaking') in the genres where they occur less frequently, i.e. news reports and conversation (see also 1.2.3 above). Similarly, news reports and conversation have the lowest proportions of textually extended metaphors. Some of these findings provide empirical confirmation for assumptions that are normally made about metaphor use, such as that the creative use of metaphor (and language generally) is a central characteristic of poetry. Other findings, however, are less predictable, and provide genuinely new insights. For example, in four out of six genres in Goatly's corpus there is a higher percentage of novel metaphors involving nouns than verbs (see Goatly 1997: 315). This may be due to the fact that the metaphorical use of nouns is more salient and obvious than that of other parts of speech: nouns typically refer to entities, so that it is relatively easy to perceive a contrast between the entities they evoke when they are used literally as opposed to when they are used metaphorically (e.g. 'head' referring to a part of the body vs. the person in charge of an organization) (see Goatly 1997: 82–6). Interestingly, the two genres that do not display this trend are poetry and conversation, which otherwise differ quite dramatically from each other in terms of frequency of novel metaphorical expressions. In conversation, Goatly suggests, this is mostly a consequence of slips of the tongue. In poetry, on the other hand, the fact that novel verb metaphors are (slightly) more frequent than novel noun metaphors is seen by Goatly as a characteristic of the genre, where, as he puts it, 'the general metaphoric heightening . . . spills over beyond the more obvious thing-referring nouns to verbs' (Goatly 1997: 315).[7]

In a different study, Skorczynska and Deignan (2006) focused on how the form and function of metaphorical expressions vary as a consequence of differences in genre. They constructed two 400,000-word corpora of business discourse, namely a 'Research corpus' containing 'scientific business discourse' (i.e. articles from specialized academic journals aimed at experts), and a 'Periodicals corpus' containing 'popular business discourse' (i.e. articles for a more general audience in magazines such as *The Economist*). Two 30,000-word samples were analysed manually in order to identify relevant metaphorical expressions, which were then concordanced in both corpora. This revealed considerable differences between the two corpora, both in terms of the metaphorical expressions that tend to be used and in terms of the source domains that appear to be dominant. The Periodicals corpus was found to contain a wider variety of metaphorical expressions drawn from a larger set of source domains than the Research corpus. In addition, the metaphorical expressions used in the Periodicals corpus tend to be part of general use (e.g. 'weapon', 'shipwreck'), while those used in the Research corpus are more genre-specific, and tend to be used repeatedly in their technical senses (e.g. 'free rider', 'bull market'). Half of the genre-specific metaphors in the Research corpus were found to be used for the purposes of modelling particular phenomena in order to provide explanations and suggest strategies. This phenomenon was found to be infrequent in the

[7] Note that these findings by Goatly apply to novel metaphorical expressions. When looking at linguistic metaphors generally in classroom interaction, Cameron (2003: 88) found that noun metaphors were relatively infrequent, especially compared with metaphors involving prepositions and verbs.

Periodicals corpus, where metaphors are used primarily to fill lexical gaps and to provide description and illustration. Bearing in mind that the corpora are similar in terms of subject matter, it appears that differences in the readership and purpose of economics articles significantly affect the use of metaphorical expressions. Skorczynska and Deignan's findings also have educational implications, since they suggest that exposure to general publications such as *The Economist* may not be adequate in order to prepare non-native speakers of English to cope with academic publications in business studies (see also chapter 4, and particularly sections 4.3.1 and 4.4).

Koller (2004b) used a corpus methodology to investigate the ideological implications of systematic metaphorical patterns in business discourse. Her study involved two 160,000-word corpora of magazine and newspaper articles on, respectively, marketing and sales on the one hand, and mergers and acquisitions on the other. On the basis of previous studies and some sample data analyses, Koller identified, for each corpus, three dominant metaphorical source domains, and a fourth 'alternative' source domain. For the marketing and sales corpus, the three main source domains were WAR, SPORTS, GAMES, while the alternative source domain was ROMANCE. For the mergers and acquisition corpus, the three main source domains were FIGHTING, MATING, FEEDING, and the alternative source domain was DANCE. Koller used various methods to compose lists of 35 expressions belonging to the lexical fields associated with each domain, and concordanced these expressions in both corpora. Her quantitative results show that WAR metaphors are used most frequently in the marketing and sales data, and FIGHTING metaphors are used most frequently in the mergers and acquisitions data. In discussing the mergers and acquisitions (M&A) corpus in particular, Koller summarizes her results as follows:

> To sum up, the media text corpus on M&A is very much characterized by an overarching EVOLUTIONARY STRUGGLE metaphor, which can be broken down into a threefold metaphor cluster of FIGHTING, MATING and FEEDING. Of these three, the FIGHTING metaphor is selected most often (almost all of the 35 items in the basic lexical fields are realized), most frequent (accounting for 70 per cent of all instances of cluster metaphors), most varied (showing the lowest type-token ratio, namely 0.07) and hence very much entrenched in the corpus. (Koller 2004b: 129)

In addition to her concordance-based quantitative analyses, Koller considers the clustering and distribution of the various sets of metaphorical expressions, and conducts some detailed analysis of representative texts from the two corpora. She concludes that her analysis provides evidence of a masculine bias in the conceptual models shared by journalists and their readers, and argues that the dominant metaphorical patterns reflect an ideology in which business transactions are viewed in terms of aggression and prevarication, and in which women are ignored and marginalized.

A similar approach is adopted by Charteris-Black (2004) in a series of corpus-based studies of political speeches, press reports and religious texts. In each study, Charteris-Black conducts sample data analyses in order to arrive at lists of significant metaphorical expressions (or 'metaphor keys'). These expressions are then concordanced in each corpus as a whole. He then uses the resulting concordances to extrapolate the dominant conceptual metaphors in each dataset, and to draw conclusions on the persuasive, emotive, and ideological functions of metaphor in different societal and cultural domains.

All these studies successfully show how the adoption of a corpus methodology does not have to result in a reductive or superficial approach to the data, as sceptics might fear. In each case, co-texts and contexts are also explored, and sample extracts are analysed in depth. All in all, this kind of work demonstrates that a corpus-based approach is not just relevant to general claims about metaphor use and conceptual metaphors, but also to the study of the rhetorical and ideological functions of metaphor, and the role it plays in particular genres and discourses.

6.3.3 Corpora and the cross-linguistic study of metaphor

Corpus-based methods are particularly relevant to the cross-linguistic study of metaphor, since comparing metaphor use across languages crucially relies on the analysis of large amounts of data.

A number of studies have focused specifically on the use of metaphors and metonymies relating to body parts in different languages. Within CMT, our physical, bodily experiences are attributed a central role in the way in which non-physical experiences are metaphorically constructed. Since human beings are biologically the same regardless of language or culture, this would suggest that metaphors involving the body should be broadly similar across languages. On the other hand, it is also normally recognized that culture affects the ways in which we perceive our bodies, including their parts and functioning. This potentially leads to cross-linguistic differences in the use of bodily metaphors (see Kövecses 2005).

Deignan and Potter (2004) investigated the use of four words referring to the same body parts in English and Italian, respectively 'nose', 'mouth', 'eye' and 'heart' in English and 'naso', 'bocca', 'occhio' and 'cuore' in Italian. These words and their various inflections were concordanced, respectively, in the Bank of English corpus and in two corpora of Italian totalling 35 million words. Deignan and Potter found both similarities and differences in the way in which these expressions are used non-literally in the two sets of data. The similarities were found to be motivated by particular aspects of bodily experiences. For example, the English expression 'look beyond the end of one's nose' has a close Italian equivalent in the expression 'vedere al di là del proprio naso'. In both cases the (positive) ability to pay attention to things that are not one's immediate concern is constructed in terms of the ability to see beyond the strict boundaries of one's body, and particularly the nose, which is the most protruding part of the human head. The metaphorical sense of both expressions, Deignan and Potter argue, results from the conventional tendencies to construct thinking as seeing, and an individual's immediate concerns as the person's body.

The differences that Deignan and Potter identified between the two sets of data could be explained, at least in part, as a consequence of differences in the main concerns and values of the two cultures. For example, the Italian corpora were found to contain a wider variety of metonymies and metaphors involving the noun 'bocca' ('mouth') than the English corpus. In the metonymic uses, 'bocca' tends to stand for eating or appetite, while in the metaphorical uses 'bocca' stands for feelings or behaviour. For example, the expression 'riempirsi la bocca di' ('filling one's mouth with') can be used to indicate that someone speaks in a grand manner about a topic they do not in fact feel strongly about. This greater variety of conventional metonymies and metaphors involving 'bocca' could be seen as a reflection of the central role of eating and food in Italian as opposed to British culture. Overall, Deignan and Potter's study raised some questions for metaphor theory, but also revealed considerable similarities between the two languages. For example, both languages appear to share the same underlying set of metaphorical mappings from the source domain of BODY onto that of MIND. Similarly, metonymic expressions involving parts of the body are more frequent than metaphorical expressions in both sets of data. While Deignan and Potter's study involved two languages that are historically related, Charteris-Black (2003) adopted a corpus-based approach to investigate two more distant languages and cultures, English and Malay. His analysis revealed a number of important differences in the way speakers of English and Malay use metaphors and metonymies involving parts of the body.

Studies like Deignan and Potter's are the cross-linguistic equivalent of the general corpus-based work on metaphor in individual languages described in 6.3.1 above. Corpus-based methods have also been applied in the cross-linguistic equivalent of the studies described in 6.3.2, namely to investigate the metaphors used in different languages within particular genres and in relation to particular topics. These studies typically involve smaller and more specialized corpora, and aim to investigate differences in historically bound views and attitudes, as well as general cultural differences.

For example, in Semino (2002b) I compared the use of metaphors for the joint European currency, the euro, in two parallel corpora of British and Italian newspaper articles. The articles were collected over a period of three weeks spanning the official introduction of the euro on 1 January 1999. I concordanced in each corpus a set of relevant metaphorical expressions that were derived from a detailed analysis of representative samples from the data. This revealed a number of patterns that were roughly similar in the two corpora, such as the metaphorical description of the introduction of the euro in terms of 'birth'/'nascita' and 'arrival'/'arrivo'. The metaphorical patterns that were specific to each corpus, however, reflected the different attitudes that dominated public opinion and a large part of the political spectrum in each country. The Italian corpus contained several metaphorical patterns that indicated the difficulty and importance of meeting the Maastricht criteria and being admitted into the eurozone: for example, admission into the euro was described as an 'esame' ('test') and as a 'battaglia' ('battle'). In contrast, the English corpus contained several uses of metaphor that reflected the general euroscepticism that had kept the United Kingdom out of the euro: for example, the new interest rates set by the European bank for all eurozone countries were described as 'one size fits all', which suggests that they may in fact be appropriate for none of the individual countries (see Musolff 2004 for a broader analysis of two corpora containing British and German newspaper articles on the European Union from the fall of the Berlin Wall to the end of the twentieth century). In other words, this kind of study is particularly concerned with comparing views and attitudes at particular historical junctures, as well as more general cultural differences.

Having provided an overview of the main methods and results of corpus-based approaches to metaphor, I now turn to a specific case study.

6.4 Case study: the metaphorical construction of communication as physical aggression in the British press

One of the areas of human experience that is often constructed metaphorically is verbal communication, or, in other words, the sophisticated processes whereby we use language to communicate meanings, attitudes, emotions, interpersonal relationships and so on. Indeed, the first conceptual metaphor that Lakoff and Johnson (1980b) discuss in *Metaphors We Live By* is ARGUMENT IS WAR: a metaphor where the target domain is a type of communicative interaction. Lakoff and Johnson extrapolate this conceptual metaphor from conventional linguistic expressions such as 'His criticisms were right on target' and 'He shot down all my arguments,' and claim that this metaphor does not simply provide a way of talking about arguments, but rather structures the way in which we conceive of and perform arguments (Lakoff and Johnson 1980b: 4). This particular conceptualization of arguments, they argue, is grounded in our experience of physical conflict, which is a basic component of both animal and human interaction, and which human beings have 'institutionalized . . . in a number of ways, one of them being war' (Lakoff and Johnson 1980b: 62; see also Kövecses 2002: 74–5).

In discussing the experiential grounding of ARGUMENT IS WAR, Lakoff and Johnson make repeated references to the general domain of 'physical conflict' and 'physical combat', which includes a wide range of violent activities, from fist-fights to military attack. However, the formulation of the conceptual metaphor ARGUMENT IS WAR restricts the source domain to military activities, and has been recently criticized for not accounting properly for the range of metaphorical expressions that construct verbal conflict in terms of physical conflict. Ritchie (2003), for example, notes that many of the metaphorical expressions that are normally subsumed under ARGUMENT IS WAR can also be explained in terms of other source domains, such as SPORTS, or GAMES like chess and bridge. Indeed, Lakoff and Johnson's original list of linguistic realizations of ARGUMENT IS WAR included the expression 'I've never won an argument with him', where 'win' could just as easily be related to the source domain of SPORTS (see also Kövecses 2002: 74–5, for the close connection between the conceptual domains of WAR and SPORTS). Ritchie suggests that the source domain that is conventionally applied to arguments should be seen as a broader conceptual field including a wide variety of types of physical conflict, from games to fist-fights to all-out war (Ritchie 2003: 135). Indeed, Vanparys (1995) had previously carried out a dictionary-based study of what he calls 'metalinguistic metaphors', and had proposed that ARGUMENT IS WAR should be replaced with the broader conceptual metaphor VERBAL AGGRESSION IS PHYSICAL AGGRESSION.

In a corpus-based study of metaphors for communication, I have also found that a more general formulation is needed in order to capture the different ways in which conflict in communication is conventionally talked about in terms of physical conflict. I begin by describing the results of a small-scale study that have already been presented elsewhere (Semino 2005, 2006c; Heywood and Semino 2007). I then provide further evidence by exploiting a larger corpus. In both cases, I focus on how verbal conflict is metaphorically constructed in the British press.

6.4.1 Communication as physical aggression in a small annotated corpus of British news reports

The first part of this case study involves the analysis of an 83,000-word corpus of newspaper news reports that were published in the British press in the 1990s. The corpus contains 40 text samples of approximately 2,000 words each, which were extracted in equal proportions from 'popular' tabloid newspapers (e.g. *The Daily Mail*) and from 'quality' broadsheet newspapers (e.g. *The Guardian*). As part of a larger project (see Semino and Short 2004) this small press corpus had been systematically annotated for references to spoken or written communication, including particularly: 'reporting clauses' of speech or writing (e.g. 'he said', 'she wrote'); references to the illocutionary force or speech act value of utterances or texts (e.g. 'senior Tory figures openly questioned the Prime Minister's judgment'), and minimal references to the occurrence of communication via speech or writing (e.g. 'Each week Fergie would talk to fortune-teller

Rita Rogers'). In other words, the corpus is annotated for expressions relating to the target domain of COMMUNICATION. I was therefore able to concordance the annotations in order to obtain large numbers of references to speech and writing. The concordances were then analysed in order to identify relevant metaphorical expressions, and to group them according to the source domains they relate to.

For example, in the expression 'senior Tory figures openly questioned the Prime Minister's judgment', the verb 'question' is used nonmetaphorically to refer to the verbal activities of a group of politicians. In contrast, the example below involves a metaphorical reference to communication:

6.12 amid renewed backbench sniping at the Blair style of leadership (*The Guardian*, 13 May 1996)

The basic meaning of the noun 'sniping' (which is derived from the verb 'snipe') is to do with armed attack from a hidden position aimed at causing injury and death. In examples such as extract 6.12, the noun is used metaphorically to refer to potentially damaging criticisms made in private rather than in the presence of the person who is being criticized. In other words, a particular kind of criticism is metaphorically constructed in terms of physical aggression involving the use of weapons.

Out of the 2,238 references to speaking (2,146) and writing (92) that were extracted from the press corpus, 536 (i.e. 23.9 per cent) were analysed as involving metaphorical expressions. These were further divided into groups according to the metaphorical source domains that they seem to relate to (e.g. MOTION, TRANSFER OF OBJECTS). In this section, I concentrate on the 62 examples where communication is metaphorically constructed in terms of physical aggression and conflict, and consider the extent to which they can be adequately captured via the conceptual metaphor ARGUMENT IS WAR. The other metaphorical patterns which were discovered in the data are discussed in some detail in Semino (2005, 2006c) and Heywood and Semino (2007) (see also a brief summary in section 6.3.1 above).

In a few examples from the corpus, verbal arguments are talked about via expressions that can fairly straightforwardly be subsumed under the source domain of WAR (the *relevant* metaphorical expressions are underlined):

6.13 Mr Major . . . has warned his party's warring factions (*The Daily Telegraph*, 5 December 1994)

6.14 The Chancellor, Kenneth Clarke, yesterday stepped up his guerrilla warfare against the Tory right by insisting that . . . (*The Guardian*, 13 May 1996)

However, examples such as these cannot be neatly separated from a wider range of expressions whose basic meanings relate to different types of physical conflict. Consider the examples below:

6.15 [O]nce again we were firing questions (*The Daily Mirror*, 13 May 1996)

6.16 Last night M. Delors attacked M. Balladur's idea of a 'Europe of circles' in which each member country could progress at its own speed. (*The Daily Telegraph*, 12 December 1994)

6.17 The Chancellor also defended his stand on a European single currency. (*The Daily Star*, 13 May 1996)

6.18 Crime victims hit out yesterday over plans to give thugs a five-star Christmas in jail. (*The Sun*, 5 December 1994)

The metaphorical use of the verb 'fire' in relation to questions in extract 6.15 could conceivably be related to the WAR source domain. However, the notion of firing shots or using firearms is not necessarily part of war, but rather part of armed violence more generally. The metaphorical uses of 'attack' and 'defend' in extracts 6.16 and 6.17 can be explained in terms of physical conflict and aggression generally, with or without the use of weapons (e.g. the non-metaphorical use of 'defend' in: 'Michael told the Old Bailey he had tried to defend his brother Lee, 13, before his father turned on him', from the BNC). In extract 6.18, the use of 'hit out' metaphorically constructs the expression of anger and criticism in terms of the delivery of physical blows, rather than in terms of armed violence.

Cumulatively, these examples show that some aspects of communication are conventionally constructed metaphorically in terms of physical conflict and aggression, ranging from fisticuffs through armed attack to full-blown war. Rather than trying to impose boundaries within this group of expressions, I would suggest that they all relate to the general source domain of PHYSICAL CONFLICT, or, following Vanparys (1995), PHYSICAL AGGRESSION.[8] The differences in meaning among the different metaphorical expressions can be accounted for, in part at least, in terms of the different scenarios that are subsumed under the broad PHYSICAL AGGRESSION domain. For example, the fact that 'sniping' in extract 6.12 indicates criticisms that are not made openly can be explained with reference to a SNIPING scenario, in which shooting occurs from a hidden position. In addition, the above examples show that the relevant target domain is also broader than suggested by the conceptual metaphor ARGUMENT IS WAR. Several examples do involve arguments, although not necessarily face-to-face (e.g. extracts 6.13, 6.14 and 6.17). However, other examples are to do more generally with the expression of criticisms (e.g. extracts 6.12, 6.16, 6.18 and 6.19), or with an aggressive, forceful attitude in communication (e.g. extract 6.15). I have therefore suggested that the pattern observed in the corpus is indeed best captured in terms of a conceptual metaphor

[8] In the second edition of *Metaphors We Live By*, Lakoff and Johnson (2003: 265) suggest that ARGUMENT IS WAR arises from a more basic 'primary' metaphor ARGUMENT IS STRUGGLE, which arises from the experience of young children in their physical contact with parents (see Grady 1997a for the notion of primary metaphor).

that is more general than ARGUMENT IS WAR, and that I have expressed as ANTAGONISTIC COMMUNICATION IS PHYSICAL AGGRESSION (see Semino 2005, Heywood and Semino 2007). In other words, the results of the corpus analysis confirm the suggestions made by Vanparys (1995) and Ritchie (2003), and arguably capture Lakoff and Johnson's own examples more adequately than ARGUMENT IS WAR.

After introducing ARGUMENT IS WAR, Lakoff and Johnson (1980b: 4–5) consider the implications of this conceptual metaphor by comparing it to a hypothetical alternative metaphor where an argument is viewed as a dance. This comparison highlights the fact that the source domain of PHYSICAL AGGRESSION emphasizes the confrontational, competitive, aggressive and potentially destructive effects of arguments, and, more generally, of antagonistic communication. Within this metaphorical conceptualization of communication, participants in arguments are constructed as opponents and enemies, whose goal is to ensure that their own views prevail, and that others are thwarted in their goals and damaged in their image. Similarly, criticism is viewed as an activity that results in humiliation and loss of face (constructed as physical damage). All this downplays the possibility that communication may lead to the formulation of new, shared views, and that it might enhance mutual understanding (other metaphors are more suitable here, such as, for example, ARGUMENT IS A JOURNEY; Kövecses 2002: 80). A comparison of my press data with similar amounts of data from other genres has suggested that PHYSICAL AGGRESSION metaphors for communication are particularly frequent in newspaper reports, where they are used to emphasize conflict in communication between newsworthy individuals (notably politicians) and hence to enhance the newsworthiness of the communication itself (see Semino 2006c). In particular, the majority of PHYSICAL AGGRESSION metaphors were found in the tabloid section of the corpus, where they seem to be part of a general tendency to dramatize and sensationalize (verbal) events.

A limitation of the corpus I have discussed so far, however, is that it is rather too small for strong conclusions to be drawn. In the next section, I discuss the results of a further study that was carried out on larger quantities of corpus data. For the sake of clarity, I will refer to the press corpus discussed so far as the 'small' corpus.

6.4.2 *Communication as physical aggression in a larger British press corpus*

In order to investigate in more depth the patterns discussed in the previous section, I turned to the BNC, which includes several million words of press data. More specifically, I accessed the online BNC web (http://escorp.unizh.ch/) and constructed two subcorpora that fitted my purposes, namely: a 'Broadsheet subcorpus' containing 1,860,134 words from two 'quality' or 'elite' newspapers:

The Independent and *The Guardian*; and a 'Tabloid subcorpus' containing 1,977,335 words from two 'popular' newspapers: the *Daily Mirror* and *Today* (NB: the latter is no longer being published). I then selected a set of linguistic metaphors that construct communication in terms of PHYSICAL AGGRESSION and concordanced them in both subcorpora.

The set of linguistic metaphors I investigated were drawn from two sources. First, I included a group of expressions that were identified as relevant in the analysis of the small corpus discussed in the previous section. These were: 'attack' (all verb forms), 'blast' (all verb forms), 'bombard' (all verb forms), 'fire' (all verb forms), 'flak', 'hit back', 'hit out', 'rap' (all verb forms), 'slam' (all verb forms), 'snipe' (all verb forms), 'swipe' (as a noun), 'warfare', 'warring'. Secondly, I included a smaller group of expressions that are mentioned in Lakoff and Johnson (1980b: 4) as examples of linguistic realizations of ARGUMENT IS WAR. These were: 'indefensible', 'right on target', 'shoot' and 'shoot/shot down'. As should be clear from these lists, in some cases I only concordanced specific expressions as strings of letters, as in the case of 'right on target'. In other cases, I exploited the concordancing software to search for a particular 'lemma', such as all forms of a particular verb. In the case of the verb 'attack', for example, a concordance of the lemma includes the following forms: 'attack', 'attacks', 'attacking' and 'attacked'. Having obtained a series of concordances from each subcorpus, I analysed each concordance in order to identify any metaphorical uses of the relevant expressions that relate to communication. This means that I did not consider any other conventional metaphorical senses of the various expressions (e.g. the use of the verb 'fire' in expressions such as 'fire the imagination'). From now on, when I refer to 'occurrences' or 'relevant occurrences' of particular expressions, I mean occurrences of metaphorical uses in relation to communication.

The only expressions for which I found no relevant occurrences in either subcorpus were part of the set I had derived from Lakoff and Johnson's examples, namely: 'shoot' and 'right on target'. As for 'shoot down', only one occurrence was identified in the Tabloid subcorpus. Even allowing for differences between British and American English, this emphasizes the importance of using naturally occurring examples, and, ideally, corpus data, when providing linguistic evidence for conceptual metaphors. Of the Lakoff and Johnson set of expressions, however, the adjective 'indefensible' did have a number of relevant occurrences (12) in the two subcorpora. In fact, in this case, almost all occurrences of the adjective related to communication generally and arguments in particular, as in: 'The Labour leader, Mr Neil Kinnock, said she was trying to defend the indefensible'. In contrast, all 13 expressions I had derived from my analysis of the small corpus had between 4 and 165 relevant occurrences in the two subcorpora (I should point out that the expression with the highest number of relevant occurrences, 'attack', is also included in one of Lakoff and Johnson's examples).

Table 6.1 *Number of occurrences and frequency of* PHYSICAL AGGRESSION *metaphorical expressions for communication in two press subcorpora of the BNC.*

Expressions searched in subcorpora	No. of metaphorical uses in relation to communication in Broadsheet corpus *(and frequency per million words)*	No. of metaphorical uses in relation to communication in Tabloid corpus *(and frequency per million words)*
Attack (all verb forms)	92 *(49.45)*	73 *(36.91)*
Blast (all verb forms)	1 *(0.53)*	111 *(56.13)*
Bombard (all verb forms)	2 *(1.07)*	7 *(3.54)*
Fire (all verb forms)	4 *(2.15)*	8 *(4.04)*
Flak	4 *(2.15)*	12 *(6.06)*
Hit back	3 *(1.61)*	39 *(19.72)*
Hit out	1 *(0.53)*	25 *(12.64)*
Indefensible	10 *(5.37)*	2 *(1.01)*
Rap (all verb forms)	3 *(1.61)*	20 *(10.11)*
Slam (all verb forms)	1 *(0.53)*	72 *(36.41)*
Snipe (all verb forms)	3 *(1.61)*	5 *(2.52)*
Swipe	4 *(2.15)*	7 *(3.54)*
Warfare	2 *(1.07)*	2 *(1.01)*
Warring	3 *(1.61)*	8 *(4.04)*
Totals	133 *(71.50)*	391 *(197.74)*

Table 6.1 provides the results of my analysis of the concordances for these 13 expressions, as well for the adjective 'indefensible' from the Lakoff and Johnson set. For each expression (or, where appropriate, verb lemma) I provide the total number of relevant occurrences in each subcorpus, and, within round brackets, the frequency per million words. In my discussion, I do not focus on the characteristic behaviour of each metaphorical expression (see Deignan forthcoming), but rather on the differences and similarities between the two subcorpora.

A few relatively infrequent expressions have similar numbers of relevant occurrences in the two subcorpora, namely 'snipe' (3 and 5 occurrences), 'swipe' (4 and 7 occurrences) and 'warfare' (2 occurrences per subcorpus). A larger set of expressions have more than twice as many relevant occurrences in the Tabloid as the Broadsheet subcorpus. Where the relevant figure for each subcorpus is 12 occurrences or less (i.e. six instances per million words or less), it is difficult to draw strong conclusions about differences between the tabloid and broadsheet press. This applies to 'bombard', 'fire', 'flak' and 'warring'. It is nonetheless interesting to notice that all these expressions are used more frequently in relation to communication in the Tabloid subcorpus than in the Broadsheet subcorpus, since the same pattern was also observed in the analysis of the small corpus. The only relatively infrequent expression that has more relevant occurrences in the Broadsheet corpus is 'indefensible'. Interestingly, this expression is slightly different from the ones I have considered so far, in that it is a relatively formal adjective, and it is to do with defence, rather than attack. It may therefore be less appropriate for the relatively informal and rather sensationalist style that is associated with tabloid journalism.

With the exception of the verb 'attack', all remaining expressions included in table 6.1 are considerably more frequent in the Tabloid than the Broadsheet subcorpus. This applies to: 'blast' (respectively, 1 and 111 relevant occurrences), 'hit back' (3 and 39 relevant occurrences), 'hit out' (1 and 25 relevant occurrences), 'rap' (3 and 20 relevant occurrences), 'slam' (1 and 72 relevant occurrences). Below I provide examples of relevant occurrences of 'blast', 'hit back', 'rap' and 'slam' from the Tabloid corpus, since their metaphorical use in relation to communication has not yet been exemplified:

6.19 Former model Christie Brinkley, 39, has blasted CNN bosses after being sacked from her TV Lifestyles show.

6.20 But Downing Street hit back immediately with a stinging rebuke, plunging Anglo–French relations to a new low.

6.21 British Rail will be rapped today for not doing an immediate drug test on a train driver after a crash that killed two and injured 500.

6.22 Motoring organisations slammed senseless drivers for travelling too fast.

What these results suggest is that tabloid newspapers fairly regularly employ a set of PHYSICAL AGGRESSION metaphorical expressions for communication that are barely used in the broadsheets. All but one of these five expressions, however, have basic meanings to do with unarmed physical scuffles or blows, rather than with armed violence or war (this applies to 'hit back', 'hit out', 'rap' and 'slam').[9] In other words, the Tabloid corpus shows a tendency to construct arguments or the expression of criticism in terms of fisticuffs among the people involved. This actually parallels a tendency to report episodes of literal violence of the same kind among sportspeople or show-business personalities. In contrast, the verb 'blast' is the only expression that metaphorically presents communication in terms of explosions, and that can therefore potentially be related to war. However, 'blast' can also be used nonmetaphorically to indicate destruction that is not to do with armed conflict or war, as in 'Certainly the galleries where the slate is blasted, which go down 1,500 ft in

[9] The basic meanings of some of these expressions fall less neatly than others under the domain of PHYSICAL AGGRESSION. The basic meaning of 'rap' includes both the action of hitting objects and that of hitting someone, usually on the knuckles, as a form of punishment. It is the latter basic meaning that best accounts for metaphorical uses such as extract 6.21. As for the verb 'slam' in extract 6.22 , its basic meaning is to do with hitting objects, such as doors. I have included it here because this basic meaning is nonetheless to do with aggressive behaviour. In fact, according to the OED, the verb 'slam' was in the past used to indicate blows against people as well as objects.

giant steps, have a dramatic quality of their own,' from the BNC. By and large, therefore, the analysis of the Tabloid corpus reveals a pattern whereby antagonistic communication is described via expressions that are relatively informal, monosyllabic words of Germanic origin, and that evoke scenarios of fisticuffs or physical destruction. This arguably lends some element of hyperbole and, potentially, entertainment to the representation of verbal behaviour.

The fact that the relevant use of the verb 'attack' is slightly more frequent in the Broadsheet than the Tabloid subcorpus (92 and 73 occurrences respectively) is not necessarily in contradiction with what I have noted so far. The metaphorical use of 'attack' in relation to communication is highly conventional, and is indeed well represented in both subcorpora. However, 'attack' is less informal and, crucially, much less specific, than the expressions favoured by the tabloids: it does not necessarily evoke a specific scenario, but rather indicates physical aggression in a rather generic way. This may explain why, in this case, the number of relevant occurrences is higher in the broadsheets, since the tabloids seem to favour more specific and evocative expressions (in fact, my concordances suggest that the tabloids often use 'blast' where the broadsheets would use 'attack'). Interestingly, the same considerations apply, *mutatis mutandis*, to 'indefensible': this adjective is also relatively formal and, by indicating a quality rather than a process, does not strongly evoke a specific violent scenario.

Overall, my analysis of the two subcorpora of the BNC has confirmed the existence of a conventional metaphorical pattern whereby some aspects and types of communication are constructed in terms of physical conflict. The most frequently used expressions, however, are in fact not to do with war or armed violence, which supports the suggestion that this pattern is best captured in terms of a general conceptual metaphor, such as ANTAGONISTIC COMMUNICATION IS PHYSICAL AGGRESSION.[10] The analysis has also shown that, overall, tabloid newspapers used PHYSICAL AGGRESSION metaphors for communication more frequently than broadsheet newspapers. However, this discrepancy is primarily due to expressions that indicate low-level physical conflict, which appear to be part of tabloid style, such as 'hit back/out', 'slam', and 'rap'. Other more general and relatively more formal expressions, notably 'attack' and 'indefensible', actually have more relevant occurrences in the Broadsheet than in the Tabloid subcorpus. The differences between the

[10] Here I am arguing that this formulation successfully captures the conventional tendency to construct communication in terms of physical conflict and violence. In fact, some of the expressions I have analysed are conventionally used metaphorically in relation to other target domains, as is the case for the verb 'attack' in the expression 'the infection attacks the lymphatic system', from the BNC. These phenomena are best captured in terms of primary metaphors, which often underlie more complex conceptual metaphors such as ANTAGONISTIC COMMUNICATION IS PHYSICAL AGGRESSION (see Grady 1997a; Semino 2005; Deignan forthcoming).

two subcorpora could be explained in terms of ideological differences between broadsheet and tabloid newspapers: while the same general metaphor for communication is exploited in both types of newspapers, its particular use in the tabloids can be seen to reflect a world-view in which interpersonal relationships are predominantly aggressive, and in which an opposition can often be established between 'good guys' and 'bad guys', or 'us' and 'them'.

Finally, the Totals row in table 6.1 shows not only that PHYSICAL CONFLICT metaphors are considerably more frequent in the Tabloid corpus, but that, overall, these metaphorical expressions occur between 71 and 197 times per million words. This corresponds to approximately one occurrence every 14,000 words in the Broadsheet corpus and one occurrence every 5,000 words in the Tabloid corpus. The frequency in the small corpus was much higher than this: 62 occurrences of PHYSICAL CONFLICT metaphors in approximately 83,000 words correspond to approximately one occurrence every 1,300 words. There are two main reasons for this difference, one accidental and one substantial. The accidental reason is that the small corpus was analysed manually, so that a wider variety of metaphorical expressions was included. The two BNC subcorpora, in contrast, were analysed by means of concordances, so that only a proportion of PHYSICAL AGGRESSION metaphors were counted. More substantially, the small corpus consists entirely of news reports, many of which involve verbal communication as the main item of news (e.g. political debates, diplomatic initiatives and so on). The two BNC subcorpora contain extracts from all sections of the newspapers (i.e. including editorials, leisure pages, arts pages, etc.), and therefore contain fewer texts that are concerned with verbal communication in particular.

Overall, I hope to have shown that corpora can be exploited with relatively low levels of technical know-how to investigate both general metaphorical patterns and more specific differences between genres or texts intended for different readerships.

6.5 Summary

I started this chapter by showing how corpora can be exploited to test, and, where appropriate, challenge, the claims made in theories such as CMT on the basis of insufficient linguistic evidence. I then went on to discuss how corpus-based methods can be used to investigate metaphorical patterns in a particular language, in specific genres or across different languages. The case study exploited different corpora to suggest an alternative formulation of Lakoff and Johnson's (1980b) conceptual metaphor ARGUMENT IS WAR, and to compare the use of PHYSICAL AGGRESSION metaphors for communication in British broadsheet and tabloid newspapers.

7 Conclusions

The approach to metaphor I have adopted in this book brings together the concerns and methodological strengths of different, but, in my view, complementary, research traditions, including particularly:

- Cognitive Metaphor Theory (CMT), and its concern for the relationship between conventional patterns of metaphorical expressions in language and conventional patterns of thought.
- Stylistics, and its concern for the relationship between linguistic choices and patterns on the one hand, and a variety of (primarily aesthetic) effects on the other.
- Critical Discourse Analysis, and its concern for the relationship between linguistic choices and patterns on the one hand and the maintenance and negotiation of power relationships and ideologies on the other.
- Corpus linguistics, and the tools it provides for investigating conventional patterns of language use.

I have combined the close analysis of the use of particular expressions in specific contexts (which is typical of both Stylistics and Critical Discourse Analysis) with a consideration of how individual uses relate to conventional metaphorical patterns (which is typical of CMT). I have also shown how such patterns can best be investigated via the exploitation of language corpora (for a similar approach to metaphor see also Charteris-Black 2004; Koller 2004b; Musolff 2004).

Overall, my discussion and analyses throughout this book have, I hope, demonstrated the following main points:

- A proper understanding of the phenomenon of metaphor in general requires both a consideration of its manifestations and functions in language, images, etc. and a consideration of its general role as a cognitive tool.
- A proper understanding of metaphor in discourse requires both a detailed analysis of specific uses within particular texts, genres and discourses, and a consideration of how specific uses relate to general metaphorical patterns and to potential underlying conceptual metaphors.
- Metaphor plays an important role in a wide variety of genres. Its main overarching function is to do with the representation or 'framing' of some aspect

of experience (including explanation, modelling, persuasion, etc.), but it can also have interpersonal functions (e.g. humour, emotional involvement) and textual functions (e.g. contributing to the internal coherence of a text, foregrounding its main points).

- While it can be argued that metaphor has different dominant functions in different genres (e.g. persuasion in political speeches, explanation in educational materials), metaphorical expressions are used for a variety of purposes within individual texts and genres. For example, in scientific articles metaphors are used for the purposes of persuasion and, occasionally, humour, as well as modelling and explanation.
- In many spheres of activity (e.g. education, medicine), people should ideally be able to view phenomena and experiences in terms of several different metaphors, so that they can opt for the metaphor that is most appropriate to them, or benefit from the different perspectives offered by different metaphors.
- An interplay between conventionality and creativity in the linguistic realization of metaphor is a characteristic of many different texts and genres, rather than being an exclusively or primarily literary phenomenon; I have shown, for example, how this applies not just to political speeches or advertising, but also to scientific writing, including both expert and non-expert genres.
- The forms and meanings of metaphorical expressions in authentic linguistic data cannot always be fully explained in terms of the broad cross-domain mappings considered in CMT, but often require explanations in terms of smaller, more specific mental representations that can be described as 'scenes' or 'scenarios' (see Grady 1997a, 1997b, 1998; Musolff 2004, 2006).
- In spite of the existence of a relatively small set of wide-scope metaphorical source domains (e.g. MOVEMENT/JOURNEYS and WAR), creative uses of metaphor may involve the exploitation of a much wider range of normally unused domains or scenarios, including invented, *ad hoc* scenarios. In some cases, the choice of source domain or scenario may be inspired by the topic of the text or by the situational context in which communication takes place.
- Corpora provide an invaluable resource for the investigation of metaphorical patterns in language and for the extrapolation of conceptual metaphors from linguistic evidence. In fact, their increasing availability and accessibility make it less and less acceptable to use artificially constructed examples in order to make claims about (metaphorical) language use.

In the rest of this chapter I first consider the implications of the previous chapters for the study of creativity in metaphor use, and then reflect on two related phenomena that have proved to be more frequent and relevant than I had initially anticipated: topic-triggered and situationally triggered metaphors.

7.1 Final reflections on metaphorical creativity

As I mentioned in chapter 2 (section 2.2), it is increasingly being recognized that creativity in language use is a widespread phenomenon, which has a variety of functions and manifestations in different genres and communicative contexts (Carter 2004; Carter and McCarthy 2004). My analyses in the course of this book have demonstrated that creativity in the use of metaphor in particular is also both widespread and multifunctional. I have shown, for example, how creative metaphors can be used in order to convey prototypically ineffable subjective experiences (e.g. the ANIMAL metaphor for migraine in section 2.1), support particular arguments (e.g. the TRAIN metaphor for the euro in section 3.4.1), and model complex phenomena in an accessible and vivid way (e.g. the OCTOPUS metaphor for neural networks in section 4.5).

I have also argued throughout the book that a proper account of creativity in metaphor use needs to consider both the linguistic and the conceptual levels of metaphor. In multi-modal texts, the non-verbal elements also need to be taken into account, as well as their interaction with the verbal elements (e.g. my analysis of the Lucozade advertisement in section 5.2.1). As readers, you may also have noticed, however, that I have used the term 'creative' or 'novel' for a wide range of metaphorical phenomena, that differ both in terms of degree and the kind of creativity that is involved.

The choice of a particular metaphorical expression in a particular context may be described as creative because the metaphorical meaning of that expression is not part of the conventional range of meanings normally included in dictionaries. This captures both metaphorical uses that are simply infrequent or rare, and uses that can be regarded as unique. In addition, I have described as potentially creative the establishment of salient patterns of metaphorical expressions within and across texts, involving repetition, recurrence, textual extension, intertextual references, and so on (see section 1.2.3). Following Lakoff and Turner (1989), I have also distinguished between creative metaphorical expressions that can be related to conventional conceptual metaphors, and metaphorical expressions that seem to realize unconventional or radically novel conceptual mappings.

What I wish to focus on here is the fact that many of the examples of metaphorical creativity I have discussed involve the creative exploitation of what are best described as different types of scenarios.

7.1.1 Metaphorical scenarios and creativity

As I have already mentioned, many of my analyses support some recent work in metaphor theory that explains conventional uses of metaphor with reference to source mental representations such as 'scenes' or 'scenarios', rather than solely in terms of broad conceptual domains. On the one hand, it can be useful to formulate conceptual metaphors in terms of sets of mappings between complex source domains, as in the case, for example, of LIFE IS A JOURNEY. This is particularly appropriate when investigating the way in which a particular target domain is conventionally constructed metaphorically, as in the case of my study of the COMMUNICATION target domain in section 6.4 above. On the other hand, however, the individual meanings and uses of particular expressions are often best explained with reference to smaller and more specific mental representations that relate to particular situations and the settings, entities, actions and goals associated with those situations. In his theory of 'primary metaphors' Grady (1997a) explains some important phenomena in metaphor use as the result of basic mappings involving what he calls 'primary scenes', which correspond to simple, basic sensorimotor experiences such as PHYSICAL CLOSENESS or ARRIVING AT A DESTINATION. In analysing media reports on the EU, Musolff (2004, 2006) considers richer and more complex source 'scenarios', such as BIRTHDAY CELEBRATIONS and TRAIN JOURNEY, and shows how they provide the appropriate kind of mental category to explain the rhetorical uses of metaphor in his data. Musolff also argues that scenarios provide story lines which can be exploited to project narrative structures onto the situations that function as targets. Both Grady and Musolff relate scenes and scenarios to larger conceptual domains and to more complex conceptual metaphors, albeit in different ways.[1]

My textual analyses in the course of this book suggest that the notion of scenario is also particularly useful in describing many creative uses of metaphor. Consider, for example, the following cases that were introduced in previous chapters: Bono's MOUNTAIN CLIMBING metaphor for the G8 summit in chapter 1 (section 1.1.1), McEwan's ANIMAL metaphor for migraine in chapter 2 (section 2.1), the TRAIN metaphor for the euro in chapter 3 (section 3.4.1), Kosslyn and Koenig's OCTOPUS metaphor for neural networks in chapter 4 (section 4.5), and the description of cancer treatment as attack and counterattack in chapter 5 (section 5.3). In all cases, the writer/speaker uses a combination of conventional and novel metaphorical expressions that creatively exploit very specific source scenarios, in order to provide a particular representation of the situation that functions as target. Similarly, in each case the source scenario provides a narrative line that is exploited to structure the target in terms of sequences of actions with a beginning, a middle and an end: for example, a migraine attack is presented in terms of a sequence of actions performed by an animal, and the future of Euroland is presented in terms of a journey that

[1] Grady's 'scenes' and Musolff's 'scenarios' are roughly comparable to the mental representations discussed in classic works in cognitive psychology, such as 'scripts' (Schank and Abelson 1977) and 'frames' (Minsky 1975; Goffmann 1975). The term 'scene' is also used by Schank (1982, 1999) and the term 'scenario' by Johnson-Laird and Garnham (1979).

potentially ends in derailment. In chapter 5, I also pointed out that the authors of scientific texts aimed at non-expert audiences make greater use of the narrative potential of source scenarios than the authors of texts aimed at specialist audiences (see sections 4.3 and 4.4).

There is also considerable variation, however, in the kinds of scenario that may be creatively exploited. Some of the examples I have just mentioned involve scenarios that are conventionally used metaphorically, and that may be related both to basic metaphors involving primary scenes or image schemata, and to more complex metaphors involving larger conceptual domains. This applies, for example, to Bono's MOUNTAIN CLIMBING scenario, which has its basis in the PATH image schema and can be seen as part of the general JOURNEY source domain. Similarly, the ATTACK and COUNTERATTACK scenarios evoked by the military description of cancer treatment in section 5.3 can be related to Grady's primary metaphor DIFFICULTIES ARE OPPONENTS (Grady 1997a), as well as to the wide-scope source domain of WAR. In such cases, creativity results from the use of novel metaphorical expressions and from the exploitation of aspects of the relevant scenario that are not conventionally used metaphorically, such as the notion of looking down at the valley in Bono's MOUNTAIN CLIMBING metaphor and the notion of barbed wire in the ATTACK metaphor for cancer treatment. Creativity may also result from the use of metaphorical expressions that combine different conventional scenarios. In extract 1.12 above (section 1.2.3), for example, the state of the UK Conservative Party is metaphorically described by combining an ILLNESS scenario with a BATTLE scenario. All these examples broadly support Lakoff and Turner's (1989) claim that novel metaphors may involve the creative exploitation of conventional metaphors, even though Lakoff and Turner do not explicitly consider the role of scenarios in this process.

In other cases, however, the choice of metaphorical scenario is either unrelated or loosely related to conventional conceptual metaphors, and specific scenarios may even be invented *ad hoc* for the purposes of particular metaphorical descriptions. Indeed, several of the examples I have discussed throughout the book involve fantastic, unrealistic or even impossible situations. In the case of McEwan's ANIMAL metaphor, the source scenario is, in a way, relatively familiar, since it involves a creature waking up, moving within an enclosed space, and finally leaving that space. However, the fact that this enclosed space corresponds to the head of a migraine sufferer lends an element of impossibility to the metaphorical description of the character's experience of pain. An unrealistic scenario is more clearly evoked by Kosslyn and Koenig's metaphor for neural networks, which involves a coven of octopi that join and wave their tentacles in order to signal the presence of fish to the birds flying above. In these two cases, creativity is much more radical than in the examples mentioned in the previous paragraph, both in linguistic and conceptual terms. The EURO

AS TRAIN metaphor discussed in 3.4.1 shares some of the characteristics of both the less striking and the more radical examples of creativity. On the one hand, the TRAIN source scenario can be related to conventional JOURNEY and MACHINE metaphors; on the other hand, however, it is rather improbable, since it involves a train where each car has a separate engine and engineer. As with the OCTOPUS metaphor, the source scenario is an imaginary situation that is invented in order to match the representation of the target that the writer wishes to convey.[2]

It is also important to point out that these examples of metaphorical creativity are not exclusive to literature, but are drawn from a variety of genres, including novels, newspaper articles, science textbooks and so on. As I have already mentioned, however, the functions of creative uses of metaphor can vary considerably depending on the genre, and there are also crucial differences in the extent to which writers constrain the interpretation of creative metaphors via explicit commentary. Unlike literary writers, for example, scientists tend to spell out in great detail how they intend their metaphors to be interpreted. This is particularly the case with new creative metaphors, which do not yet have conventional interpretations within the scientific community.

7.2 Final reflections on topic-triggered and situationally triggered metaphors

In the course of the book I have repeatedly discussed examples of metaphorical expressions where the choice of the source domain or scenario appears to be inspired by some aspect of the topic under discussion or of the communicative situation. Koller (2004a) has called the former kind of metaphor 'topic-triggered'; similarly, I have labelled the latter kind of case 'situationally triggered' metaphors (see sections 1.2.3 and 3.4.7). Kövecses (2005: 236–41) has also noted how the choice of metaphorical source domain may be influenced by the topic or by aspects of the communicative situation, as a result of what he calls 'pressure of coherence'. On the whole, however, these phenomena have so far received little attention. I will therefore provide an overview of their main manifestations and functions in the texts I have discussed in the course of this book.

Topic-triggered metaphors involve the use of some aspect of the topic under discussion as source domain or scenario. This applies, for example, when a newspaper headline includes a metaphorical expression whose basic meaning relates directly to the topic of the article itself. In 1.2.3 above, I mentioned an article on the breakdown of diplomatic relations between two African countries

[2] The creative process that underlies this kind of metaphor can be accounted for in terms of the merging of different mental representations, as in Fauconnier and Turner's (2002) blending theory.

over the control of part of the Sahara region, which was introduced by the headline 'Diplomatic desert'. The basic meaning of 'desert' applies literally to the topic of the article, but the noun is used metaphorically in the headline to suggest lack of diplomatic relationships. Similarly, the headline 'Visionary or fortune teller? Why scientists find diagnoses of "x-ray" girl hard to stomach' was used to introduce an article concerning a Russian teenager who was allegedly able to 'see' inside people's bodies and diagnose their illnesses (*Guardian Unlimited*, 25 September 2004). The expression 'hard to stomach' is conventionally used to describe something that is difficult to accept. However, the basic meaning of 'stomach' applies literally to the topic of the article, since the young woman in question was supposed to be able to see people's internal organs, including their stomachs. As I have pointed out before, this kind of topic-triggered metaphor involves the production of puns, and primarily has a humorous and attention-grabbing function, which is particularly appropriate in newspaper headlines.

In chapter 3, however, I suggested that topic-triggered metaphors may also be exploited in less obvious ways to reinforce and exploit existing associations between source and target domains (see section 3.4.7). This applied, for example, to Rudolph Giuliani's description of Saddam Hussein as 'a weapon of mass destruction' to justify the 2003 invasion of Iraq: Saddam's presumed possession of weapons of mass destruction had been the main official motivation for the war, but these weapons had not in fact been found. However, Giuliani emphasizes Saddam's past crimes, including the fact that he had *used* weapons of mass destruction. Hence, the use of the notion of weapon of mass destruction as source concept in the description of Saddam himself may be perceived as particularly apt by Giuliani's audience at the 2004 Republican Party conference, who may be persuaded that a metaphorical weapon could justify the war just as much as literal weapons would have done.

My other examples of topic-triggered metaphors in politics were much less noticeable, and involved more conventional metaphorical expressions. For example, the anti-asylum BNP leaflet I discussed in section 3.7 explicitly establishes a strong real-world connection between asylum seekers and terrorist attacks in Europe, and also consistently describes the effects of the arrival of asylum seekers in Britain via metaphorical references to bombs, explosions and physical destruction. In cases such as this, there is no punning or obvious word play between the literal and metaphorical meanings of the relevant expressions. However, the choice of topic-triggered metaphors may increase the rhetorical force of the text for particular audiences, as these metaphors rely on pre-existing, non-metaphorical and highly evaluative associations between source and target domains. This phenomenon has been noted in other studies of metaphors used in relation to immigrants, who tend to be (negatively) described metaphorically in terms of characteristics that are 'literally' associated with them by at least some section of the public. O'Brien (2003), for example, discusses the metaphors used in the immigration restriction debate in the USA at the beginning of the twentieth century, and makes the following point about the frequency of metaphorical expressions that present immigrants as germs or organisms that cause disease:

> Moreover, immigrants have always been rightly feared as carriers of disease, and thus the public was conditioned to think of them in such a way. The earliest immigration restriction policies were passed in response to the very real fear of the spread of disease from incoming foreigners . . . Once the connection between disease and immigrants was formed, it became linguistically easy to describe all immigrants as potentially diseased organisms who threatened the integrity of the nation. (O'Brien 2003: 36)

Similar considerations apply to what I have called 'situationally triggered metaphors', where the chosen of source domain or scenario is linked to some aspects of the relevant communicative situation. The Lucozade advertisement I discussed in chapter 5, for example, is meant to be viewed in service stations, and exploits the process of refuelling vehicles to describes the product: in other words, the concepts and scenario that function as metaphorical sources are an important part of the setting in which the advertisement is physically located. In the Barclays Bank advertising mailshot that I also described in chapter 5, it is the health conditions associated with a particular time of year that inspire the choice of metaphor. The mailshot was sent in early January, and was particularly aimed at people whose excessive eating, drinking and spending in the recent holiday period had negatively affected their health and finances. The loans offered by the bank are therefore metaphorically described as a health-promoting detoxification programme. In such cases, the choice of metaphor may be perceived as witty and humorous (rather like the headlines described above), but also strategically exploits real-world associations in order to present the consumption of the product as an essential and 'natural' part of, respectively, stopping at service stations and starting a 'new' life at the beginning of the year.

As with topic-triggered metaphors, the use of situationally triggered metaphors in political discourse has a predominantly persuasive function. In chapter 3 (section 3.4.7) I mentioned Silvio Berlusconi's frequent and creative use of football metaphors at the beginning of his political career in 1994, including the choice of name and flag of the political party he had created (*Forza Italia*). In this case, the choice of source domain is linked to the activities of the speaker himself, who was well known for his success as owner of the football club AC Milan. As mentioned in 3.4.7, Berlusconi explicitly suggested on several occasions that he could do for Italy what he had done for his football team, and that the citizens of Italy should follow the example of the AC Milan team (see also Semino and Masci 1996). In this case a situationally triggered metaphor very clearly functions as a rhetorical tool, particularly in the effort to legitimize Berlusconi as a capable and trustworthy politician.

The choice of topic-triggered or situationally triggered metaphors may not always be deliberate, however. Boers (1999), for example, considered the use of metaphorical expressions in a corpus of articles from *The Economist*, and noted that HEALTH metaphors were used more frequently during the cold winter months (in the northern hemisphere), i.e. at a time of year when the high frequency of viral infections makes people more aware of their bodies and their state of health. He concluded that, when a number of conventional metaphors are potentially available for the same target domain, 'a source domain is more likely to be used for metaphorical mapping as it becomes more salient in everyday experience' (Boers 1999: 55).

These examples suggest that topic-triggering and situational triggering in the use of metaphor may be more frequent than one would conclude from the scarcity of studies in this area. I would argue that these phenomena are relevant to metaphor scholars in two respects. On the one hand, they strongly indicate that the choice of metaphor may be influenced, among other things, by experiences that are currently salient and mental representations that are currently active, whether they relate to the topic under discussion, the speaker/writer, the time of year and so on. Secondly, many of my examples show that the choice of a source domain/scenario that is linked to the topic or the communicative situation may be a deliberate strategy aimed not just at entertaining, but also at persuading and influencing behaviour, especially in advertising and politics. As a consequence, these phenomena are worthy of further, more systematic investigation.

I should point out in conclusion that the texts I have discussed in detail throughout this book were selected for their intrinsic interest, and do not therefore cumulatively form a balanced and representative corpus of data. This means that my claims about the pervasiveness, distribution and frequency of particular phenomena (e.g. the use of creative metaphorical expressions, or of topic-triggered metaphors) can only be tentative, and require further and more systematic corpus-based investigations. Nonetheless, I hope to have shown that the study of discourse requires an understanding of the manifestations and functions of metaphor, and to have provided some guidance for readers who need to deal with the complexities of metaphor use in real data.

Glossary

Chains (of linguistic metaphors) – The occurrence of several related metaphorical expressions throughout a text. Chains normally result from a combination of repetition, recurrence and extension. *See also* entries for these terms.

Clusters (of linguistic metaphors) – The occurrence of several different metaphorical expressions drawing from different source domains in close proximity to one another.

Collocate – A word or expression that tends to co-occur with a particular word or expression, according to tests of statistical significance.

Combination (of metaphors) – The use of metaphorical expressions evoking different conceptual metaphors in close proximity to one another.

Conceptual domain – Knowledge about a particular area of experience, normally including rich and complex networks of elements and relations, such as our knowledge about war, life, journeys, illness and so on. Conceptual domains are a type of mental representation. *See also* Mental representation.

Conceptual mappings – Correspondences between elements of source and target domains in conceptual metaphors. For example, in the conceptual metaphor LIFE IS A JOURNEY, the person living their life corresponds to a traveller.

Conceptual metaphor – The cognitive phenomenon whereby one conceptual domain (the target domain) is understood in terms of another (the source domain). Conceptual metaphors involve mappings, or sets of correspondences, from source to target domain. They are usually expressed in terms of A IS B equivalences, such as LIFE IS A JOURNEY. *See also* Conceptual mappings.

Concordance – A list of instances of a particular linguistic expression extracted from a corpus, with part of the preceding and following co-text.

Conventional conceptual metaphor – A set of mappings across two different conceptual domains that explains a numbers of conventional linguistic metaphors in a particular language, and that can therefore be said to be part of the shared ways in which speakers of that language conceptualize the domain that functions as target. For example, the conceptual metaphor LIFE IS A JOURNEY can be described as conventional because it explains conventional linguistic metaphors such as 'I'm at a crossroads in my life' and 'I need a change of direction'. *See also* Conceptual metaphor.

Conventional linguistic metaphor – A linguistic metaphor can be described as conventional when it has one or more metaphorical meanings that occur frequently, so that they are normally included in dictionary entries alongside nonmetaphorical meanings. For example, the noun 'crossroads' is conventionally used metaphorically to refer to situations where one has to make a decision, and this meaning is normally included in dictionaries alongside the nonmetaphorical meaning of a place where two roads cross. Conventionality is a matter of degree. *See also* Linguistic metaphor.

Corpus – A large collection of machine-readable texts.

Creativity (in metaphor use) – *See* Novel linguistic metaphor and Novel conceptual metaphor.

Discourse (as a count noun, with 'discourses' as plural) – Ways of speaking or writing about particular topics (e.g. medical discourse) or in particular settings (e.g. classroom discourse), usually from particular perspectives.

Discourse (as a non-count noun, without plural) – Naturally occurring language use in authentic situations.

Discourse systematicity (of metaphors) – The conventional use of a set of related metaphorical expressions in a particular genre or discourse (see Cameron 1999).

Elaboration (of conceptual metaphors) – The unconventional use of some aspect of the source domain in the realization of a conventional conceptual metaphor, for example by specifying the characteristics of the source domain in an unusual way (see Lakoff and Turner 1989).

Etymological metaphors – Words that are metaphorical in origin, but that no longer exhibit a contrast between (conventional) metaphorical and nonmetaphorical meanings, since the original nonmetaphorical meanings have become obsolete or only existed in the language from which the word was borrowed.

Extension (of conceptual metaphors) – The exploitation of normally unused elements of the source domain in the realization of a conventional conceptual metaphor (see Lakoff and Turner 1989).

Extension (of linguistic metaphors) – The occurrence of several metaphorical expressions evoking the same source domain and describing the same target domain in close proximity to one another in a text.

Foregrounding – The phenomenon whereby some stretches of text are perceived to be particularly noticeable, salient, interesting and memorable, usually as a result of creative uses of language such as deviation and parallelism.

Genre – Any conventionalised use of language that is linked to a particular activity, such as newspaper articles, novels, print advertisements, lectures and informal conversations. An alternative term for 'genre' is 'text type'.

Global systematicity (of metaphors) – The conventional use of a set of related metaphorical expressions in a language generally, across different genres and discourses (see Cameron 1999).

Ideology – A system of beliefs and values consisting of the sets of mental representations shared by a particular group.

Image metaphor – A metaphor that involves the mapping of visual images.

Image schema – A basic and skeletal mental representation of recurring aspects of experience, such as PATH and CONTAINER.

Key word – A word or expression that is more frequent in a particular dataset as compared with a reference corpus according to tests of statistical significance.

Linguistic metaphor – A linguistic expression that, in context, is used to mean something that contrasts with (one of) its more basic meaning(s). This applies, for example, to the use of the expression 'battle' in the phrase 'her battle against cancer'. Here the contextual meaning of 'battle' (someone's brave attempt to recover from or cope with cancer) contrasts with the basic meaning (a physical fight involving weapons). The contextual and basic meanings of a metaphorical expression belong to different conceptual domains, and the contextual meaning can be understood in terms of the basic meaning. In the case of the expression above, a difficult enterprise is understood in terms of a physical fight.

Locally systematicity (of metaphors) – The use of a set of related metaphorical expressions in a particular text (see Cameron 1999).

Mental representation – An organised packet of information about a particular aspect of experience, involving knowledge about entities, actions, situations, relationships, goals, and so on. Mental representations vary in their degree of basicness, complexity, generality and so on. A variety of terms have been used to capture different types of mental representations, such as 'schema', 'frame', 'script', 'mental space', 'domain', 'image schema', 'scene' and 'scenario'.

Metaphor – The phenomenon whereby we talk and think about one thing in terms of another, as when a difficult enterprise is described as a 'battle'. *See also* Conceptual metaphor and Linguistic metaphor.

Metaphor key – A metaphorical expression that is found to be particularly frequent and important in a particular dataset (see Charteris-Black 2004).

Metaphorical expression – *See* Linguistic metaphor.

Metonymy – The phenomenon whereby we refer to one thing in terms of something else that is closely associated (or contiguous) with it, as when the expression 'The White House' is used to refer to the US President and administration.

Novel conceptual metaphor – A set of mappings across two different conceptual domains that is not linguistically realized by conventional metaphorical expressions, and that can therefore be said to provide a new perspective on the domain that functions as target. An example is the metaphorical conceptualization of the target domain of CONSCIOUSNESS in terms of the source domain of FAME (see section 5.1).

Novel linguistic metaphor – A linguistic metaphor can be described as novel when its metaphorical meaning is not one of the meanings that are normally associated with that expression and included in dictionary entries. For example, Sylvia Plath's use of the nouns 'loaf' and 'prawn' to refer metaphorically to a foetus (in the poem 'You're') can be described as novel, since these nouns are not normally used metaphorically in this way. Like conventionality, novelty is a matter of degree. In particular, novel linguistic metaphors differ depending on whether they can be related to conventional conceptual metaphors or rather realize novel mappings.

Personification – A type of metaphor whereby non-human entities are constructed in terms of the characteristics and activities of human beings.

Primary metaphor – A simple, basic metaphorical mapping that involves a primary scene, has a strong basis in experience, and explains metaphorical expressions that can be applied to many different domains of experience (see Grady 1997a). For example, the primary metaphor ASSISTANCE IS SUPPORT is based on the physical correlation between physical support and the continued functionality of entities, and motivates metaphorical expressions that apply to a variety of target domains, such as 'financial support', 'emotional support' and so on.

Primary scene – A mental representation that captures a recurring and basic type of experience, such as moving forward or being physically close to someone (see Grady 1997a).

Questioning (of conceptual metaphors) – Commenting explicitly on the limitations of conventional conceptual metaphors.

Recurrence (of linguistic metaphors) – The occurrence of two or more metaphorical expressions drawing from the same source domain at different points in a text.

Repetition (of linguistic metaphors) – The occurrence of two or more instances of the same metaphorical expression in a text.

Scenario – Knowledge about a particular type of situation, including a setting, entities, participants, goals and actions, such as our knowledge of travelling on a train or being at a party. Scenarios are a type of mental representation (*see also* Mental representation).

Signalling (of metaphor) – The use of expressions that potentially suggest the presence of metaphorical expressions in the co-text, such as 'sort of', 'as it were', 'metaphorically speaking'. These expressions are also known as 'tuning devices'.

Simile – The explicit linguistic formulation of a comparison between two unlike entities, usually signalled by expressions such as 'like' or 'as if', as in 'Marriage is like a prison'.

Situationally triggered metaphor – A metaphor where the source domain is closely related to the situation in which the text is produced and/or interpreted.

Source domain – A conceptual domain that is used to think and talk metaphorically about another conceptual domain. In the conceptual metaphor LIFE IS A JOURNEY, JOURNEY is the source domain. Other types of mental representations, such as scenes and scenarios, can also function as sources in conceptual metaphors.

Target domain – A conceptual domain that is metaphorically thought and talked about in terms of another conceptual domain. In the conceptual metaphor LIFE IS A JOURNEY, LIFE is the target domain. Other types of mental representations, such as scenes and scenarios, can also function as targets in conceptual metaphors.

Text – Any individual and relatively self-contained instance of language use, whether written or spoken (e.g. a newspaper article, a lecture).

Topic-triggered metaphor – A metaphor where the source domain is closely related to the topic of the text.

References

Abrams, M. H., Donaldson, E. T., Smith, H., *et al.* (1979). *The Norton Anthology of English Literature*. New York: W. W. Norton & Co.

Allbritton, D. W. (1995). When metaphors function as schemas: some cognitive effects of conceptual metaphors. *Metaphor and Symbolic Activity,* 10 (1), 33–46.

Allen, G. (2000). *Intertextuality*. London: Routledge.

Avise, J. C. (2001). Evolving genomic metaphors: a new look at the language of DNA. *Science,* 294 (5540), 86–7.

Baars, B. J. (1988). *A Cognitive Theory of Consciousness*. Cambridge: Cambridge University Press.

Baker, P. and McEnery, T. (2005). A corpus-based approach to discourses of refugees and asylum seekers in UN and newspaper texts. *Journal of Language and Politics*, 4 (2), 197–226.

Balbus, I. (1975). Politics as sport: the political ascendancy of the sports metaphor in America. *Monthly Review*, 26 (10), 26–39.

Barcelona, A. (1995). Metaphorical models of romantic love in *Romeo and Juliet*. *Journal of Pragmatics*, 24 (6), 667–88.

Barthes, R. (1981). *Image, Music, Text*. Glasgow: Fontana Press.

Belkaid, Y. and Rouse, B. T. (2005). Natural regulatory T cells in infectious disease. *Nature Immunology*, 6 (4), 353–60.

Biber, D., Conrad, S. and Reppen, R. (1998). *Corpus Linguistics: Investigating Language Structure and Use*. Cambridge: Cambridge University Press.

Black, M. (1962). *Models and Metaphors: Structure in Language and Philosophy*. Ithaca, N.Y.: Cornell University Press.

(1993). More about metaphor. In A. Ortony (ed.), *Metaphor and Thought*, pp. 19–41. Cambridge: Cambridge University Press.

Boers, F. (1999). When a bodily source domain becomes prominent: the joy of counting metaphors in the socio-economic domain. In R. W. Gibbs, Jr. and G. J. Steen (eds.), *Metaphor in Cognitive Linguistics*, pp. 47–56. Amsterdam: John Benjamins.

Boyd, R. (1993). Metaphor and theory change: What is 'metaphor' a metaphor for? In A. Ortony (ed.), *Metaphor and Thought*, pp. 481–532. Cambridge: Cambridge University Press.

Bradley, M. and Sunley, C. (2005). *GCSE Physics Revision Guide*. London.

Brown, P. and Levinson, S. C. (1987). *Politeness: Some Universals in Language Usage*. Cambridge: Cambridge University Press.

Brown, T. L. (2003). *Making Truth: Metaphor in Science*. Urbana, Ill.: University of Illinois Press.

Cameron, L. (1999). Operationalising 'metaphor' for applied linguistic research. In L. Cameron and G. Low (eds.), *Researching and Applying Metaphor*, pp. 3–28. Cambridge: Cambridge University Press.

(2003). *Metaphor in Educational Discourse*. London: Continuum.

Cameron, L. and Deignan, A. (2003). Combining large and small corpora to investigate tuning devices around metaphor in spoken discourse. *Metaphor and Symbol*, 18 (3), 149–60.

Cameron, L. and Low, G. (2004). Figurative variation in episodes of educational talk and text. *European Journal of English Studies*, 8 (3), 355–73.

Cameron, L. and Stelma, J. H. (2004). Metaphor clusters in discourse. *Journal of Applied Linguistics*, 1 (2), 107–36.

Canter, D. (1988). How do we know that it works? Therapeutic outcome as negotiation. *Complementary Medical Research*, 2 (3), 98–106.

Capra, F. (1996). *The Web of Life: A New Synthesis of Mind and Matter*. New York: Anchor Books.

Carter, R. (2004). *Language and Creativity: The Art of Common Talk*. London: Routledge.

Carter, R. and McCarthy, M. (2004). Talking, creating: interactional language, creativity, and context. *Applied Linguistics*, 25 (1), 62–88.

Carter, R. and Nash, W. (1990). *Seeing through Language: A Guide to Styles of English Writing*. Oxford: Basil Blackwell.

Chabot, C. N. (1999). *Understanding the Euro: The Clear and Concise Guide to the New Trans-European Economy*. New York: McGraw-Hill.

Chantrill, P. A. and Mio, J. S. (1996). Metonymy in political discourse. In J. S. Mio and A. N. Katz (eds.), *Metaphor: Implications and Applications*, pp. 171–84. Mahwah, N. J.: Lawrence Erlbaum Associates.

Charteris-Black, J. (2003). Speaking with forked tongue: A comparative study of metaphor and metonymy in English and Malay phraseology. *Metaphor and Symbol*, 14 (4), 289–310.

(2004). *Corpus Approaches to Critical Metaphor Analysis*. Basingstoke: Palgrave Macmillan.

(2005). *Politicians and Rhetoric: The Persuasive Power of Metaphor*. Basingstoke: Palgrave Macmillan.

Chew, M. K. and Laubichler, M. D. (2003). Natural enemies – metaphor or misconception? *Science*, 301 (5629), 52–3.

Chiappe, D., Kennedy, J. M. and Smykowski, T. (2003). Reversibility, aptness, and the conventionality of metaphors and similes. *Metaphor and Symbol*, 18(2), 85–105.

Childs, P. (1999). *The Twentieth Century in Poetry: A Critical Survey*. London: Routledge.

Chilton, P. (1985). *Language and the Nuclear Arms Debate: Nukespeak Today*. London: Pinter.

(1996). *Security Metaphors: Cold War Discourse from Containment to Common House*. New York: Peter Lang.

(2004). *Analysing Political Discourse: Theory and Practice*. London: Routledge.

Chilton, P. and Schäffner, C. (2002). Introduction: themes and principles in the analysis of political discourse. In P. Chilton and C. Schäffner (eds.), *Politics as Talk and Text: Analytic Approaches to Political Discourse*, pp. 1–41. Amsterdam: John Benjamins.

Ching, M. K. L. (1993). Games and play: pervasive metaphors in American life. *Metaphor and Symbolic Activity*, 8 (1), 43–65.

Combs, G. and Freedman, J. (1990). *Symbol, Story, and Ceremony: Using Metaphor in Individual and Family Therapy*. New York and London: Norton.

Conquest, R. (1962). *New Lines*. London: Macmillan.

Cook, G. (1994). *Discourse and Literature: The Interplay of Form and Mind*. Oxford: Oxford University Press.

(2001). *The Discourse of Advertising*. London: Routledge.

Cooper, L. (2005). *Aristotle on the Art of Poetry*. Whitefish, Mont.: Kessinger Publishing.

Corts, D. P. and Pollio, H. R. (1999). Spontaneous production of figurative language and gesture in college lectures. *Metaphor and Symbol*, 14 (2), 81–100.

Crisp, P. (1996). Imagism's metaphors: a test case. *Language and Literature*, 5 (2), 79–92.

(2001). Allegory: conceptual metaphor in history. *Language and Literature*, 10 (1), 5–19.

(2003). Conceptual metaphor and its expressions. In J. Gavins and S. Gerard (eds.), *Cognitive Poetics in Practice*, pp. 99–113. London: Routledge.

Croft, W. and Cruse, D. A. (2004). *Cognitive linguistics*. Cambridge: Cambridge University Press.

Czechmeister, C. A. (1994). Metaphor in illness and nursing: a two-edged sword. *Journal of Advanced Nursing*, 19, 1226–33.

Darian, S. (2000). The role of figurative language in introductory science texts. *International Journal of Applied Linguistics*, 10 (2), 163–86.

(2003). *Understanding the Language of Science*. Austin, Tex.: University of Texas Press.

De Souza, L. H. and Frank, A. O. (2000). Subjective pain experience of people with chronic back pain. *Physiotherapy Research International*, 5 (4), 207–19.

Deane, P. D. (1995). Metaphors of centre and periphery in Yeats' *The Second Coming*. *Journal of Pragmatics*. 24 (6), 627–42.

Deignan, A. (1995). *Collins Cobuild Guides to English 7: Metaphor.* London: Harper Collins.

(1999). Corpus-based research into metaphor. In L. Cameron and G. Low (eds.), *Researching and Applying Metaphor*, pp. 177–99. Cambridge: Cambridge University Press.

(2000). Persuasive uses of metaphor in discourse about business and the economy. In C. Heffer and H. Sauntson (eds.), *Words in Context: A Tribute to John Sinclair on His Retirement*, pp. 156–68. Birmingham: English Language Research Discourse Analysis Monographs.

(2003). Metaphorical expressions and culture: an indirect link. *Metaphor and Symbol*, 18 (4), 255–71.

(2005). *Metaphor and Corpus Linguistics*. Amsterdam: John Benjamins.

(forthcoming). Linguistic data and conceptual metaphor theory. In M. Cavalcanti, M. Zanotto and L. Cameron (eds.), *Confronting Metaphor in Applied Linguistics*. Amsterdam: John Benjamins.

Deignan, A. and Potter, L. (2004). A corpus study of metaphors and metonyms in English and Italian. *Journal of Pragmatics*, 36 (7), 1231–52.

Dennett, D. (2001). Are we explaining consciousness yet? *Cognition*, 79 (1–2), 221–37.

Dickens, C. (1994). *Hard Times*. London: Penguin.

Dirven, R., Frank, R. M. and Pütz, M. (2003). *Cognitive Models in Language and Thought*. Hawthorne, N. Y.: Mouton de Gruyter.

Drew, P. and Holt, E. (1998). Figures of speech: figurative expressions and the management of topic transition in conversation. *Language in Society*, 27 (4), 495–522.

El Refaie, E. (2001). Metaphors we discriminate by: naturalized themes in Austrian newspaper articles about asylum seekers. *Journal of Sociolinguistics*, 5 (3), 352–71.

Emmott, C. (2002). 'Split selves' in fiction and in medical life stories: cognitive linguistic theory and narrative practice. In E. Semino and J. Culpeper (eds.), *Cognitive Stylistics: Language and Cognition in Text Analysis*, pp. 153–81. Amsterdam: John Benjamins.

Encyclopaedia Britannica (1999). CD-ROM. Chicago, Ill.: Encyclopaedia Britannica Inc.

Eubanks, P. (2000). *A War of Words in the Discourse of Trade: The Rhetorical Constitution of Metaphor*. Carbondale: Southern Illinois University Press.

Eysenck, M. W. and Keane, M. T. (2000). *Cognitive Psychology: A Student's Handbook*. Hove: Psychology Press.

Fairclough, N. (1992). *Discourse and Social Change*. Cambridge: Polity Press.

Fauconnier, G. and Turner, M. (2002). *The Way We Think: Conceptual Blending and the Mind's Hidden Complexities*. New York: Basic Books.

Fontenot, J. D. and Rudensky, A. Y. (2005). A well adapted regulatory contrivance: regulatory T cell development and the forkhead family transcription factor Foxp3. *Nature Immunology*, 6 (4), 331–7.

Forceville, C. (1996). *Pictorial Metaphor in Advertising*. London: Routledge.

Forster, E. M. (1924). *A Passage to India*. London: Edward Arnold.

Freeman, D. C. (1993). 'According to my bond': King Lear and re-cognition. *Language and Literature*, 2 (1), 1–18.

(1995). 'Catch[ing] the nearest way': Macbeth and cognitive metaphor. *Journal of Pragmatics*, 24 (6), 689–708.

(1999). 'The rack dislimns': schema and metaphorical pattern in Anthony and Cleopatra. *Poetics Today*, 20 (3), 443–60.

Freeman, M. H. (1995). Metaphor making meaning: Emily Dickinson's conceptual universe. *Journal of Pragmatics*, 24 (6), 643–66.

(2000). Poetry and the scope of metaphor: toward a cognitive theory of literature. In A. Barcelona Sánchez (ed.), *Metaphor and Metonymy at the Crossroads: A Cognitive Perspective*, pp. 253–81. Berlin: Mouton de Gruyter.

Gems, D. and McElwee, J. J. (2005). Broad spectrum detoxification: the major longevity assurance process regulated by insulin/IGF-1 signaling? *Mechanisms of Ageing and Development*, 126 (3), 381–7.

Gentner, D. and Bowdle, B. F. (2005). The career of metaphor. *Psychological Review*, 112 (1), 193–216.

Gentner, D. and Gentner, D. R. (1983). Flowing waters or teeming crowds: mental models of electricity. In D. Gentner and A. L. Stevens (eds.), *Mental Models*, pp. 447–80. Hillsdale, N. J.: Elrbaum.

Gentner, D. and Grudin, J. (1985). The evolution of mental metaphors in psychology: a 90-year retrospective. *American Psychologist*, 40 (2), 181.

Gentner, D. and Jeziorski, M. (1993). The shift from metaphor to analogy in Western science. In A. Ortony (ed.), *Metaphor and Thought*, pp. 447–80. Cambridge: Cambridge University Press.

Gibbs, R. W. Jr. (1994). *The Poetics of Mind: Figurative Thought, Language, and Understanding*. Cambridge: Cambridge University Press.

Giora, R. (2003). *On Our Mind: Salience, Context, and Figurative Language*. Oxford: Oxford University Press.

Glucksberg, S. (2001). *Understanding Figurative Language: From Metaphors to Idioms*. Oxford: Oxford University Press.

Goatly, A. (1997). *The Language of Metaphors*. London: Routledge.

(2002). Conflicting metaphors in the Hong Kong special administrative region educational reform proposals. *Metaphor and Symbol*, 17 (4), 263–94.

(2007). *Washing the Brain: Metaphor and Hidden Ideology*. Amsterdam: John Benjamins.

Goddard, A. (1998). *The Language of Advertising*. London: Routledge.

Goffmann, E. (1975). *Frame Analysis: An Essay on the Organization of Experience*. Harmondsworth: Penguin.

Goossens, L., Pauwels, P., Rudzka-Ostyn, B., Simon-Vandenbergen, A.-M. and Vanparys, J. (1995). *By Word of Mouth: Metaphor, Metonymy and Linguistic Action in a Cognitive Perspective.* Amsterdam: John Benjamins.

Grady, J. (1997a). Foundations of meaning: primary metaphors and primary scenes. Unpublished PhD thesis. Berkeley: University of California.

(1997b). THEORIES ARE BUILDINGS revisited. *Cognitive Linguistics*, 8 (4), 267–90.

(1998). The ‘Conduit’ metaphor revisited: a reassessment of metaphors for communication. In J.-P. Koenig (ed.), *Discourse and Cognition: Bridging the Gap*, pp. 205–18. Stanford, Calif.: CSLI Publications.

(1999). A typology of motivation for conceptual metaphor: correlation vs. resemblance. In R. W. Gibbs Jr. and G. Steen (eds.), *Metaphor in Cognitive Linguistics*, pp. 79–100. Amsterdam: John Benjamins.

Green, T. F. (1993). Learning without metaphor. In A. Ortony (ed.), *Metaphor and Thought*, pp. 610–20. Cambridge: Cambridge University Press.

Greer, S. (1991). Psychological response to cancer and survival. *Psychological Medicine*, 21 (11), 43–9.

Halliday, M. A. K. (1978). *Language as Social Semiotic: The Social Interpretation of Language and Meaning*. London: Edward Arnold.

(2004). *The Language of Science*. London: Continuum.

Halliday, M. A. K. and Hasan, R. (1985). *Language, Context, and Text: Aspects of Language in a Social-semiotic Perspective*. Victoria: Deakin University.

Hamilton, C. (1996). Mapping the mind and the body: on W. H. Auden’s personifications. *Style*, 36, 408–27.

(2003). Genetic roulette: on the cognitive rhetoric of biorisk. In R. Dirven, F. Roslyn and M. Pütz (eds.), *Cognitive Models in Language and Thought*, pp. 353–93. Berlin: Mouton de Gruyter.

Hardie, A., Koller, V., Rayson, P. and Semino, E. (2007). Exploiting a semantic annotation tool for metaphor analysis. *Proceedings of Corpus Linguistics 2007*, University of Birmingham.

Harris, J. (1999). *Chocolat*. London: Doubleday.

Heywood, J. and Semino, E. (2007). Metaphors for speaking and writing in the British press. In S. Johnson and A. Esslin (eds.), *Language in the Media: Representations, Identities, Ideologies*, pp. 25–47. London: Continuum.

Hiraga, M. (1999). 'Blending' and an interpretation of haiku: a cognitive approach. *Poetics Today,* 20, 461–82.

(2005). *Metaphor and Iconicity: A Cognitive Approach to Analysing Texts*. Basingstoke: Palgrave Macmillan.

Hobbes, T. (1651). *Leviathan, or, The Matter, Forme & Power of a Common-Wealth Ecclesiasticall and Civill.* London: Andrew Crooke.

Hoffman, R. R., Cochran, E. L. and Nead, J. M. (1990). Cognitive metaphors in experimental psychology. In D. E. Leary (ed.), *Metaphors in the History of Psychology*, pp. 173–229. Cambridge: Cambridge University Press.

Howe, N. (1988). Metaphor in contemporary American political discourse. *Metaphor and Symbolic Activity,* 3 (2), 87–104.

Jäkel, O. (1999). Kant, Blumenberg, Weinrich: some forgotten contributions to the Cognitive Theory of Metaphor. In R. W. Gibbs Jr. and G. J. Steen (eds.), *Metaphor in Cognitive Linguistics*, pp. 9–27. Amsterdam: John Benjamins.

Jakobson, R. (1956). Two aspects of language and two types of aphasic disturbances. In R. Jakobson and M. Halle (eds.), *Fundamentals of Language,* pp. 53–82. The Hague: Mouton.

(1960). Closing statement: linguistics and poetics. In T. A. Sebeok (ed.), *Style and Language*, pp. 350–77. Cambridge, Mass.: Massachussetts Institute of Technology Press.

Jansen, S. C. and Sabo, D. (1994). The sport/war metaphor: hegemonic masculinity, the Persian Gulf war and the New World Order. *Sociology of Sports Journal*, 11, 1–17.

Jennings, E. (1979). *Selected Poems.* Manchester: Carcanet.

Johnson, M. (1987). *The Body in the Mind: The Bodily Basis of Meaning, Imagination, and Reason.* Chicago: University of Chicago Press.

Johnson-Laird, P. N. and Garnham, A. (1979). Descriptions and discourse models. *Linguistics and Philosophy,* 3, 371–93.

Kangas, I. (2001). Making sense of depression: perceptions of melancholia in lay narratives. *Health,* 5 (1), 76–92.

Keller, E. F. (1995). *Refiguring Life: Metaphors of Twentieth-century Biology.* New York: Columbia University Press.

Kesey, K. (1973). *One Flew Over the Cuckoo's Nest.* London: Picador.

Kittay, E. F. (1987). *Metaphor: Its Cognitive Force and Linguistic Structure.* Oxford: Clarendon.

Knowles, M. and Moon, R. (2006). *Introducing Metaphor.* London: Routledge.

Knudsen, S. (2003). Scientific metaphors going public. *Journal of Pragmatics,* 35 (8), 1247–63.

Koller, V. (2002). 'A shotgun wedding': co-occurrence of war and marriage metaphors in mergers and acquisitions discourse. *Metaphor and Symbol,* 17 (3), 179–203.

(2003). Metaphor clusters, metaphor chains: analysing the multifunctionality of metaphor in text. *Metaphorik.de,* 5, 115–34.

(2004a). Businesswomen and war metaphors: 'possessive, jealous and pugnacious?' *Journal of Sociolinguistics,* 8 (1), 3–22.

(2004b). *Metaphor and Gender in Business Media Discourse: A Critical Cognitive Study.* Basingstoke: Palgrave Macmillan.

Kosslyn, S. M. and Koenig, O. (1992). *Wet Mind: The New Cognitive Neuroscience.* New York: Free Press.

Kövecses, Z. (2000). *Metaphor and Emotion: Language, Culture, and Body in Human Feeling.* Cambridge: Cambridge University Press.

(2002). *Metaphor: A Practical Introduction.* Oxford: Oxford University Press.

(2005). *Metaphor in Culture: Universality and Variation.* Cambridge: Cambridge University Press.

Kress, G. R. and van Leeuwen, T. (2006). *Reading Images: The Grammar of Visual Design.* London: Routledge.

Lakoff, G. (1987). *Women, Fire, and Dangerous Things: What Categories Reveal about the Mind.* Chicago: University of Chicago Press.

(1991). Metaphor and war: the metaphor system used to justify war in the Gulf. *Journal of Urban and Cultural Studies,* 2 (1), 59–72.

(1993). The contemporary theory of metaphor. In A. Ortony (ed.), *Metaphor and Thought*, pp. 202–51. Cambridge and New York: Cambridge University Press.

(1996). Sorry, I'm not myself today: the metaphor system for conceptualizing the self. In G. Fauconnier and E. Sweetser (eds.), *Spaces, Worlds and Grammar*, pp. 91–123. Chicago: University of Chicago Press.

(2001). September 11, 2001. *Metaphorik.de.* www.metaphorik.de/aufsaetze/lakoff-september11.htm

Lakoff, G. and Johnson, M. (1980a). The metaphorical structure of the human conceptual system. *Cognitive Science*, 4, 195–208.

(1980b). *Metaphors We Live By.* Chicago: University of Chicago Press.

(1999). *Philosophy in the Flesh: The Embodied Mind and its Challenge to Western Thought.* New York: Basic Books.

(2003). *Metaphors We Live By.* Second edition. Chicago: University of Chicago Press.

Lakoff, G. and Turner, M. (1989). *More than Cool Reason: A Field Guide to Poetic Metaphor.* Chicago: University of Chicago Press.

Lascaratou, C. (2007). *The Language of Pain: Expression or Description.* Amsterdam: John Benjamins.

Leary, D. E. (1990a). *Metaphors in the History of Psychology.* Cambridge: Cambridge University Press.

(1990b). Psyche's muse: the role of metaphor in the history of psychology. In D. E. Leary (ed.), *Metaphors in the History of Psychology*, pp. 1–78. Cambridge: Cambridge University Press.

Leech, G. N. (1966). *English in Advertising: A Linguistic Study of Advertising in Great Britain.* London: Longman.

(1969). *A Linguistic Guide to English Poetry*. London: Longman.

Lindop, G. (2001). Elizabeth Jennings. *The Guardian Newspaper*, 31 October 2001.

Lipsky, R. (1981). *How We Play the Game: Why Sports Dominate American Life.* Boston, Mass.: Beacon Press.

Littlemore, J. and Low, G. (2006). *Figurative Thinking and Foreign Language Learning.* Basingstoke: Palgrave Macmillan.

Lodge, D. (1977). *The Modes of Modern Writing: Metaphor, Metonymy, and the Typology of Modern Literature.* London: Edward Arnold.

(2001). *Thinks.* London: Secker & Warburg.

(2002). *Consciousness and the Novel.* London: Secker & Warburg.

Low, G. (2003). Validating metaphoric models in applied linguistics. *Metaphor and Symbol,* 18 (4), 239–54.

(2005). Explaining evolution: the use of animacy in an example of semi-formal science writing. *Language and Literature,* 14 (2), 129–48.

MacCormac, E. R. (1985). *A Cognitive Theory of Metaphor.* Cambridge, Mass.: Massachusetts Institute of Technology Press.

Macmillan English Dictionary for Advanced Learners (2002). London: Macmillan.

Mahon, J. E. (1999). Getting your sources right: what Aristotle didn't say. In L. Cameron and G. Low (eds.), *Researching and Applying Metaphor,* pp. 69–80. Cambridge: Cambridge University Press.

Margolin, U. (2003). Cognitive science, the thinking mind, and literary narrative. In D. Herman (ed.), *Narrative Theory and the Cognitive Sciences*, pp. 27–94. Stanford: CSLI Publications.

Mason, Z. (2004). CorMet: a computational, corpus-based conventional metaphor extraction system. *Computational Linguistics,* 30 (1), 23–44.

Mayer, R. E. (1993). The instructive metaphor: metaphoric aids to students' understanding of science. In A. Ortony (ed.), *Metaphor and Thought*, pp. 561–78. Cambridge: Cambridge University Press.

McArthur, F. (2005). The competent horseman in a horseless world: observations on a conventional metaphor in Spanish and English. *Metaphor and Symbol,* 20 (1), 71–94.

McCarthy, J. (1959). *Symposium on the Mechanization of Thought Processes*. London: HMSO.

McEnery, T. and Wilson, A. (2001). *Corpus Linguistics: An Introduction.* Edinburgh: Edinburgh University Press.

McEwan, I. (2001). *Atonement.* London: Jonathan Cape.

McMullen, L. M. and Conway, J. B. (2002). Conventional metaphors for depression. In S. R. Fussell (ed.), *The Verbal Communication of Emotions: Interdisciplinary Perspectives,* pp. 167–81. Mahwah, N. J.: Lawrence Erlbaum Associates.

Miller, D. B. (1988). The nature–nurture issue: Lessons from the Pillsbury Doughboy. *Teaching of Psychology,* 15 (3), 147.

Minsky, M. (1975). A framework for representing knowledge. In P. E. Winston (ed.), *The Psychology of Computer Vision*, pp. 211–77. New York: McGraw-Hill.

Mio, J. S. (1996). Metaphor, politics and persuasion. In J. S. Mio and A. N. Katz (eds.), *Metaphor: Implications and Applications,* pp. 127–46. Mahwah, N. J.: Lawrence Erlbaum Associates.

(1997). Metaphor and politics. *Metaphor and Symbol,* 12 (2), 113–33.

Mithen, S. J. (1998). *Creativity in Human Evolution and Prehistory.* London and New York: Routledge.

Moon, R. (1998). *Fixed Expressions and Idioms in English: A Corpus-based Approach.* Oxford: Clarendon Press.

Mukařovský, J. (1970). Standard language and poetic language. In D. C. Freeman (ed.), *Linguistics and Literary Style,* pp. 40–56. New York: Holt, Rinehart and Winston.

Musolff, A. (2004). *Metaphor and Political Discourse: Analogical Reasoning in Debates about Europe*. Basingstoke: Palgrave Macmillan.

(2006). Metaphor scenarios in public discourse. *Metaphor and Symbol,* 21 (1), 23–38.
Myers, G. (1990). *Writing Biology: Texts in the Social Construction of Scientific Knowledge*. Madison, Wis.: University of Wisconsin Press.
(1994). *Words in Ads.* London: Arnold.
Nelkin, D. (2001). Molecular metaphors: the gene in popular discourse. *Nature Review Genetics,* 2 (7), 555–9.
Nerlich, B. and Clarke, D. (2000). Clones and crops: the use of stock characters and word play in two debates about bioengineering. *Metaphor and Symbol,* 15 (4), 223–39.
Nerlich, B. and Dingwall, R. (2003). Deciphering the human genome: the semantic and ideological foundations of genetic and genomic discourse. In R. Dirven, F. Roslyn and M. Pütz (eds.), *Cognitive Models in Language and Thought,* pp. 395–427. Berlin: Mouton de Gruyter.
Nerlich, B. and Halliday, C. (2007). Avian flu: the creation of expectations in the interplay between science and the media. *Sociology of Health and Illness*, 29 (1), 46–65.
Nerlich, B., Dingwall, R. and Clarke, D. (2002). The book of life: how the completion of the Human Genome Project was revealed to the public. *Health: An Interdisciplinary Journal for the Social Study of Health, Illness and Medicine,* 6 (4), 1363–93.
Nowottny, W. (1962). *The Language Poets Use.* London: Athlone Press.
O'Brien, G. V. (2003). Indigestible food, conquering hordes, and waste materials: metaphors of immigrants and the early immigration restriction debate in the United States. *Metaphor and Symbol,* 18 (1), 33–47.
Ortony, A. (1993). The role of similarity in simile and metaphor. In A. Ortony (ed.), *Metaphor and Thought,* pp. 342–56. Cambridge: Cambridge University Press.
Parker, S. (1987). *The Body and How it Works.* London: Dorling Kindersley.
Petrie, H. G. and Ortony, A. (1993). Metaphor and learning. In A. Ortony (ed.), *Metaphor and Thought*, pp. 579–609. Cambridge: Cambridge University Press.
Plath, S. (1965). *Ariel.* London: Faber and Faber.
Popova, Y. (2002). The Figure in the Carpet: discovery or re-cognition. In E. Semino and J. Culpeper (eds.), *Cognitive Stylistics: Language and Cognition in Text Analysis,* pp. 49–71. Amsterdam: John Benjamins.
Pragglejaz Group (2007). MIP: A method for identifying metaphorically used words in discourse. *Metaphor and Symbol,* 22 (1), 1–39.
Reddy, M. J. (1993). The conduit metaphor: a case of frame conflict in our language about language. In A. Ortony (ed.), *Metaphor and Thought,* pp. 164–201. Cambridge: Cambridge University Press.
Reisfield, G. M. (2004). Use of metaphor in the discourse on cancer. *Journal of Clinical Ontology,* 22 (19), 4024–7.
Richards, I. A. (1936). *The Philosophy of Rhetoric.* Oxford: Oxford University Press.
Ritchie, D. (2003). 'ARGUMENT IS WAR' – Or is it a game of chess? Multiple meanings in the analysis of implicit metaphors. *Metaphor and Symbol,* 18 (2), 125–46.
Rohrer, T. (1991). To plow the sea: metaphors for regional peace in Latin America. *Metaphor and Symbolic Activity,* 6 (3), 163–81.
Romaine, S. (1996). War and peace in the global greenhouse: metaphors we die by. *Metaphor and Symbol,* 11 (3), 175–94.
Sakaguchi, S. (2005). Naturally arising Foxp3-expressing CD25+CD4+ regulatory T cells in immunological tolerance to self and non-self. *Nature Immunology.,* 6 (4), 345–52.

Schank, R. C. (1982). *Dynamic memory: A Theory of Reminding and Learning in Computers and People.* Cambridge: Cambridge University Press.

(1999). *Dynamic Memory Revisited.* Cambridge: Cambridge University Press.

Schank, R. C. and Abelson, R. P. (1977). *Scripts, Plans, Goals and Understanding: An Inquiry into Human Knowledge Structures.* Hillsdale, N. J.: Lawrence Erlbaum Associates.

Schrödinger, E. (1944). *What is Life?: The Physical Aspect of the Living Cell.* Cambridge: Cambridge University Press.

Schwartz, R. H. (2005). Natural regulatory T cells and self-tolerance. *Nature Immunology,* 6 (4), 327–30.

Scott, M. (1999). *WordSmith Tools.* Oxford: Oxford University Press.

Searle, J. R. (1997). *The Mystery of Consciousness.* London: Granta Books.

Segrave, J. O. (1994). The perfect 10: 'sportspeak' in the language of sexual relations. *Sociology of Sports Journal,* 11, 95–113.

Semino, E. (1997). *Language and World Creation in Poems and Other Texts.* London: Longman.

(2002a). A cognitive stylistic approach to mind style in narrative fiction. In E. Semino and J. Culpeper (eds.), *Cognitive Stylistics: Language and Cognition in Text Analysis*, pp. 95–122. Amsterdam: John Benjamins.

(2002b). A sturdy baby or a derailing train? Metaphorical representations of the euro in British and Italian newspapers. *Text,* 22 (1), 107–39.

(2005). The metaphorical construction of complex domains: the case of speech activity in English. *Metaphor and Symbol,* 20 (1), 35–69.

(2006a). Blending and characters' mental functioning in Virginia Woolf's 'Lappin and Lapinova'. *Language and Literature*, 15 (1), 55–72.

(2006b). Fictional characters and individual variation in metaphor use. In R. Benczes and S. Csábi (eds.), *The Metaphors of Sixty: Papers Presented on the Occasion of the 60th Birthday of Zoltán Kövecses*, pp. 227–35. Budapest: Eötvös Loránd University.

(2006c). A corpus-based study of metaphors for speech activity in British English. In A. Stefanowitsch and S. T. Gries (eds.), *Corpus-Based Approaches to Metaphor and Metonymy*, pp. 35–60. Berlin: Mouton de Gruyter.

Semino, E. and Masci, M. (1996). Politics is football: metaphor in the discourse of Silvio Berlusconi in Italy. *Discourse and Society,* 72, 243–69.

Semino, E. and Short, M. (2004). *Corpus Stylistics: Speech, Writing and Thought Presentation in a Corpus of English Writing.* London: Routledge.

Semino, E. and Steen, G. (forthcoming). Metaphor in literature. In W. J. Gibbs Jr. (ed.), *Handbook of Metaphor*, Cambridge: Cambridge University Press.

Semino, E. and Swindlehurst, K. (1996). Metaphor and mind style in Ken Kesey's *One Flew over the Cuckoo's Nest. Style,* 30 (1), 143–66.

Semino, E., Heywood, J. and Short, M. (2004). Methodological problems in the analysis of a corpus of conversations about cancer. *Journal of Pragmatics,* 36 (7), 1271–94.

Short, M. (1996). *Exploring the Language of Poems, Plays and Prose*. London: Longman.

Silberstein, S. (2002). *War of Words: Language, Politics, and 9/11.* London: Routledge.

Simon-Vandenbergen, A.-M. (1993). Speech, music and de-humanisation in George Orwell's *Nineteen Eighty-Four*: a linguistic study of metaphors. *Language and Literature*, 2, 157–82.

Skorczynska, H. and Deignan, A. (2006). Readership and purpose in the choice of economics metaphors. *Metaphor and Symbol*, 21 (2), 105–20.

Skott, C. (2002). Expressive metaphors in cancer narratives. *Cancer Nursing,* 25 (3), 230–35.

Smith, Z. (2005). *On Beauty.* London: Penguin.

Sobolev, D. (2003). Hopkins's rhetoric: between the material and the transcendent. *Language and Literature,* 12 (2), 99–115.

Sontag, S. (1979). *Illness as Metaphor.* London: Allen Lane.

(1988). *AIDS and its Metaphors.* London: Penguin.

Sperber, D. and Wilson, D. (1995). *Relevance: Communication and Cognition.* Oxford: Blackwell.

Spiro, D., Feltovitch, P., Coulson, R. and Anderson, D. (1989). Multiple analogies for complex concepts: antidotes for analogies-induced misconceptions in advanced knowledge acquisition. In S. Vosniadou and A. Ortony (eds.), *Similarity and Analogical Reasoning*, pp. 498–531. Cambridge: Cambridge University Press.

Steen, G. (1994). *Understanding Metaphor in Literature: An Empirical Approach.* London: Longman.

(1999). From linguistic to conceptual metaphor in five steps. In R. W. Gibbs Jr. and G. J. Steen (eds.), *Metaphor in Cognitive Linguistics*, pp. 57–77. Amsterdam: John Benjamins.

Steen, G. J., Biernacka, E. A., Dorst, A. G., Kaal, A. A., López-Rodríguez, I. and Pasma, T. (forthcoming). Pragglejaz in practice: finding metaphorically used words in natural discourse. In L. Cameron (ed.), *Researching and Applying Metaphor in the Real World.*

Stefanowitsch, A. (2006). Words and their metaphors: A corpus-based approach. In A. Stefanowitsch and S. T. Gries (eds.), *Corpus-Based Approaches to Metaphor and Metonymy,* pp. 63–105. Berlin: Mouton de Gruyter.

Stefanowitsch, A. and Gries, S. T. (2006). *Corpus-based Approaches to Metaphor and Metonymy.* Berlin: Mouton de Gruyter.

Stern, J. (2000). *Metaphor in Context.* Cambridge, Mass.: Massachusetts Institute of Technology Press.

Sternberg, R. J. (1990). *Metaphors of Mind: Conceptions of the Nature of Intelligence.* Cambridge: Cambridge University Press.

Sunderland, J. (2004). *Gendered Discourses.* Basingstoke: Palgrave Macmillan.

Swan, J. (2002). 'Life without parole': metaphor and discursive commitment. *Style,* 36 (3), 446–65.

Sweetser, E. (1990). *From Etymology to Pragmatics: The Mind-as-Body Metaphor in Semantic Structure and Semantic Change*. Cambridge: Cambridge University Press.

Taber, K. S. (2001). When the analogy breaks down: modelling the atom on the solar system. *Physics Education,* 36 (3), 222–6.

Thompson, A. and Thompson, J. O. (1987). *Shakespeare: Meaning and Metaphor.* Brighton: Harvester.

Thompson, S. (1996). Politics without metaphor is like a fish without water. In J. S. Mio and A. N. Katz (eds.), *Metaphor: Implications and Applications*, pp. 185–202. Mahwah, N. J.: Lawrence Erlbaum Associates.

Toolan, M., Bhaya Nair, R. and Carter, R. (1988). Clines of metaphoricity, and creative metaphors as situated risktaking. *Journal of Literary Semantics,* 17 (2), 20–40.

Traugott, E. C. and Dasher, R. B. (2002). *Regularity in Semantic Change*. Cambridge: Cambridge University Press.

Tsur, R. (1992). *Toward a Theory of Cognitive Poetics.* Amsterdam: Elsevier Science Publishers.

(2003). *On the Shore of Nothingness: A Study in Cognitive Poetics.* Thorverton: Imprint Academic.

Tudge, C. (1999) The language of the future. *Index on Censorship*, 28 (3), 172–80.

Turney, J. (2005). Why humans grow old grungily. *New Scientist,* (2499), 44.

van Dijk, T. A. (1987). *Communicating Racism: Ethnic Prejudice in Thought and Talk.* London: Sage.

(1998). *Ideology: A Multidisciplinary Approach.* London: Sage.

(2002). Ideology: political discourse and cognition. In P. Chilton and C. Schäffner (eds.), *Politics as Talk and Text: Analytic Approaches to Political Discourse*, pp. 143–69. Amsterdam: John Benjamins.

van Peer, W. (1986). *Stylistics and Psychology: Investigations of Foregrounding.* London: Croom Helm.

van Teeffelen, T. (1994). Racism and metaphor: the Palestinian–Israeli conflict in popular literature. *Discourse and Society,* 5 (3), 381–405.

Vanparys, J. (1995). A survey of metalinguistic metaphors. In L. Goossens, P. Pauwels, B. Rudzka-Ostyn, A.-M. Simon-Vandenbergen and J. Vanparys (eds.), *By Word of Mouth: Metaphor, Metonymy and Linguistic Action in a Cognitive Perspective*, pp. 1–34. Amsterdam: John Benjamins.

von Boehmer, H. (2005). Mechanisms of suppression by suppressor T cells. *Nature immunology*, 6 (4), 338–44.

Walsh, C. (2003). From 'capping' to intercision: metaphors/metonyms of mind control in the young adult fiction of John Christopher and Philip Pullman. *Language and Literature,* 12 (3), 233–51.

Watson, J. D. and Crick, F. (1953). Genetical implications of the structure of deoxyribonucleic acid. *Nature*, 171, 964–7.

Weigman, K. (2004). The code, the text and the language of God. *Embo Reports,* 5 (2), 116–18.

Werth, P. (1999). *Text Worlds: Representing Conceptual Space in Discourse.* London: Longman.

Whorf, B. L. (1956). *Language, Thought, and Reality: Selected writings of B. L. Whorf.* Edited by John B. Carroll. Cambridge, Mass.: Technology Press of Massachusetts Institute of Technology.

Wodak, R. (2001). The discourse-historical approach. In R. Wodak and M. Meyer (eds.), *Methods of Critical Discourse Analysis,* pp. 63–95. London: Sage.

(2002). Fragmented identities: redefining and recontextualizing national identity. In P. Chilton and C. Schäffner (eds.), *Politics as Talk and Text: Analytic Approaches to Political Discourse,* pp. 143–69. Amsterdam: John Benjamins.

Wodak, R. and Meyer, M. (eds) (2001). *Methods of Critical Discourse Analysis.* London: Sage.

Wodak, R., de Cillia, R., Reisigl, M. and Liebhart, K. (1999). *The Discursive Construction of National Identity.* Edinburgh: Edinburgh University Press.

Wolf, H.-G. and Polzenhagen, F. (2003). Conceptual metaphor as ideological stylistic means: An exemplary analysis. In R. Dirven, F. Roslyn and M. Pütz (eds.), *Cognitive Models in Language and Thought,* pp. 245–74. Hawthorn, N. Y.: Mouton de Gruyter.

Zinken, J. (2003). Ideological imagination: intertextual and correlational metaphors in political discourse. *Discourse and Society,* 14 (4), 507–23.

Index